GREAT BATTLES
OF
WORLD WAR I

GREAT BATTLES
OF
WORLD WAR I

Anthony Livesey

Foreword by Major-General Sir Jeremy Moore

CHARTWELL
BOOKS, INC.

This edition first published in 2003 by
Chartwell Books, Inc.
A Division of Book Sales, Inc.
114 Northfield Avenue
Edison, New Jersey 08837

Conceived, edited and designed by Marshall Editions
The Old Brewery
6 Blundell Street
London N7 9BH
UK
www.quarto.com

ISBN–10: 0-7858-1757-3
ISBN–13: 978-0-7858-1757-4

Printed and bound in China by 1010 Printing Limited

10 9 8 7 6 5 4 3 2

Editor	Gwen Rigby
Art Director	David Goodman
Picture Research	Anne-Marie Ehrlich
Production	Anna Pauletti
Consultant	James Lucas
Main Illustrator	Harry Clow

'LEAVE'

"How long have you got Fred?"

A cartoon by Bryce Bairnsfather

Contents

Introduction

From the beginning of 'Modern War' in the seventeenth century until the early years of the present century, European armies steadily increased in size as populations grew and larger and larger proportions of them were recruited, and then conscripted, to fight for their country. Thus the concept of 'mass' came to dominate much of the thinking about war. At the same time though, the range and lethality of the weapons available to those armies also increased, until the point was reached at which their destructive power gained predominance over the battlefield.

No longer was it possible, as had been a common practice, simply to overwhelm the enemy by launching larger numbers of men at a vital point than he was able to bring to bear. Until 1914 dogged persistence, backed by sheer weight of men and materials, had been in the end an acceptable substitute for imagination, and had won wars. The turning point was reached, as with the benefit of hindsight we can all now see, in the mud, and the chaos, and the stagnation of World War I.

One part of the continuing fascination of this period for the general reader probably lies in what is perceived as a total lack of awareness, at least among the commanders, that this point in the development of warfare had been reached, though this does not seem an altogether fair assessment. Pigheadedness and lack of imagination there certainly were, but much ingenuity, resource and inventiveness in dealing with this intractable problem were also displayed at many levels.

If we examine the ideas behind the concepts, from the turning of the flank of the Central Powers at the Dardanelles to the coordinated use of the mines at Messines, from the invention of the tank to the ingenious ruses employed to cover the evacuation from Gallipoli, we see imagination being displayed at every level, from Government to front-line soldier.

None of that alters the fact that the numbers of casualties were indeed appalling, and the conditions in which men lived and fought, and died, almost defy description; this makes their spirit and persistence the more astonishing. And this spirit of sacrifice was shown, it is too easily forgotten, by men of all nations—both the Allies and the Central Powers—and again at all levels.

One possible clue to that spirit, at least as far as the British Army was concerned, and another possible cause for the abiding interest in this period, may perhaps lie in the concept, widely and popularly held at the time, that this was 'The War that will end War'. That if, somehow, we could only hold on to the end, peace and justice and right would prevail. This of course makes it all the more poignant that, despite the disillusionment and cynicism that followed the Armistice, Europe was at war again a mere 21 years later.

This latest volume in the *Great Battles* series shows that, despite our vision of the continuing stream of casualties and the persistent cloying mud of the Western Front, not all the battles of the Great War were the same. It puts Gallipoli, the Somme, Verdun and Passchendaele into context with what preceded and followed them, with what went on on the other battlefronts and farther afield. In Africa and the Levant, for instance, Lettow-Vorbeck and Allenby, freed as they were from the straightjacket of the main campaigns, were able vividly to display the flair and imagination so sadly lacking in most of battles of this war. The war at sea and in the air are also briefly covered.

Thus there are concepts to be studied over the whole range; some as stupid as is usually supposed, some less so given the context in which they were conceived, some bright, some even brilliant. And as always there are the men who carried them out, or died in the attempt. This book gives us new insights into the many and varied lessons to be learned from World War I.

Jeremy Moore

Major-General Sir Jeremy Moore, KCB, OBE, MC, was the victorious Commander of the British Land Forces in the Falkland Islands in May-July 1982. As a career soldier in the Royal Marines he saw action in Malaya, Cyprus, Brunei, Sarawak and Northern Ireland during his 35-year span of service.

Europe goes to War *August 1914*

World War I ranks high among the disasters to have afflicted mankind. The war's complex origins—political and economic—date from the 1870s, when Germany defeated France and caused lasting resentment by seizing Alsace and Lorraine. Germany then rapidly emerged as the greatest industrial and military power in Europe, an object of fear and envy to other states.

Alliances fluctuated over the years but by 1914 the alignment was clear: on one side Germany and Austria-Hungary, the 'Central Powers'; and on the other the 'Allies', Great Britain, France and Russia. This alignment, designed by diplomats to maintain the balance of power and thus ensure peace in Europe, was in fact potentially inflamatory. By 1914 it needed only a spark to start the conflagration. In the event, as historians have observed, the spark was trivial—a man's signature on his marriage contract.

The Archduke Franz Ferdinand, heir to the throne of Austria-Hungary, had in 1900 married the Countess Sophie Chotek. Her rank, though high, did not meet the level protocol demanded of a future empress. She was not accorded the title of archduchess, nor could she appear with her husband as an equal in public. This never ceased to aggrieve the Archduke, but he found a way publicly to show his love for his wife.

He was a field marshal and, when acting in his military capacity as Inspector General of the Imperial forces, his wife could accompany him in public. To enable her to drive through the streets with him in an open carriage and be jointly greeted at receptions, he decided in 1914 that, on the anniversary of his marriage, he would inspect the army in Bosnia, of which the capital was Sarajevo. Thus his marriage certificate became also his death warrant.

Bosnia and Herzegovina had both been administered by Austria-Hungary since 1878 but had been formally annexed only in 1908. The people of the area were Bosnians, Croats and Slavs. A Serbian minority wanted to join Serbia, and deeply resented Austrian annexation. On 28 June 1914, as the Archduke and his wife drove through Sarajevo, a student with nationalistic sympathies, Gavrilo Princip, encouraged by a Serbian secret society called the 'Black Hand', shot both of them dead.

Austria-Hungary, supported by her more powerful ally, Germany, sought redress and proof that the government of

Kaiser Wilhelm, with the Archduke Franz Ferdinand on his right, *below*, at army manoeuvres in 1909. Germany had for many years been preparing for war, and manoeuvres were regular events, even social occasions.

Two women at their ease on an English beach, *bottom*, are oblivious of the newspaper boy behind them, with his placard announcing hostilities. In 1914 most people in Britain thought the war would 'be over by Christmas'.

The wall painting, *below right*, by Albert Herter of French soldiers leaving for the front, appears in the booking hall of the Gare de l'Est in Paris.

Scenes like this were repeated all over France, where the potential horror of war was more keenly realized. All too soon the trains would be returning loaded with scores of wounded.

Serbia had instigated a plot. None could be found; nevertheless, on 23 July the Imperial government sent Serbia an ultimatum, so worded as to be unacceptable. Serbia, however, abjectly stomached the terms, save for two which violated her status as an independent country. Austria-Hungary broke off diplomatic relations and mobilized. European diplomacy had begun its ponderous, grimly inevitable march to war.

Russia, self-proclaimed protector of the Balkan Slavs, could not permit Serbia to be overrun; she, too, mobilized. But Russia mobilized as a political bluff, playing a card to trump Austria-Hungary's. Others, however, could also bluff. Germany sent an ultimatum to Russia, demanding that she demobilize within 12 hours. Russia refused, and on 1 August Germany declared war on her and, shortly afterward, without pretext, on France.

Great Britain, bound by treaty to maintain Belgian independence, declared war on Germany when German troops crossed that country's border. World War I, the most avoidable but most terrible of wars, had begun. In the following weeks, Montenegro and Japan joined the Allies, the Turkish Empire the Central Powers, with whom it had a secret treaty; Italy and Portugal were later to join the Allies.

The combatants were—on paper, at least—evenly matched. The German Army, with the Prussians at the core, had been emerging since the Napoleonic Wars as the supremely efficient fighting machine. By the Franco-Prussian War of 1870 it had become the most professional in Europe. Conscripts were trained to a high pitch and could be called upon in war, not merely as reserves but as front-line troops. In this way, Germany in 1914 was able to throw into her initial onslaughts far greater numbers of trained fighting men than the Allies had thought possible.

Germany's ally, Austria-Hungary, was not so formidable. A conglomerate of disparate races and ridden with bureaucracy, Austria-Hungary, since the time of Napoleon, had, in the main, a history of military ineptitude. Conscription, though operated on the German model, produced more problems than solutions, since units of a racial group had to be allocated to positions where they would not have to engage their kinsmen across the border. Troop dispositions were, therefore, made for ethnic, rather than strictly military, considerations.

Allied armies were raised differently. France, with a much smaller manpower than Germany (at most some 6 million potential servicemen to Germany's nearly 10 million), also employed conscription but with a different object, for the French regarded their conscripts principally as reserves for such tasks as garrison duty, while relying on the professional army of some 1 million men quickly to win an opening campaign and then the war.

Russia, for her part, was possessed of almost limitless manpower, but this was in large measure negated by her chronically inefficient rail system, so large numbers of men could be transported across country only with difficulty and by laborious stages. The conscript troops were, however, generally fervent and courageous, and many senior and middle-rank officers had gained valuable military experience in the war against Japan (1904–5), which the Austrians lacked.

Telephone and other communication systems were both inadequate in number and doubtful in operation. Nor did Russia possess the industrial might of Germany. She had to rely largely on imports from her allies (notably Great Britain) brought over long and hazardous distances.

Great Britain was in another category. She was traditionally a great, indeed the leading, sea power; she had neither conscription nor a large standing army, and her original expeditionary force numbered a mere 160,000. This comprised, however, in the historian Basil Liddell Hart's felicitous phrase, 'a rapier among scythes', for of all the European armies Britain's alone had seen repeated, though limited, action in the colonial campaigns.

ALBERT HERTER

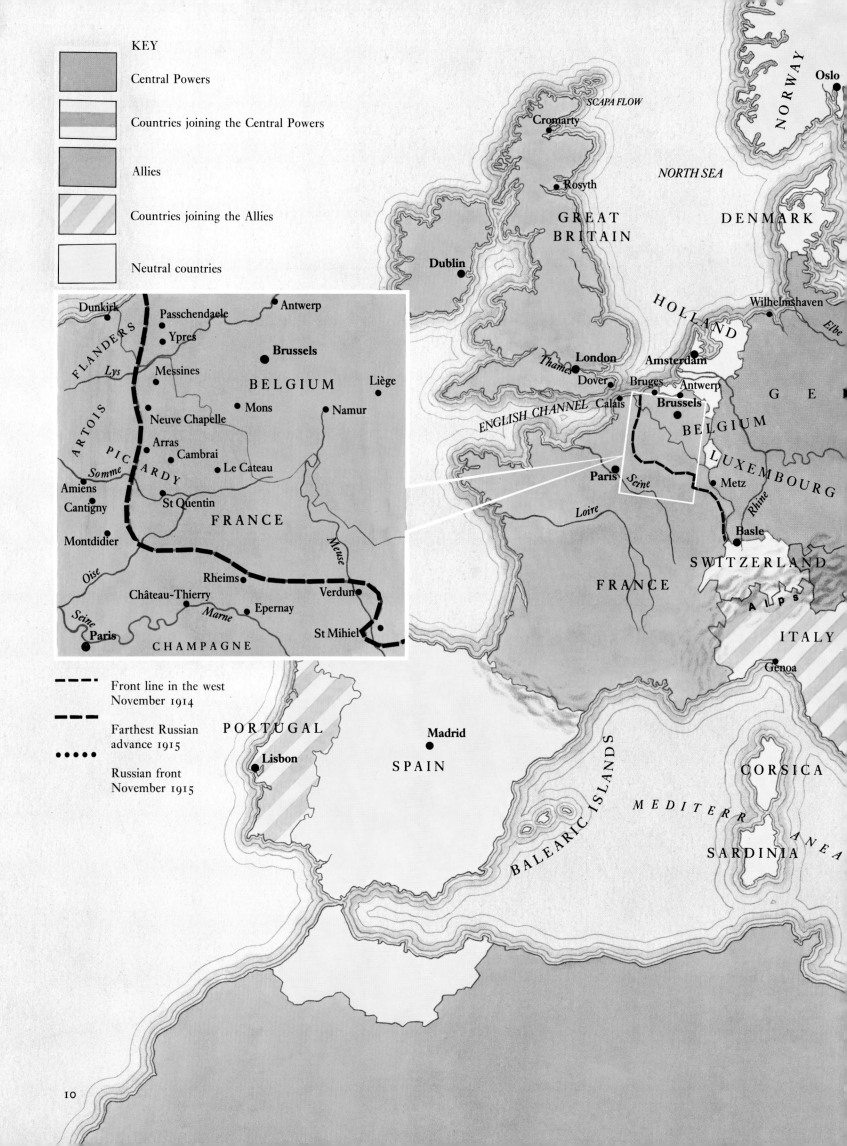

KEY

Central Powers

Countries joining the Central Powers

Allies

Countries joining the Allies

Neutral countries

- - - Front line in the west
November 1914

- - - Farthest Russian
advance 1915

· · · · · Russian front
November 1915

OSLO

NORWAY

SCAPA FLOW

NORTH SEA

Cromarty

Rosyth

GREAT
BRITAIN

DENMARK

Dublin

HOLLAND

Wilhelmshaven

Elbe

London

Amsterdam

Thames

Dover

Bruges

Antwerp

GER

ENGLISH CHANNEL

Calais

Brussels

BELGIUM

LUXEMBOURG

Paris

Seine

Metz

Rhine

Loire

Basle

SWITZERLAND

FRANCE

Alps

ITALY

Genoa

PORTUGAL

Madrid

Lisbon

SPAIN

CORSICA

BALEARIC ISLANDS

MEDITERRANEA

SARDINIA

Inset map

Dunkirk

Antwerp

Passchendaele

FLANDERS

Ypres

Lys

Messines

BELGIUM

Brussels

ARTOIS

Neuve Chapelle

Mons

Namur

Liège

PICARDY

Arras

Cambrai

Somme

Le Cateau

Amiens

Cantigny

St Quentin

FRANCE

Montdidier

Oise

Meuse

Rheims

Verdun

Château-Thierry

Marne

Epernay

St Mihiel

Seine

Paris

CHAMPAGNE

SWEDEN

Stockholm

BALTIC SEA

openhagen

Königsberg

Danzig

Tannenberg

Gumbinnen

Masurian Lakes

Berlin

Vistula

Brest Litovsk

Warsaw

POLAND

San

Pinsk

Lutsk

Lemberg

Galicia

Przemsyl

Cracow

Carpathians

Czernowitz

Bukovina

Danube

Prague

Vienna

AUSTRIA-HUNGARY

Budapest

Caporetto

Trieste

enice

ADRIATIC SEA

MONTENEGRO

Belgrade

Sarajevo

SERBIA

Transylvania

ROMANIA

Bucharest

Dobrudja

BULGARIA

Sofia

Petrograd

Moscow

RUSSIA

Riga

Minsk

Kiev

Dnieper

Dniester

Crimea

BLACK SEA

Rome

ALBANIA

Tirana

Salonika

Gallipoli

DARDANELLES

GREECE

AEGEAN SEA

Athens

Constantinople

TURKEY

Kizil Irmak

Euphrates

Tigris

Aleppo

SYRIA

SICILY

SEA

MALTA

CRETE

CYPRUS

Beirut

Megiddo

Damascus

Jerusalem

Amman

Alexandria

PALESTINE

Cairo

SUEZ CANAL

EGYPT

LIBYA

Nile

Sinai

Akaba

Germany declared war on France on 1 August 1914; she invaded Luxembourg on the 2nd and the following day Belgium. On 4 August, Great Britain, with the overwhelming support of her people, declared war on Germany for violating Belgian sovereignty. By the 6th, Germany had reached maximum deployment against Belgium and France, and some 550 trains carrying men and munitions were crossing the bridges of the Rhine every day. Within a week, one and a half million men, with abundant supplies, were in position for a massed attack.

Deployed near Aix-la-Chapelle in northeast Belgium was the First Army (General Alexander von Kluck), with the Second Army (General Bernard von Bülow) assembled near Limburg on its left. These two armies comprised the German right wing, entrusted with the task of encircling Paris. On the left of Bülow's army lay the Third Army (General von Hausen) and the armies of Duke Albrecht of Württemberg, of Crown Prince Wilhelm of Prussia, and of Crown Prince Rupprecht of Bavaria.

The German left wing was held by the army of General von Heeringen. As the German advance progressed, however, these formations were modified. Von Kluck on the right wing was to strike at the French left, through Brussels, Mons and Le Cateau, toward the River Somme near Amiens, while Bülow wheeled south of Liège, up the River Sambre. The armies of the centre group were to move through the Ardennes in the direction of Rheims, the central Meuse and Verdun, and Heeringen's force was to repel any French offensive into Alsace.

By the afternoon of 4 August, leading formations of Kluck's First Army were before the great city of Liège, with its ring of six major and six minor forts. It was here that the Germans experienced their first unpleasant surprise of the campaign.

The assault was stiffly resisted and at no time in their planning had the Germans calculated that the Belgians would do anything other than tamely submit. Though the city itself was speedily taken, the forts held out stubbornly, obliging the attackers to bring up heavy howitzers,

German cavalry and artillery limbers, *right*, moving through Brussels, which was captured on 20 August during the Germans' sweep to the west.

Courageous Belgian resistance aroused admiration in Great Britain, and many postcards, *far right*, were produced that expressed this sentiment.

Rival German and French plans

German strategy in 1914 was based on a plan devised by Field Marshal Count Alfred von Schlieffen (1833–1913), Chief of the German Great General Staff 1891–1905. His plan, accepted in 1905, was designed to solve Germany's potential problem of having to fight simultaneously on two fronts, west and east. A massive blow, delivered at maximum speed, was to knock France out of the war in the first six weeks; then, using Germany's efficient interior rail system, the victorious troops were to be rushed east to destroy the Tsar's armies before Russia's cumbersome mobilization could be completed.

Schlieffen planned to leave his left wing in Alsace and Lorraine lightly manned, while an immensely strong right wing was to execute a rapid enveloping movement through Flanders and Picardy—'brushing the Channel with their sleeves'—and lay siege to Paris from the west. The beauty of this strategy lay in the fact that, if the opening manoeuvre were successful, the Germans would take the French centre and right wing armies in rear, with the added bonus that these troops would then have to fight with their backs to their own line of fortifications along the German border.

The plan had one drawback: the advancing Germans would violate Belgian and Dutch neutrality, guaranteed by Great Britain, Austria, France, Germany and Russia, thus bringing Great Britain into the war on the Allied side.

Schlieffen was dead by 1914 (his dying words are reported to have been, 'It must come to a fight. Only make the right wing

KEY:
Schlieffen's planned attack
Actual German attack

strong'), and his successor as Chief of Staff, General Helmuth von Moltke, while broadly adopting Schlieffen's plan, had already fatally modified it through timidity.

Fearing that a weak German left flank might enable the French to invade the Fatherland (which Schlieffen had been prepared temporarily to tolerate), Moltke allocated eight of his nine new divisions to the left flank and added only one to the right—precisely the reverse of what Schlieffen had intended. Moreover, his nerve deserted him when Russia invaded East Prussia, and he transferred two army corps from France to the East. These modifications virtually ensured that Germany could not win the ensuing battle and would ultimately lose the war.

The French General Staff were utterly astonishing in their misreading of the situation. Following France's defeat by Germany in the war of 1870–1 and her loss of Alsace and Lorraine, her strategists had devised numerous plans in the event of another war. All hinged on the newly strengthened eastern frontier forts, such as Verdun, and a strategy of an initial defensive campaign, followed, when opportune, by a powerful counter-stroke.

But in the last few years before the war, a new military mentality had dominated French planning, the leading exponent of which was Colonel de Grandmaison, Director of Military Operations. His Plan 17 rejected any form of defensive strategy, claiming that the French national character was more suited to attack, in the manner of Napoleon.

An attack to the utmost—*offensive à l'outrance*—was to be made into Lorraine by the First and Second armies, while the Third and Fifth armies, on their left, would take the offensive north of Metz or, if the Germans did indeed come down through Belgium, strike them in flank.

Plan 17 ignored all historical evidence of the militarily possible, particularly in French miscalculation of German strength: in the first week of conflict, the French counted only 45 German front-line divisions while, in fact, 83 were deployed. All experience showed that an attack had some prospect of success only if it had numerical superiority in a ratio of at least 3:1. And at this time the Germans outnumbered the French on the Western Front 3:2.

BRAVE
LITTLE BELGIUM

No. 2456b

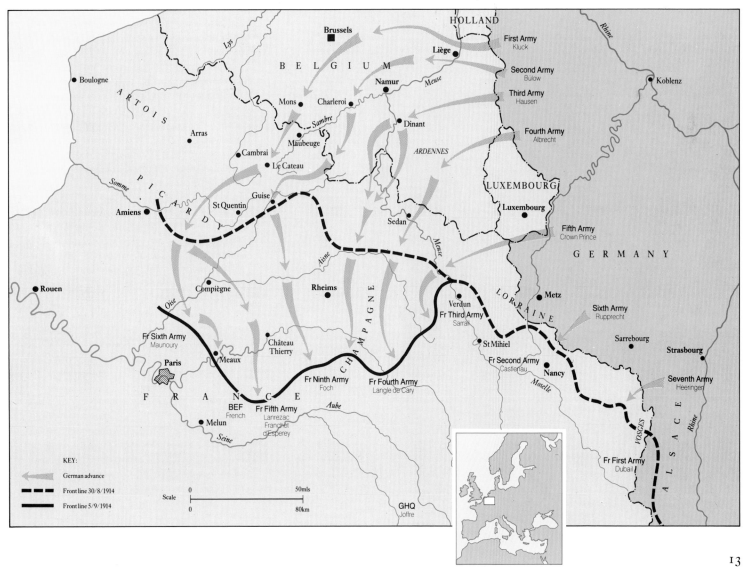

A private of the **Royal Hampshire Regiment, 1914**. The khaki service cap was later replaced by a soft-topped version with ear flaps; steel helmets were not in general issue until 1916. Troops wore a standard tunic above pantaloons and puttees. The rifle is a short magazine Lee-Enfield Mk 4.

'Les 4 fils Aymon', by Raoul Dufy, portrays Tsar Nicholas, King Albert, French and Joffre as Charlemagne's knights, whose heroic deeds were extolled in a medieval ballad.

The British Expeditionary Force

In 1914, the BEF comprised some 160,000 men, formed into six infantry divisions, one cavalry division, two additional unattached cavalry brigades and a complement of services troops. By comparison with the vast conscript armies of Europe, the BEF was indeed small—'a contemptible little army' in the Kaiser's words—but it was the most professional in the world. The men were volunteers who had undergone a long and thorough training, and most had also had battle experience in South Africa, India and Egypt.

The aim of British governments had, for a century, been to possess a small, highly professional army of volunteers, with a second-line volunteer citizen army intended for home defence. But the real defence lay with the supremely powerful Royal Navy.

Between 9 and 22 August 1914, the BEF was safely ferried across the Channel under the watchful guardianship of the navy. Of this the Germans were unaware, and their astonishment was great when, on the 23rd, they found themselves opposed at Mons by the entire BEF. The force was virtually destroyed in its gallant endeavours at Mons and the First Battle of Ypres, with losses amounting to 95,654 by the end of 1914. Thereafter, the British relied on 'Kitchener's Army'—hundreds of thousands of volunteers, all of whom required training—and Empire troops.

READY!

ENTENTE CORDIALE

A. T. PARIS

whose huge, destructive, armour-piercing shells swiftly demolished the concrete and steel fortifications and turned them into death traps. Belgian resistance in the last of the untaken forts continued until 15 August. This delayed the advance of the German right wing but—of even more importance—it revealed to the Allies the full and deadly impact of the hitherto unknown and undeployed German howitzers.

The brave Belgian resistance gave rise to two further factors of the greatest importance. Additional time in which to gather forces to resist the invasion was granted to the French, and the Belgian Army, without support from her allies, was forced aside and, on 20 August, took refuge in the fortress town of Antwerp. Thus placed, however, it remained a potential danger to the right and rear of the advancing German Army.

On the same day, the invaders appeared before the fortified city of Namur, the last citadel barring the route up the Meuse into France. Having learned their lesson at

Postcards with patriotic themes were produced in great number by both sides. The British lion stands defiantly on guard on the white cliffs of Dover, while Britannia and Marianne dance in friendly accord.

A private of the 9th Regiment of Grenadiers, 1914. All units of the German Army wore field grey, with brass or silvered buttons. The spiked helmet was replaced in 1916 by a steel helmet. Trousers were tucked into boots. The rifle is a Mauser, model 1898.

The German Army

The German army system of 1914 dated from the reorganization of the Prussian Army after its defeat by Napoleon at the Battle of Jena in 1806. It was based on the principle of 'a nation in arms', much as Napoleon had employed a *levée en masse*.

Every able-bodied male was liable for conscription, from the age of 17, for two years' full-time training in the infantry, three in the cavalry or horse artillery. Subsequently, although a civilian, the German conscript was still obliged to serve in the Regular Reserve for four or five years, according to his arm. He next went into the 'first levy' of the *Landwehr* for five years, then the 'second levy' up to the age of 39, and the *Landsturm* until he was 45.

The army was organized into 25 army corps, each comprising a unit of staff, two infantry divisions of two brigades, two regiments of field artillery, a battalion of riflemen, cavalry, and corps troops. On mobilization, the first-line army for an offensive operation would have numbered some 761,000 men, with a second line of about 1 million. But far greater numbers were available: the total figure for both fully and partially trained troops was around 2,398,000, with a further 2–3 million available if needed. Masterminding this great force were the best brains in Germany, for the military profession carried a prestige unequalled by any other.

Liège, the Germans immediately used howitzers and took the city in two days.

While these momentous events were unfolding in Belgium, on 7 August the French had improvidently launched their long-planned assault into Upper Alsace and on 14 August a greater force—the First and Second armies—thrust into Lorraine, south of Metz. These formations, 19 divisions in all, were broken within a week at the Battle of Morhange–Sarrebourg by the machine-gun, the second weapon to emerge in great numbers; with it, entire ranks of advancing men could be cut down. More than 300,000 French soldiers were killed, maimed or taken prisoner in this futile exercise.

By repelling the French attack, the Germans had, however, in some measure abandoned their potentially lethal Schlieffen Plan, for the late Chief of Staff's intention had been to offer only weak resistance in this area, so luring the French forward. Moltke, by reinforcing his left wing at the expense of his right, had given it sufficient strength to resist attack but insufficient to mount a crushing counter-attack.

Thus the French were here driven back to their defensive fortifications but no farther. Moreover, benefiting from their interior railway network, the French were able to move troops from this area to the now crucial sector of the campaign: the threatening German swing through Belgium and northeast France. This was to have decisive consequences

Meanwhile, the British Expeditionary Force (BEF) had been safely ferried to France under the watchful eye of the British Navy. Between 12 and 17 August, about 80,000 soldiers, together with their equipment, ammunition and horses, had been landed at the channel ports of Le Havre and Boulogne, and at Rouen on the River Seine.

There had been much dispute in the British Cabinet, and among the higher ranking military, as to where this relatively small but experienced and professional army should be deployed. Some, including Field Marshal Lord Roberts, at one time Commander-in-Chief of the British Army, were for landing at Antwerp to sustain the Belgian Army and pose an inhibiting threat to the German right wing. Others, notably Field Marshal Lord Kitchener, newly appointed Secretary of State for War, advocated concentrating it around Amiens.

In the end, however, the view of Field Marshal Sir John French, the BEF's commander, prevailed. It was decided that the British should move forward, as

Great Britain, unlike the European powers, had only a small professional army, so recruits were needed quickly. They came forward in great numbers, as the line, *above*, of volunteers waiting to enlist testifies.

Men of D Company, 1st Cameronians, *far right*, marched confidently through the town of Maretz on their way to the front in the early days of August.

But only a few weeks later they, and the rest of the BEF, were forced to retreat before the German onslaught. This exhausting manoeuvre was, however, carried out in similar good order, as is shown by the view of cavalry withdrawing, *right*.

agreed with the French High Command some years earlier, to latch on to the extreme left wing of the French Army: at this time General Charles Lanrezac's Fifth Army.

Lanrezac had moved his force forward to the northeast into the angle formed by the Rivers Sambre and Meuse, roughly between Givet and Charleroi. The BEF was, therefore, concentrated in a strip of country some 40km/25mls wide between Maubeuge and Le Cateau to the southwest, on the left of Lanrezac's army.

The flaw in this disposition was that the advancing Germans were not only more numerous than the Allies had supposed but they were also moving in a more extended arc than had been expected. The ten divisions of the French Fifth Army and the four divisions of the BEF had, therefore, on the instructions of General Joseph Joffre, virtually put their heads into a noose, for they could easily be assailed from the north by the German First and Second armies and by the Third Army from the east. This perilous situation was unrecognized at the French Supreme Headquarters, but was swiftly

Early air reconnaissance

In 1914 many senior commanders could see no military role for aircraft. Indeed, only a month before war began, General Haig stated that it would be foolish to think 'that aeroplanes will be able to be usefully employed for reconnaissance'; he believed that only cavalry could gather information.

The value of aircraft in this capacity was, in fact, at once proved, when the Royal Flying Corps monitored the German offensive in August. As soon as machines landed, pilots' written reports were sent by dispatch rider or telephoned through to GHQ. In this way, Sir John French was warned of

large-scale German movements to his front before the Battle of Mons and later of Kluck's attempts to envelop the BEF. Crucially, it was air reconnaissance that informed the Allies, on 3 September, of Kluck's change of direction from west to east of Paris. German reconnaissance was less reliable, and Kluck was largely misled as to Allied movements.

The RFC machines—mainly BE2s, Blériots and Henri Farmans—operated individually and came under attack not by enemy aircraft but by artillery, and even by rifle fire from their own troops.

apparent to the watchful and questioning Lanrezac. To avoid strangulation, retreat was the only option.

The four divisions of the BEF had moved up to Mons on 22 August, in full expectation of forming part of an offensive on the Allied left wing. On arrival, however, Sir John French heard that Lanrezac's Fifth Army had been attacked

the previous day and was no longer able to cross the River Sambre. The next day, Lanrezac was warned that Namur was about to fall and the German Third Army appeared at Dinant, on his exposed right flank. This led him, correctly, to withdraw at once. But Joffre thought Lanrezac lacked fighting spirit and dismissed him on 3 September.

On 26 August 1914, the anniversary of Edward III's famous English victory at Crécy in 1346, the 2nd Corps of the BEF, under General Sir Horace Smith-Dorrien, turned and made a stand against the German First Army at Le Cateau, during the retreat from Mons.

The action was a delaying tactic to gain time so that the bulk of the BEF could withdraw unmolested.

The day dawned hot and still as the men of 13th and 14th Infantry Brigades took cover in the fields, and the guns of the Royal Field Artillery (RFA) opened up.

Advancing Germans pinned the British down by constant heavy fire and threatened to envelop their right wing. By 01.45 the British position was critical.

Le Cateau (9) lay astride the steep-sided valley of the River Selle, in open, cultivated country. Although much of the wheat had been cut, sugar beet and clover were still standing, giving some cover to the British soldiers.

Men of the 2nd Battalion King's Own Scottish Borderers had scraped shallow trenches along the Cambrai road (4); farther up the slope, near the Roman Road (6), the 2nd Battalion King's Own Yorkshire Light Infantry and the 1st Royal West Kents (12) had dug in. They came under constant fire from German heavy guns (8) on the high ground near Montay.

The 18-pounders of 122, 123 and 124 batteries (5, 3) of 28th RFA replied, firing on German troops who had gained the wood west of Le Cateau.

By 13.45 the Germans had reached the cutting east of the crossroads, where they set up at least nine machine-guns (7), with more along the Cambrai road. The British had a single machine-gun (11).

East of the Roman Road, the 18-pounders of 11, 52 and 80 batteries and 37 Battery's howitzers (10) had also been pounding the enemy, who by now were beginning to gather south of the town.

Some of the shells brought up for the howitzers were short of fuses, and a motor-cyclist (1) was sent by brigade HQ (2) to fetch a supply.

German artillery had unerringly established the range of the RFA's guns, putting many out of action; so at 14.00 orders were given to try to retrieve the guns. The situation of 122, 123 and 124 batteries especially was so exposed that this was extremely hazardous, but Captain R.A. Jones of 122 Battery called for volunteers, and soon six teams of horses and men were ready to attempt the daunting task.

Captain Jones led the teams down the shell-torn slope toward the guns. A storm of machine-gun fire was loosed on men and horses. In the first minute, eight men, including the captain, were killed and 11 injured; 20 horses fell.

The rest of the teams reached the guns and succeeded in limbering up three of them, but one team was at once shot down in the road. The other two teams galloped up the slope through the lines of the West Kents, who stood up and cheered wildly. As one officer said, 'It was a very fine sight.'

The guns of 123 and 124 batteries could not be moved, so the men smashed the sights and withdrew the breech blocks before retiring. Four guns of 11 battery, five of 80 and four howitzers of 37 were also saved. In all, 2nd Corps lost 38 guns.

Encirclement now seemed certain unless British troops were withdrawn, and by 17.00 all of 2nd Corps had begun to retreat. In one eye-witness's words, there was 'confusion, but no disorganization; disorder, but no panic'; another likened it to 'a crowd leaving a race meeting'.

The gallant stand by the British at Le Cateau disjointed the German attack, and despite the loss of 8,000 men, 2nd Corps had, said Smith-Dorrien, put up 'a real good fight'.

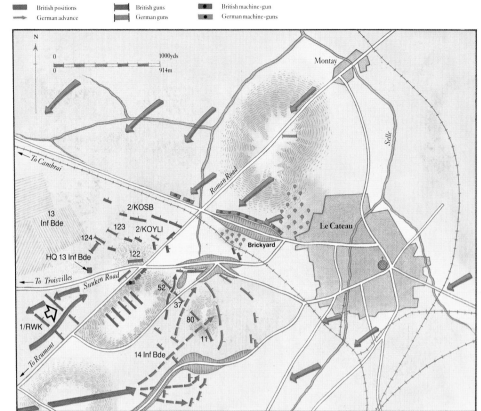

British positions
German advance
British guns
German guns
British machine-gun
German machine-guns

N

0   1000yds
0   914m

Montay

Selle

To Cambrai

Roman Road

13 Inf Bde

2/KOSB

123   2/KOYLI

124

Le Cateau

122

Brickyard

HQ 13 Inf Bde

To Troisvilles   Sunken Road

52

37

To Reumont   80

11

1/RWK

14 Inf Bde

7

8

9

10

11

12

The BEF, having stubbornly resisted repeated German attacks at Mons, was now in a dangerously exposed position and was likewise obliged to withdraw. This move was executed overnight, with little time to spare, for Kluck, believing both French and British forces already defeated, was still marching westward at maximum speed and would shortly have been able to envelop the BEF's left flank. Although Joffre, who seems at this time not to have been in touch with military reality, even now expected his left wing to advance and halt the invasion.

The Western Allies' retreat had, however, been saved from degenerating into panic and rout by the intervention of the Russians on the Eastern Front. On any sound military precept, the Russians should have withdrawn eastward until the mobilization of their limitless manpower

had been achieved. Instead, at the urgent appeal of the French, on 17 August they had loyally struck not only at Austria but into East Prussia. Their reward was to be defeated at the Battle of Tannenberg, but this gallant westward thrust had an overwhelming impact on the timorous and unsure Moltke. As Winston Churchill was to write: 'Honour must ever be done to the Tsar and Russian nation for the noble ardour and loyalty with which they hurled themselves into the war.'

Moltke's nerve failed him, and on 25 August—when the campaign in the west was reaching its decisive moment—he removed two army corps and a cavalry division from the German right wing for dispatch to the east. It was a foolhardy decision: these formations arrived too late in the east to affect events there, but their transfer so weakened the German thrust in

Praise and respect for the '75' was unbounded, as this postcard shows. One correspondent wrote: 'To every French civilian and to every French soldier . . . the Soixante-Quinze is the real hero of the war.'

Field artillery

The purpose of field artillery is both to destroy enemy assaults and to support one's own infantry as it attacks. The field artillery weapons with which the combatants entered the war in 1914 had been designed also for use in short-range battles. Thus the standard British field gun, the 18-pounder, had a range of only 6,400m/7,000yds; the range of equivalent guns in the French, Austrian, German and Russian armies was similar.

To demolish enemy fortifications, heavy guns had also been developed. Of these, the Austrian 30.5cm Skoda was by far the most versatile. In 1914 batteries of these weapons were lent by Austria to Germany's right-wing armies to reduce the Belgian fortress-cities. The corresponding German guns—the 30.5cm and the large 42cm—lacked the mobility of the Austrian pieces, which were those most frequently used during the war of movement in the early months of the conflict.

Guns increased in size and range during the war to enable targets far behind the front line to be hit. On the Somme in 1916, the British used 15in weapons, while in 1918 the Germans produced a long-range gun with which to bombard Paris. Toward the end of the war, many artillery pieces were of such a size and weight that they could only be moved around on specially strengthened railway freight wagons.

The French '75', *right above*, seen in action during the Battle of the Marne. An observer monitors the fall of shot. The limber held 80 spare rounds, but these were quickly expended in battle.

The French 75mm had a buffer recoil action, enabling it to be fired repeatedly without re-laying. Range: 8,230m/9,000yds. Rate of fire: 15 rounds/min; maximum 30.

The British 18-pounder was developed from experience gained during the Boer War of 1899–1902. Range: 6,400m/7,000yds. Rate of fire: 8 rounds/min. Elevation −5 to +6 degrees.

the west as to make material success in that theatre improbable.

That, however, was not immediately evident on a map. On that day, 25 August, the Germans had seemed on the point of victory. Although the French right-wing armies held their stations, those of the centre and left, including the BEF (shortly to comprise five divisions) were retreating steadily south toward Paris. But Moltke's misgivings now began to grow. True, his western armies were pushing forward rapidly as planned, but danger lay even in this, for the troops were becoming exhausted and famished as they moved far ahead of their supply trains. Moreover, Lanrezac's army had put up a stiff resistance at Guise, and the British (the unexpected joker in the pack, for German calculations had contemputuously dismissed their strength and effectiveness) had inflicted great slaughter as they turned on their tormentors at Mons, Le Cateau, Néry and Villers-Cottérêts.

Moltke, initially so confident of quick and overwhelming victory, now had uncertainty added to his natural timidity. 'Where are the prisoners?' he is reported to have asked. There was another worrying sign on his map. Not only did the Belgian Army remain threateningly ensconced in Antwerp, but Winston Churchill, First Lord of the Admiralty, had ordered a brigade of 3,000 British Marines to Ostend on 17 August. Their presence was given the utmost publicity, and soon their numbers (and the numbers of a mythical Russian landing force) menacing his armies' rear, had multiplied in Moltke's fretful imagination into a mighty host. These anxieties were shortly to lead to his mental collapse.

Events were now reaching the crisis point. Joffre, calm and impassive— still enjoying his two massive daily meals, consumed at leisure and followed by deep slumber—planned to counter-attack sooner or later. But when? Plan 17 was in tatters and, to stem the German advance and prepare for a decisive riposte, a new French army (the Sixth, under General Michel Maunoury) was still assembling near Amiens.

The troops comprising this army were largely those brought by rail from the area of the eastern fortresses, and their designated task was the defence of Paris. But soon this force also was obliged to retreat and thus came within the grasp of a new figure, General Joseph Galliéni, the recently appointed Military Governor of the French capital and the man who, above all, was to save France from conquest.

The Germans were now faced with an insoluble strategic problem, perceived but not resolved by von Schlieffen: they had insufficient strength to wheel west of Paris and subdue it. Kluck, therefore, decided to march east of the capital to strike the French centre and right armies in rear and destroy them. This decision to pass obliquely across the Paris defences became evident to the French on the morning of 3 September, when British air reconnaissance revealed that his First Army was no longer moving toward Paris but had wheeled southeast toward Compiègne.

Kluck's was a fateful decision, and Galliéni, studying maps and reports in his Paris headquarters, saw at once the manner in which to deliver a decisive blow. 'It is too good to be true', he is reported to have said in astonished delight, for he now had in Paris the new French Sixth Army, and Kluck, by his change of direction, would shortly expose his right flank and rear to shattering attack from the west.

In the early evening of 3 September, Galliéni asked Joffre's permission to make the attack, despite the fact that the Sixth Army was designated specifically for the defence of Paris and nothing else. But even more was required. The French, along the whole line from Paris to Verdun, must turn and counter-attack; and Galliéni needed also the active cooperation of the BEF. But Sir John French, already disheartened by the news that the French Government was leaving Paris for new headquarters at Bordeaux, was thinking of retreat to the Channel ports.

Galliéni went by motorcar to French's headquarters, where he saw only Major-General Sir Archibald Murray, Chief of Staff, who declined to make a decision in his superior's name. Galliéni returned to

An 18-pounder being repositioned in action, *above*. The Austrian 30.5cm, *left*, was moved by road. Many of these howitzers, borrowed by the Germans, were used to subdue the forts of Liège, Namur and Maubeuge. They could fire a 810-kg/1,786-lb shell every six minutes.

Paris, but later again reached Joffre by telephone and, with passionate argument, finally wrung from the Commander-in-Chief acceptance for his plan to strike north of the River Marne. It was now Joffre's turn to convert the doubters, and on 4 September he went to BEF headquarters at Melun and in an emotional meeting won French's support for the proposed attack.

Kluck, meanwhile, had lost contact with both the BEF and the French armies and, supposing them still in retreat, was reluctant to obey Moltke's instructions of 4 September to stand fast. Consequently his First Army continued its advance south of the River Marne.

The Battle of the Marne—if it can be called a battle—began at about 14.30 on the afternoon of 5 September, when the advance guard of Maunoury's Sixth Army encountered a corps on Kluck's flank, north of Meaux. But it was 6 September before all the Allied left-wing armies could turn about and launch a full-scale attack on the invaders.

Belatedly aware of the grave situation in

Joffre
et sa rivière la Marne

Joffre depicted by Guy Arnoux in 1915 beside 'his' River Marne. During the early stages of the war, Joffre was held in affectionate esteem and was known in France as 'Papa' Joffre.

An anonymous painting of a French counter-attack at Châtillon-sur-Morin, Belgium, in September 1914. The number of fallen is an early indication of the terrible power of the machine-gun.

which he had foolishly placed himself, Kluck now had no option but to turn his army to face westward to counter Maunoury's ever-growing threat. This manoeuvre, however, opened a gap of some 48km/30mls between the German First and Second armies, inviting disaster.

Meanwhile, all attacks by the German centre, west of Verdun and at Nancy, had been halted with heavy loss. Since these armies could not break through, the crucial sphere of activity became the gap that had developed between Kluck's and Bülow's armies, and which the Germans had no reserves to fill. Into this gap were now marching 20,000 highly trained men in five columns—the counter-attacking

Galliéni: defender of Paris

Debate continues as to whether General Joffre or General Joseph Galliéni (1849–1916) deserves most credit for the Allied victory on the Marne. Galliéni, who was senior to Joffre, had been offered the supreme command, a post he turned down on the grounds that all his experience had been as a colonial soldier and administrator. On 25 August 1914 he was, however, appointed Military Governor of Paris, and its defence became entirely his responsibility.

During the Franco-Prussian War of 1870–1, in 1914 still within living memory, Paris had been besieged for four months and forced to surrender. Mindful of this, Galliéni took immediate precautions to prevent its happening again. He knew that the city was unready, and its defences inadequate, to withstand a siege, despite the two rings of forts and redoubts, which had been constructed after the débâcle of 1871 but neither properly maintained nor modernized.

Galliéni, therefore, ordered huge amounts of munitions to be stockpiled; all roads, rail tracks, even sewers leading into the city were barricaded, and bridges prepared for demolition. Farm animals were brought into the woods and parks to provide food if Paris were to suffer a prolonged siege. Nevertheless, when the Government removed to Bordeaux, many thousands of civilians also fled.

In the event, Paris was saved because Galliéni recognized that the moment had come to strike at the Germans when Kluck, wheeling northeast of the city, exposed his right flank to the Sixth Army. Galliéni was posthumously made a marshal of France in recognition of his great services.

General Joseph Galliéni, portrait by Georges Scott. General mobilization order and Galliéni's proclamation issued when the Government left Paris.

The **taxicabs** of Paris were commandeered by Galliéni to take half a French infantry division to the front during the crucial battle on 7 September. In all, some 600 cabs—many of them Renaults—made two 74-km/45-ml trips in convoy transporting 6,000 men in all.

The military effect of this unconventional procedure was limited, but the psychological effect great: the war became a 'people's war'.

GOUVERNEMENT MILITAIRE DE PARIS

Armée de Paris, Habitants de Paris,

Les Membres du Gouvernement de la République ont quitté Paris pour donner une impulsion nouvelle à la défense nationale.

J'ai reçu le mandat de défendre Paris contre l'envahisseur.

Ce mandat, je le remplirai jusqu'au bout.

Paris, le 3 Septembre 1914

Le Gouverneur Militaire de Paris, Commandant l'Armée de Paris,

GALLIÉNI

ARMÉE DE TERRE ET ARMÉE DE MER

ORDRE

MOBILISATION GÉNÉRALE

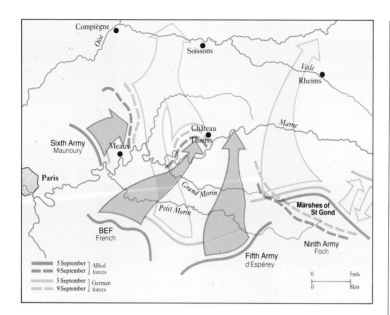

General Joseph Joffre (1852–1931), later created marshal, became Chief of Staff of the French Army in 1911.

A slow, nerveless man, his impenetrable calm helped to sustain the armies' morale in the grim days of 1914. He was relieved of the supreme command after Verdun and appointed chief military adviser to the government, but soon resigned.

'Attack! Attack! Attack!'

Some of the most decisive fighting in the battle of the Marne took place in the centre of the line, in the St Gond Marshes, where Foch's Ninth Army was stationed. The left wing of General von Bülow's Second Army mounted a bayonet attack on Foch's forces at dawn on 5 September, capturing the French outposts and driving back their advance units. But spurred on by their determined commander, whose reaction was 'My flanks are turned; my centre gives way; I attack!', the hardpressed French rallied and held. Gradually they gained the upper hand and after almost a week of savage fighting the Germans began to fall back.

It was during this time that Foch showed his unshakeable courage. As one of his staff officers later wrote, Foch conceived of war as 'essentially a struggle between moral forces'. 'Victory', Foch asserted, 'means will-power. . . . The day will be carried by the side which holds out longest. Battles are won with remnants.'

General Helmuth von Moltke (1848–1916), nephew of the military genius of the same name, had fought in the Franco-Prussian War and served as his uncle's adjutant. However, he entirely lacked strategic talent. The Crown Prince wrote of the 'serious, high-minded' Moltke that he utterly lacked 'those traits of character which make a man a leader in the field.'

General Ferdinand Foch (1851–1929) was director of the École de Guerre (1908–11) and took part in the Somme campaign of 1916. In 1917 he became Chief of the General Staff and in April 1918 was created marshal and appointed generalissimo of the combined French, British and American armies in France.

After the war, in July 1919, King George V presented Foch with the baton of a field marshal in the British Army, a rare honour.

General Alexander von Kluck (1846–1934) came of a military family and followed the conventional career of a landowner. He was educated at Cadet School and then joined a Guards regiment. He was later appointed to the General Staff and rose to become a corps commander. In 1914 he was given command of the 1st Army. Kluck was wounded in 1915.

BEF and left-wing formations of the French Fifth Army, under its new commander General Franchet d'Espèrey. This advance could, in fact, have placed the BEF in a dangerous salient, for strategists did not yet comprehend the crippling defensive effectiveness of machine-guns and artillery.

Moltke, studying the situation on his maps, seems to have collapsed mentally. Colonel Bauer, a German staff officer, wrote: 'He sat with a pallid face gazing at the map, dead to all feeling, a broken man.' The actors in this moment of high drama at German headquarters in Luxembourg are all long since dead and much of their discussions cannot be verified. What is certain, however, is that Moltke, on 8 September, for the second time instructed a young staff officer, Lieutenant-Colonel Hentsch, to visit the command centres of all the German armies to assess the situation. If it were found that the BEF was indeed across the River Marne and moving into the gap between Kluck and Bülow, then Bülow should retreat to the River Aisne.

British movements in that direction were verified, and on 9 September Bülow ordered the Second Army to withdraw. Once this had been resolved upon, Kluck's position became untenable and he, too, was obliged to withdraw to the Aisne. By afternoon the Battle of the Marne was over, but the slow-moving Allies failed to consolidate their gains.

Sir Basil Liddell Hart, the military historian, justly describes the Marne as 'The battle that was not, yet turned the tide.' He observed: 'For the profoundest truth of war is that the issue of battles is usually decided in the minds of the opposing commanders, not in the bodies of their men.' Moltke lost his nerve, Joffre and Galliéni did not.

Though widely reported, it is uncertain whether on 10 September Moltke, in fact, informed the Kaiser, 'Majesty, we have lost the war'; if so, it showed a flash of strategic prescience that he displayed at no other moment in his military career.

French infantrymen march through a village in the Marne area, watched by the local priest.

The French staff acheived a remarkably rapid and orderly redeployment of large bodies of men during the days of retreat and crisis. Although some troops were moved by train, trucks and requisitioned buses, most had to cover long distances on foot.

Germany's missed opportunity

The consequences of the First Battle of the Marne were profound; arguably they were decisive. In retrospect one can easily detect the miscalculations of the German staff: exaggerating the defensive potential of France's great concrete and steel fortresses, underestimating both the courageous tenacity of Belgian resistance and the ability of Russia to debouch early into East Prussia. Although the Schlieffen Plan, if faultlessly executed, might just have brought about the fall of France, in the event it failed because Moltke depleted, rather than strengthened, his right flank, and because, at the crucial moment, he lost his nerve.

The price Germany had to pay was dreadful. Total defeat might yet be averted; military successes elsewhere might lead to a negotiated peace, but the chance of quick and absolute victory was gone forever. It had been a chance perhaps worth taking to violate Belgian neutrality, but this had brought Great Britain, with her Empire and her naval supremacy into the War, with the inevitable result that Germany would, by blockade, eventually be brought to starvation. This could only be averted by unrestricted use of submarine warfare, which in turn would bring an enraged United States into the conflict. Now the Germans had little choice but to dig trenches and hope to win a war of attrition: a forlorn expectation, with the enemy ranks gathering against them.

Moreover, the Germans had made a further—and fateful—error: they had omitted to occupy the Channel ports, as they might easily have done, without loss, during their initial advance. Now, belatedly, they tried to take them by force, an exercise in which they failed despite the loss of tens of thousands of irreplaceable soldiers. Attempts by both Germany and the Allies to turn the other's flank, the so-called 'race to the sea' followed.

Battle of Tannenberg *August 1914*

On paper, the strategy of the Russian advance of August 1914 was sound. East Prussia, jutting out from the River Vistula almost to the centre of the River Niemen, was penned between the Baltic Sea and the northern frontier of Russian Poland and so could be attacked from either, or both, east and south.

Under the terms of a new military agreement with France, Russia was committed to fielding 800,000 men fifteen days after mobilization started. Given the size of the country and the poor communications, this was an impossibility, and by mid-August the army was still in a state

of unpreparedness, with many problems unresolved. Nevertheless, at France's repeated entreaty and in a spirit of generous cooperation, two Russian armies now advanced into East Prussia in order to honour that commitment.

General Yakov Jilinski, then in overall command of the Northwest Front Group, on 17 August directed the First Army, under General Pavel Rennenkampf, comprising six and a half infantry divisions and five cavalry divisions, north toward

Russia's war plans

Germany's principal problem at the outbreak of the war was to avoid having to fight on two fronts, east and west, at the same time. Russia's problem was strategically different but no less daunting, for though she had only one front she faced two enemies: Germany and Austria–Hungary. The Russian General Staff (Stavka) had to prepare for two eventualities, dependent on whether Germany's main opening blow was directed into France or into Russia.

Two plans were therefore devised, although Russia's military dispositions remained identical for both. The First and Second armies were to be stationed in the north, facing East Prussia, the Third, Fifth and Eighth armies in the southwest facing Austria–Hungary. The Fourth Army could

be deployed either to the northern or southern sector as circumstances dictated.

If Germany attacked in mass eastward, all Russian formations were to retire, in the manner prescribed by Field Marshal Kutuzov in the face of Napoleon's onslaught in 1812, then counter-attack when the opportunity arose. If, however, the Germans maintained a defensive stance in the east while attacking France, both army groups were to advance immediately—the northern group into East Prussia, the southern group into Galicia, where the Austro–Hungarian army was strongest. If these manoeuvres were successful, the whole might of Russia could then be redeployed for an attack on central Germany, thereby bringing the war to an end.

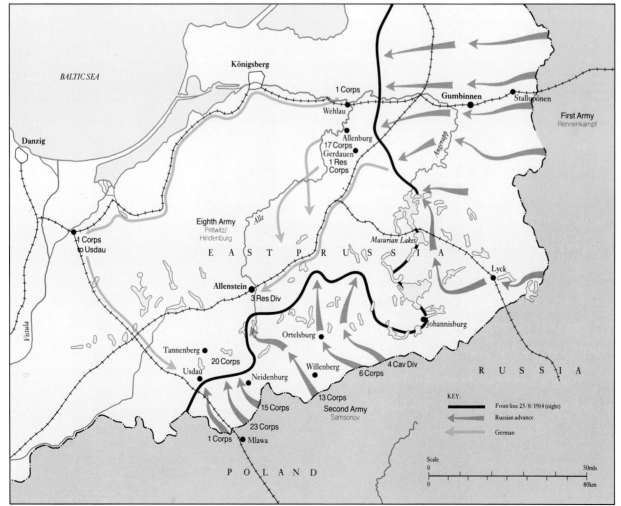

German infantry, *right*, by the Masurian Lakes at the end of August, take cover in prepared positions behind pine logs and steel firing plates. The lakes—of which there are some 2,700— posed acute tactical problems for an attacking army, since their sheer number provided ideal defensive ground.

'**Gloria Victoria**', a marching song, gave its title to a book for children with pictures of Germany's enemies: see the Cossacks, *opposite*.

On the card, *below*, Germany and Austria box Russia's ears, while her Allies wait their turn. Little Serbia pulls a toy Montenegro.

the fortified area around Königsberg. On 19 August, the Second Army, under General Aleksandr Samsonov, was ordered to advance toward Danzig (Gdansk), with the idea of cutting off the German forces from the River Vistula.

Both Rennenkampf and Samsonov had distinguished military records as cavalry commanders in Manchuria, but they had quarrelled and become bitter enemies. Indeed, so violent was their hatred for one another that, in a much-quoted scene, they actually came to blows when they met by chance on the railway platform at Mukden. This animosity boded ill for their future cooperation in East Prussia. Moreover, advancing west and northwest respectively, as the two armies were, produced a potentially calamitous separation of the two forces, for between them lay the Masurian Lakes, a complex of waters stretching some 80km/50mls north to south. Each army could, therefore, be attacked individually.

Von Schlieffen had applied his fertile brain to this eventuality and had stipulated that, since any advancing Russian armies must inevitably become divided by the lakes, first one, then the other, was to

be attacked by the full weight of German forces in East Prussia. Once one army had been crushed, the efficient German rail system was to convey the victorious troops to engage the second Russian army.

This situation, as Winston Churchill succinctly observed, was one to stimulate invention in a Marlborough or Napoleon. Unfortunately for Germany, however, the commander on the spot was the timorous

Cossacks, *below*, were mostly used for reconnaissance but the front was so long that neither they nor the Germans gleaned much information about each other's movements.

General Max von Prittwitz, who failed to exploit the opportunity through fear of his numerical inferiority. Apprehensive of defeat, he sent one reserve corps to bolster the northern sector, another to the southern sector, while holding those remaining between the two.

Rennenkampf's First Army crossed the frontier during 17–18 August, and on 19–20 August eight of his divisions encountered seven German divisions, forcing the Germans to withdraw. Although a small engagement by later standards, this battle at Gumbinnen, and the fact that Samsonov's encircling movement to the south had been detected, induced Prittwitz to call off the action. He also informed General von Moltke, Chief of the Great General Staff, that he intended to retire behind the defensive line of the River Vistula.

The reverse had a marked impact on Moltke, whose mental concentration was at that time directed to the western theatre. He was so horrified by Prittwitz's proposed withdrawal that he immediately replaced him with Generals Paul von Hindenburg and Erich Ludendorff. The battle also convinced Moltke that he had seriously underestimated Russian strength and capability. And since, up to the night of 25 August, German victory in the west seemed assured, he dispatched to the Eastern Front two corps from the supposedly invincible German right wing in France. But they reached East Prussia too late to intervene in the coming battle.

The Russians, too, misread the new strategic situation. Jilinski, now over-confident and desirous of seizing the opportunity to destroy the German Army in East Prussia, urged Samsonov and his five corps, a total of some 200,000 men, to advance at maximum speed. This in turn encouraged Samsonov to drive farther to the west than originally intended, before turning northward, in the hope of encircling even greater numbers of Germans. This mighty host crossed the German–Polish frontier during 21–22 August. But the troops were already fatigued by an unremitting nine days' marching on inadequate rations, and the communications and organization were so poor that no supplies could be brought up to them.

Samsonov's westward drive took him even farther from Rennenkampf, who after Gumbinnen had remained stationary in the north to enable Samsonov's now wider sweeping movement to complete the German encirclement.

Of all the consequences of the Battle of Gumbinnen, the most significant was the appointment of Hindenburg and

The Russian Army

The Imperial Army was a conscript force, with a peace-time strength of 1,200,000, making it by far the largest standing army in Europe. General mobilization was designed to raise the strength to $3\frac{1}{2}$ million, but this number was almost doubled in 1914. Reservists made their way by train to western Russia, picking up other reservists *en route*, and so forming the 'Russian steamroller', a great force that could, in theory, overwhelm all opposition.

The army was a mainly infantry force, with a light cavalry screen, supported by a strong artillery arm. Although multi-national and multi-lingual, it was united in loyalty to the Tsar; the cavalry was well led and the infantry competent and brave. Experience in the Russo-Japanese War had led to an understanding of modern warfare: the army was equipped with machine-guns and howitzers and knew how to use trench systems and barbed wire to effect.

Ludendorff to command, for they quickly formed a superlative military team, for a time as successful as that of Marlborough and Prince Eugène in the early years of the eighteenth century.

A special train was arranged for Ludendorff, the hero of the siege of Liège and newly appointed Chief of Staff in the east. And at 21.00 on 22 August, the day of his appointment, having been received by

the Kaiser and awarded the order *Pour le Mérite*, he left German headquarters at Coblenz for East Prussia. The train steamed at speed through the night and at 04.00 halted briefly at Hanover where, on the platform, waited the portly figure of General von Hindenburg, who had been brought out of retirement to become Commander-in-Chief. It was the first time the two men had met; they briefly

The Russian Army had 48 guns per division, more than the Austrians but fewer than the Germans' 72. *Below*, gunners pose beside their medium field guns, as if ready for action. This pre-war photograph, *top right*, shows a battery of Russian field guns on manoeuvres. Overhead flies a reconnaissance aircraft.

Max Rabes's painting, *centre right*, depicts Russian infantrymen facing an attack at Tannenberg.

Two Russian gunners, *bottom right*, pose with their tricycle and Maxim gun, which has been pivoted on a ball joint for use against aircraft.

discussed the dangerous yet promising situation in the east and then retired to their beds.

Ludendorff has widely been given sole credit for the great German victory at Tannenberg, but before he and Hindenburg had even arrived at their new post imaginative steps had been taken by Colonel Max Hoffmann, Deputy Chief of Operations of the Eighth Army, which made that victory possible. Employing his considerable powers of persuasion to the full, he convinced his superiors that the German Eighth Army should disengage from Rennenkampf's First Army near Gumbinnen, leaving merely a cavalry screen, and strike with every available man at Samsonov's advancing Second Army.

Both 1st Corps (General Hermann François) and 3rd Reserve Division, recently engaged at Gumbinnen, were to be conveyed by train to the right flank of 20th Corps, which was barring Samsonov's advance. Meanwhile, 17th Corps (General August von Mackensen) and his 1st Reserve Corps (General Otto von Below) were also to withdraw from the Gumbinnen area and march southward to take up station on 20th Corps' left.

Thus, when Ludendorff arrived at his new headquarters at Marienburg, orders had already been given for the mass of the Eighth Army to form a half-moon facing southeast, toward the centre of which Samsonov, urged on by telegrams from Jilinski, was now marching his weary men.

These movements of German troops calculatedly left an ominous and potentially fatal ingredient: Rennenkampf's First Army. If this army moved west and then south, there was no German force to prevent its taking the Eighth Army in rear and crushing it against Samsonov's Second Army. Indeed, even if Rennenkampf marched directly south and joined Samsonov, the Germans would be heavily outnumbered. But Rennenkampf did not move and one can only conjecture why.

Cossacks were the most famous Russian light cavalry. Their tasks were to scout ahead of an advancing army and to cover its rear in retreat.

They were armed with a *shashka* (a sabre without a handguard) and an M1891 pattern carbine; 30 rounds of ammunition were carried in two oilskin bandoliers. Half the riders carried a lance, a long wooden spear with a 15-cm/6-in steel point and a metal butt.

Cossacks preferred hand-to-hand fighting, considering lances a hindrance, and they were issued only to the first line in a charge.

When this broke the enemy, they would be cut down by the *shashkas* of the riders in the ranks behind.

Many have cited treason (he was of German descent) or his hatred of Samsonov. A more likely explanation is that, seeing that the Germans had vanished overnight from the field of Gumbinnen, he judged his outnumbered foe to be in full retreat, either to the fortress city of Konigsberg or over the Vistula. A comforting conclusion, but one which was wholly divorced from the actuality.

In all their subsequent movements during the campaign, the Germans were immeasurably helped by the Russian staff practice—inexplicably naive even for the militarily inept—of sending radio messages and orders 'in clear' rather than in cypher. Thus the Germans were alerted to almost every Russian tactic in the coming days.

Hindenburg and Ludendorff endorsed all Hoffman's proposed dispositions. Meanwhile, Samsonov's fully stretched men, spurred on by Jilinski, were pressing northeastward, over exhausting sand tracks through forests and between numerous lakes. In front of this already fatigued force were arrayed some of the best-equipped and best-trained troops in the world. Russia's one advantage was numerical superiority, but for this to be effective Rennenkampf's and Samsonov's armies needed to unite.

Jilinski, however, seemed oblivious to Samsonov's ever more perilous situation, and as late as 26 August—when the hapless Samsonov was just about to be

A dynamic partnership

Field Marshal Paul von Hindenburg (1847–1934) and **General Erich Ludendorff (1865–1937)** formed a uniquely successful military partnership during World War I. Hindenburg had fought in both the Austro-Prussian War (1866) and the Franco-Prussian War (1870–1). In 1878 he was appointed to the Great General Staff. He retired in 1911 but, having unrivalled knowledge of the Eastern Front and its terrain, was recalled in 1914 to assume command in the east,

with Ludendorff serving as chief of staff.

The decisive victories at Tannenberg and the Masurian Lakes gave both great prestige in Germany. In 1916, following General Erich von Falkenhayn's dismissal after the disasters of Verdun, Hindenburg was appointed commander of all German armies, with Ludendorff as Quartermaster-General, and the two became, effectively, dictators in both military and civilian affairs.

Hindenburg was elected President of the

Republic in 1925; he was re-elected in 1932 but in the following year, by then virtually senile, he was persuaded to appoint Adolf Hitler chancellor.

Ludendorff demanded an armistice in 1918, when Germany's offensive collapsed, and was summarily dismissed. He fled to Sweden but returned to Germany in 1919. He subsequently supported Hitler and took part in his abortive *putsch* in 1923. He was a National Socialist member of the Reichstag (1924–8) but later fell out with Hitler.

engulfed from all sides—he commanded Rennenkampf to employ two corps for the investment of Königsberg and with the rest of his army to press on to the Vistula. Thus, though the Russians in total outnumbered the Germans, Samsonov's Second Army was outnumbered by 180 battalions to 150.

During 23 August, Samsonov's centre (13th, 15th and 23rd corps) made contact with the German 20th Corps. Second Army was now extended over a front of some 97km/6omls, with its two wings separated from the centre. As the Russians advanced, so the German 20th Corps gave way, for the formations sent from the north by rail were not yet in position on the right. To Samsonov, all seemed to be proceeding as he most desired, and he, like Rennenkampf before him, with mistaken confidence, began to believe that the enemy were all in retreat to the Vistula.

Throughout 24 and 25 August, the gallant Russians, exhausted, without adequate provisions, and lacking the organization, communications and armament of the Germans, fought with stubborn resolve. By their greater numbers in this sector—seven divisions to half that number of German—the Russians slowly drove the German centre back.

Once again the problematical question arose as to what Rennenkampf would do. German formations from the north were now marching into position on either side of 20th Corps, but those assigned to the left wing—called by the Germans the 'Eastern Group'—might have to face about if Rennenkampf marched south. Then, acting as a screen, they would not be able to take part in the action against Samsonov. A crucial decision must be made without hesitation.

To hesitate now—to leave the Eastern Group to guard against a southward march that Rennenkampf might or might not make—was to jeopardize the encirclement of Samsonov's Second Army. As before, Hoffman's arguments were persuasive, and orders were issued for the entire Eastern Group to march southward on 25 August to be in position to attack Samsonov's right wing.

Hoffman's reading of the situation was shortly to be justified, for two Russian radio messages—again, astonishingly, sent in clear—proclaimed to the German wireless station in Königsberg that Rennenkampf, soon belatedly to be on the move again, would drive west in leisurely fashion and not reach the Gerdauen–Allenburg–Wehlau line until 26 August. Thus it became certain that Rennenkampf could not, for at least two, possibly three,

A squadron of German lancers, *left*, moves up to the front in East Prussia.

Landwehr of the 17th Corps, *left below*, prepare for a Russian attack.

German machine-gunners, *below*, wrought havoc among Russian troops in the fighting around the Masurian Lakes that followed the Battle of Tannenberg.

Prussian infantry, *bottom*, fire from a concealed position inside a farmhouse in the battle zone.

days, come to Samsonov's aid and that the entire German Eastern Group could, therefore, assail Samsonov's right wing with impunity. The scene was set for a Russian calamity.

The German 20th Corps was still slowly withdrawing in face of the Russian centre on 26 August, when, to prevent further retreat, Ludendorff ordered François's 1st Corps to smash the Russian left wing. François, however, was a commander of independent mind. He was determined to get behind the Russians and cut them off from the east. Therefore—rightly claiming that his force was as yet incomplete and most of his field guns not brought up—he made only a token attack on the Russian left, while positioning his troops as they detrained and making his own tactical preparations.

On that same day—26 August—the Russian right wing, already separated from the Russian centre, came into contact with two corps of the German Eastern Group near Lautern. The Russians were thrown back; and although they retired in reasonably good order, some became trapped with their backs to Bossau Lake, in which a number drowned. The Russian right flank guard was, in any event, beaten and fell into retreat southward until it reached Olschienen and Wallen, more than 32km/20mls away.

The next day found François, with his troops in position and his artillery and ammunition brought up, ready to attack the Russian left near Usdau. The artillery bombardment was such that the starving and bewildered Russians could not withstand it; they retreated in disorder over the frontier. François now moved in the general direction of Neidenburg to get behind the Russian rear, despite the fact that

By 30 August 1914, the central corps of General Samsonov's Second Army—the 13th, 15th and part of the 3rd—were virtually surrounded by German troops. Exhausted and starving, they surrendered in their thousands.

Only the left-hand column of 13th Corps, to the north, kept up the fight, hoping to break through to the east before the German ring could close completely.

Men of the Advanced Guard, marching in good order through the forests, early in the evening clashed with a German force armed with artillery and machine-guns. Led by Colonel Pervushin of the Nevsky Regiment, the Russians charged and captured four enemy guns.

But this determined effort took its toll, and during the night the units of 13th Corps, scattered among the trees, became inextricably mixed.

German cavalry of the 5th Hussars (**3**) had come up, meanwhile, and were preparing to ride in with the coming of day to complete the submission of the survivors.

The remnants of 13th Corps, despite their gallant actions, were rounded up and taken prisoner—some of the 122,000 men who were captured at Tannenberg. Their commander, General Samsonov, ill and in despair, had himself committed suicide on the night of 29/30 August in the forest a short distance south of Willenberg.

Before dawn the next day, 31 August, the ragged column (**1**)—neither they nor their horses had had food or water for two days—made five attempts to break out of the forest into a large clearing not far from the town of Wallendorf.

Each time, the waiting Germans of 35th Infantry Division (**2**) turned searchlights on the Russians and raked the leading ranks of men, caught in their beam, with machine-gun fire.

Each time, more men fell, and the wounded were dragged by their comrades back into the forest. Here, in the shelter of the trees, amid the wounded and dying and the panic-stricken horses, officers rallied their men for yet another assault.

Germans
Russians

THE COMMANDERS

RENNENKAMPF

SAMSONOV

MACKENSEN

FRANÇOIS

Though a fine cavalry officer and considered one of the best field commanders in the Russian Army, **General Pavel Rennenkampf (1845–1918)** made the fatal error of not marching to the aid of **General Aleksandr Samsonov (1840–1914)** at Tannenberg. The reasons for his decision are unknown, but Max Hoffmann attributed it to their personal animosity. Rennenkampf deserted his army in panic in 1915 and was dismissed. In 1918 he was murdered by Bolsheviks.

Samsonov had served in the war against Turkey (1877) and distinguished himself as leader of a cavalry division in the Russo-Japanese war. By August 1914, however, his health and mental powers were in decline.

Field Marshal August von Mackensen (1849–1945) was largely responsible for the defeat of the Russians in the Battle of the Masurian Lakes and master-minded successful German operations in Galicia, Serbia and Romania, which was occupied in 1917. Mackensen became, in effect, generalissimo of all the Austro-German forces in the south and virtual dictator of Romania until the armistice. After World War I and his retirement, he became a prominent member of a monarchist organization and later gave qualified support to Adolf Hitler.

General Hermann von François (1856–1933) joined the 3rd Guards Regiment in 1875, served in the War Academy from 1887, and then became chief of staff of Hindenburg's 4th Corps. In 1913 he was given command of 1st Corps. Later he fought at Gorlice and in 1918 led a corps on the River Aisne.

Russian soldiers, surrounded by the Germans during the fighting in East Prussia, had little option but surrender, *above.*

In all, 122,000 men were captured at Tannenberg, many of whom, *right*, were later sent westward to work as labourers in Germany.

Ludendorff had ordered him to march rapidly northeast toward Lahna.

By that evening, both his right and left flanks having been broken, Samsonov's position was untenable. He had but one course open to him: to order his reassembled flanks to attack, while he withdrew his centre corps to safety. Instead—inexplicably—he ordered his centre to strike northward again. Did he not choose to retreat when his old enemy Rennenkampf was advancing? Did he merely obey Jilinski's orders unquestioningly? Was he courting disaster with Russian fatalism? Hindenburg certainly thought the last, for he later wrote: '. . . they were no longer seeking victory, but destruction.'

The entire German Army attacked at first light on 28 August. François pushed eastward and reached Neidenburg by nightfall. He then thrust on to Willenberg to plug the Russian line of retreat, creating a string of pickets along the way to prevent any Russians escaping the trap.

The moment of Russian collapse had now arrived, for Second Army's rear was closed, its flanks broken. The entire Russian centre—13th, 15th and much of 23rd Corps—degenerated into a largely bewildered, starving, uncoordinated mêlée of ill-trained and illiterate peasants, struggling through thick forests, intent only on escape from the encircling fire of a well-fed, highly trained army.

The dissolution of the Russian centre continued throughout 29 August. That evening, absenting himself from his staff officers, Samsonov stumbled, asthmatic and exhausted, into a solitary part of the forest and shot himself.

During 29 and 30 August the desperate Russians made repeated attempts to break through the encircling enemy—only and always to be driven back by the murderous fire of François's 1st Corps, which barred the line of retreat along the route by which they had earlier advanced. Some Russians, still fighting, tried to break through, many formations led by a priest holding high a cross; all were cut down. By 31 August, all Russian troops emerging from the forest did so carrying the white flag of surrender on poles and rifles.

How many Russian soldiers were killed or later perished from their wounds in the dark glades of the forest is not precisely

German infantry moving up to the front are watched by comrades resting at the roadside. On the march, each unit was given a 10-minute break every hour.

known, but the Germans took prisoner 92,000 unwounded men, some 30,000 wounded and 500 guns. Of this total, 60,000 were taken by François and his 1st Corps. The German Eighth Army lost 10,000 to 15,000 men.

The 'Russian steamroller' in reverse

The Russian Commander-in-Chief, the Grand Duke Nicholas, was appalled by the news of Tannenberg. But even worse tidings were to follow, since, as Hoffmann wrote: 'Our hands were free to act against Rennenkampf.'

That general's position was parlous; for with the two army corps withdrawn from the Western Front, the German Eighth Army was now a force of 17 divisions. On 5 September, it made a sustained attack on Rennenkampf to hold his attention, while, on the 9th, a turning movement under François, was directed from the south through the area of the Masurian Lakes to sever Rennenkampf's communication lines to the rear.

Rennenkampf now had no option but to order First Army to retreat eastward and, but for two factors, his entire force might yet have been cut off. He ordered two divisions to counter-attack in the centre, an action that was executed with such vigour that the German 20th Corps was brought to a halt for 48 hours. This led Ludendorff to counter-order François' great northeastward thrust and turn it closer to the main body of the German army in readiness for a possible battle.

Thus the bulk of Rennenkampf's army, streaming back along the route they had earlier taken westward, contrived to escape. Even so, the Russians suffered possibly as many as 100,000 casualties and some 45,000 men taken prisoner; they also forfeited 200 guns and great quantities of supplies and ammunition they could ill afford to lose.

By a curious paradox of war, the Schlieffen Plan had been completely reversed: the Germans had been reduced to stalemate in the west while in the east they had inflicted an almost knock-out blow.

The aggressively minded General Conrad von Hötzendorff, Chief of the Austrian General Staff, had long been avid for a pre-emptive war. On the outbreak of hostilities with Russia, he intended to open an immediate offensive with the object of swiftly crushing her hastily mobilized armies.

By the twentieth day of mobilization, 18 August, Conrad calculated that Russia would be able to deploy approximately 31 divisions, including 11 cavalry divisions, to Austria's 20 infantry and 10 cavalry divisions. By 28th August, the thirtieth day of Russian mobilization, their array would, however, have increased to 52 divisions, while Austria would have no more than 39.

Conrad did not recognize that a mere equality of strength was, for an attacking army, inadequate in the face of modern, though as yet undeployed, defensive weaponry. In addition, there were imponderables, indeed miscalculations, in his planning, and most particularly in his underestimation of the speed of Russia's

mobilization and his misinterpretation of her strategic intentions.

Although the numerous rivers flowing from the Carpathian Mountains offered Conrad abundant lines of defence against any Russian invasion, it seemed to him that the sooner the Austrians attacked, the more auspicious the prospects, since they would shortly be heavily outnumbered. Also, the more likely Austria would be to avoid Germany's fate of having to fight on two fronts if neutral Italy entered the war on the Allied side.

The clinching argument for Conrad's

offensive strategy was his expectation of German aid. He assumed, as he had been led to believe at meetings with General Helmuth von Moltke immediately prior to the war, that Germany would at the outset deploy some eight corps in East Prussia. If this considerable force struck toward Siedlice, some 160km/100mls east of Warsaw, Conrad's northward drive could, in combination, cut off all Russian forces in the salient.

Russia for her part, conscious that the main German blow was directed against France, was bound by military treaty to

Russia's strategical options

The governing factor on the Eastern Front was the vast salient of Russian Poland. In the middle of this probing mass lay the fortress city of Warsaw, guarded by a ring of forts, while diagonally through the area ran the natural obstacle of the mighty River Vistula. To the north of the salient, along the Baltic shore, lay German East Prussia; to the south, the plain of Galicia, backed by the barrier of the Carpathian Mountains.

The Russian frontier, running some 1,450km/900mls from Memel on the Baltic Sea to the Bukovina in northern Romania, was highly vulnerable to a German attack

southward from East Prussia, especially if this were matched by an Austrian advance northward from Galicia.

The Russians could avoid the danger of encirclement by withdrawing entirely from the salient, or advance in overwhelming numbers to seize both East Prussia and Galicia. Their front would then run roughly straight from Danzig (Gdansk) to Cracow, enabling them to undertake an advance into either Germany or Austria.

Russia chose the latter option, and her campaign in the south was at first to have a most promising outcome.

The complex moves in the Lemberg campaign may best be compared to a revolving door. Mistaking the other's intentions, each side put most weight on its left wing to try to encircle the enemy.

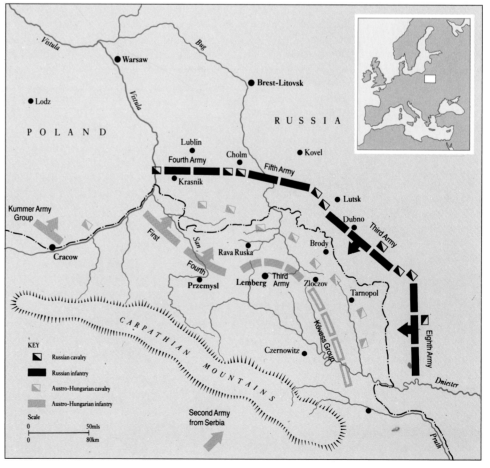

The Austro-Hungarian Army

The army of Austria-Hungary comprised three separate forces: the Imperial and Royal force, the Royal Army of Hungary and the Imperial Army of Austria, which combined in time of war.

The principal arm was the infantry, with 169 line regiments, 4 regiments of Kaiserjaeger, 33 battalions of light infantry and 4 regiments of Bosnian troops. The cavalry comprised 15 regiments of Dragoons, 26 of Hussars and 29 of Uhlans. The artillery arm was divided into four: Horse, Field, Mountain and Fortress regiments.

The peacetime strength of the army was 415,000; on mobilization this was expected to rise to 1,800,000, but in fact it grew to nearly twice that number.

The army was raised by conscription from all the countries of the empire and thus contained 11 different nationalities, with an even greater number of languages and several different religions. Despite this, and despite being equipped with largely obsolescent arms and trained principally to attack, the army fought throughout the war without major dissensions. Its cohesion stemmed entirely from the almost feudal loyalty the troops accorded the Emperor.

attack in the east. The ensuing campaign, generally known as the Battle of Lemberg, was fought over a period of three weeks (23 August–12 September) along a front of some 322kms/200mls between the rivers Vistula and Bug. It was characterized by each commander misinterpreting the intentions of his rival.

General Ivanov, who commanded the Russian armies in the south, believed the Austrians would strike eastward, and that the northern armies of his group could then march south and take the invaders in rear. Conrad, meanwhile, was marching

northward in the mistaken belief that desultory Russian mobilization would present him with little opposition from the east. In fact, a heavy Russian attack was shortly to be mounted from this direction.

Conrad's first manoeuvre was to send massed cavalry forward on 15 August to reconnoitre on a huge front, some 400km/250mls wide. Because of their ill-fitting saddles and the fact that the Austrians did not follow the practice of the British cavalry of riding for an hour and walking for an hour to rest their horses, most of the animals developed sore backs.

Russia, like all the belligerents produced propaganda postcards. *Far left*, a Russian soldier beats Germany with his belt, while he stands scornfully on the diminutive figure of Franz Joseph, the Austrian emperor.

The popular print, *Chasing the Austrians out of Lvov*, *right*, first issued with a verse beneath by the poet and propagandist Vladimir Mayakowksy, lauds the Russian capture of Lemberg.

Eleven Uhlan regiments had been on the Imperial cavalry establishment since 1784. This composite painting, dating from 1910, shows various ranks, in winter and summer dress.

Their uniforms were based on Polish peasant costume, including the extra-high boots, triangular sleeve cuffs and semi-spherical buttons.

Between the waist buttons on the back of their tunics, officers wore a gold lace border and double row of gold fringe, known as a waterfall.

The helmet, or shapka, bore a metal plate in the form of the Imperial eagle, and a horsehair plume. The number on the plate, the shapka's colour, and his buttons denoted an Uhlan's regiment. In 1884 the lance was replaced by a cavalry sabre.

Their riders had then to cover long distances on foot, leading their mounts. Such information as the reconnaissance gleaned convinced Conrad that there was inadequate Russian strength to resist him to the north. So, on 20 August, he confidently gave the order for an Austrian advance, believing there were no Russian formations to imperil his right flank.

The forces engaged in this advance were formidable: three armies with a total strength of some million men. The Austrian First Army (General Dankl) was given the task of reaching Lublin and Cholm. If this were achieved, it would sever the Warsaw-Kiev railway and also give Austria command of the road to Brest-Litovsk, thus threatening all the Russian positions to the east of Warsaw.

To the immediate right of the First Army lay the Fourth (General von Auffenberg) and to the right of that General Brudermann's Third Army. The entire mass was guarded, on its left flank, by Kummer's Army Group—in reality no more than a cavalry division, 44 infantry battalions and some artillery and bicyclists—and on the right, by the Kovess Army Group of two corps.

Arrayed in a crescent against these Austrian formations were four Russian armies, comprising some 1,200,000 men. The Fourth (General Salza) and, to its left, the Fifth (General Plehve), faced south; the Third Army (General Nikolas Ruzski), on the Fifth Army's left, southwest; while on the extreme left flank the Eighth Army of General Alexei Brusilov faced due west.

When General Dankl's First Army marched, to reach and take Lublin and Cholm, Auffenberg was to move in unison in the same direction. Brudermann's Third Army was, meanwhile, to stand fast in front of the city of Lemberg (Lvov) and guard it against any Russian threat that might materialize.

The first clash of arms in the campaign came on 23 August, when Salza's Fourth Army, moving southward in expectation of cutting off the rear of the Austrians—who he deemed to be driving east—ran into Dankl's advancing First Army at Krasnik. The Austrians, by weight of numbers, won the day; the Russians fell back and held their foe only some 18km/11mls from Lublin.

Conrad was determined to capitalize on the victory of Krasnik. On 25 August, he withdrew three divisions from the Third Army to support Auffenberg's right flank, in the hope of winning a decisive victory. General Brudermann, commanding the Third Army, although being depleted in

numbers, ordered his army, and much of the Kovess Army Group on his right, to move northeast to strike at the encircling Russian forces then marching on the town of Zloczov.

On 26 August, Brudermann ordered an advance to the Gnila-Lipa, a tributary of the River Dneister, and from there to the Zlota-Lipa, another tributary. He planned to engage what he believed to be weak Russian formations advancing from the east.

Conrad and Brudermann had seriously misjudged Russian strength and intentions, for the combined armies of Ruzski (Third) and Brusilov (Eighth), with 336 battalions, 264 squadrons and some 1,200 guns, outnumbered Brudermann by two and a half to one. And Brudermann was the only defence on the right flank of the Austrian First and Fourth armies in the north. On the 28th, the Austrian Second Army, withdrawn from Serbia, entered

Austrian Uhlans, or lancers, *top,* riding through a Polish village in Galicia, August 1914, are given a deferential welcome by the peasants.

A 30.5cm howitzer, *above,* being taken up to the front through Lemberg. These giant guns were transported in three sections.

Austrian infantry attacking at Lemberg, *right,* are supported by second-line troops with *Schwarzlose* machine-guns, while reserves await the chance to exploit a breakthrough.

the battle forming to the south of Brudermann's Third Army.

On the Russian side, the Battle of Krasnik had been a disagreeable surprise to Grand Duke Nicholas, but he persisted in the belief that Dankl's First Army was no more than an Austrian flank guard. He therefore ordered Plehve's Fifth Army to turn west to overlap and cut off the intruding and, so he supposed, insignificant Austrian thrust. This manoeuvre exposed the Russian Fifth Army's flank to Auffenberg's Fourth Army, still advancing northward, so Conrad commanded it to turn about and strike at the left flank of the Russian Third Army. At the same time, the Army Group led by Archduke Joseph Ferdinand, was to confront and hold the Russian Fifth Army, and the Austrian Second and Third armies were to strike eastward.

The Battle of Komarov that followed went largely in Austria's favour, since while Plehve was urging his army westward in accordance with the Grand Duke's instructions, the advancing Austrians were, in fact, forcing them to turn about and face south. The Austrians were not able to trap Plehve, and Conrad's plan was brought to nought, with consequences that were to prove disastrous.

The much-reduced Austrian Third Army, advancing toward the Zlota-Lipa, had been flung back by Brusilov's more numerous Eighth Army. The Austrians fell back first on the Gnila-Lipa, and many withdrew to the city of Lemberg 40km/ 25mls distant.

The Russians, needing to regroup their forces, delayed their pursuit for some 48 hours. So it was not until 30 August that

A defensive position near Lemberg, *left*, manned by Austrian infantry. The troops to the rear are braced, ready to repel any successful enemy attack.

Although Third Army on the far right of the Austro-Hungarian battle line, had been greatly depleted by the loss of three divisions to General Auffenberg's Fourth Army, their commander, General Brudermann remained sanguine.

As he began to move northeast, however, in an effort to reach the town of Zloczov, he found himself under threat from the Russian Third and Eighth armies (Ruski and Brusilov), which had crossed into Galicia intent on gaining the passes through the Carpathians.

Brudermann was instructed to make a 'short, sharp attack' on the Russians to halt their attack.

The afternoon was fine and hot, with summer storm clouds gathering on the horizon, when units of the opposing forces came in contact on 26 August 1914.

The swarthy-faced men of the 2nd Bosnian-Herzgovinian Regiment had orders to seize the high wooded ground near Gologory, prior to a further advance.

At about 15.00, they were moving out of Bortkòw (3) along the road to Gologory (7), when they became aware of the Russian soldiers, who had already established an outpost line on the heights.

The Russians (6) of Grand Duke Nicholas's Guard regiment were busy entrenching and setting up their machine-guns high among the trees on the hills overlooking the Bortkòw road.

Cossacks (5), who had been scouting near the Tarnopol to Lemberg railway (4) for information about the enemy, seeing the Austrian troops on the road, galloped back to join their comrades.

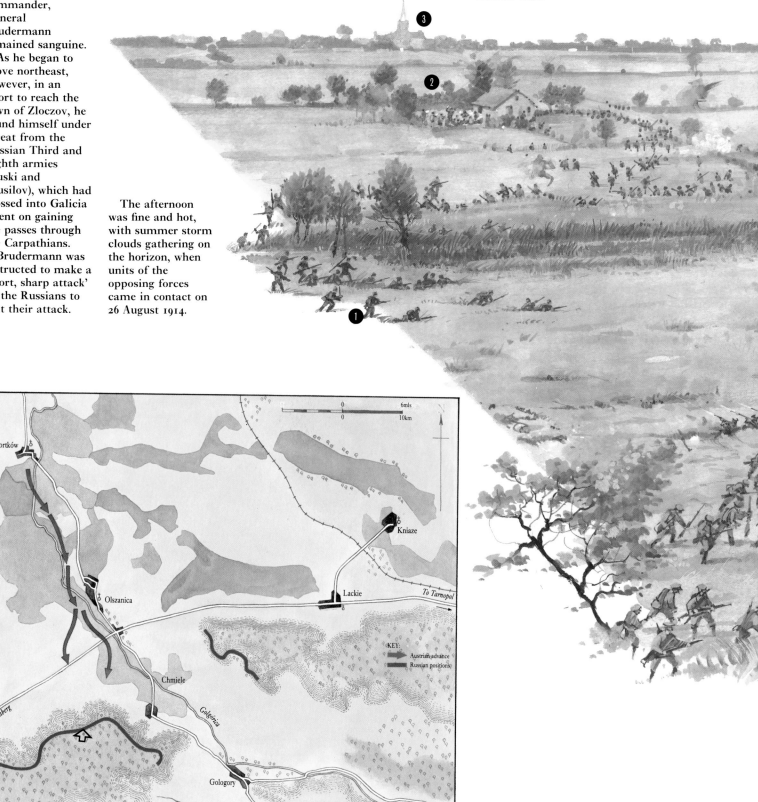

KEY:
→ Austrian advance
▬ Russian positions

The road at this point was slightly raised, for it ran through low-lying marshy meadows, and the 1st Battalion of the Bosnians advanced straight down it as if on manoeuvres. They were even played into battle by the regimental band (2), concealed behind a farm building.

Machine-gun fire took a terrible toll of the Bosnians, but some units managed to deploy (1) into the water meadows either side of the road and reached Russian lines. Fierce hand-to-hand fighting developed, but the result was never really in doubt.

The Bosnian's attack on Russian-held high ground was finally repelled and, since the rest of the division had not yet come up in support, the 1st Battalion was forced to retire. This formed only part of a more general retreat, and within days the Third Army had fallen back as far as Lemberg.

Brusilov struck hard at the Austrian right, causing it to collapse and its formations to retreat westward in panic and confusion. On 3 September, Conrad was obliged to order the evacuation of Lemberg.

But all was not yet lost, in Conrad's sanguine view, for his armies had been victorious in the north. By 30 August Auffenberg was behind Plehve's flanks and Dankl was thrusting deep between the Russian Fourth and Fifth armies—and a successful and decisive conclusion might yet be arrived at. He resolved to push on, despite the fact that Ruzski and Brusilov, though advancing tardily, were now at most 48km/30mls from severing the northern Austrian armies from their line of retreat, and Plehve had succeeded in

THE COMMANDERS

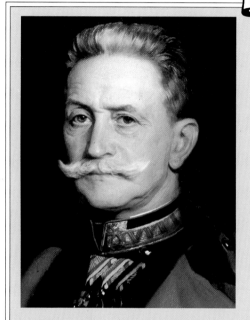

CONRAD VON HÖTZENDORFF

Field Marshal Conrad von Hötzendorff (1852–1925), although an outstanding strategist, came to ruin largely because the Austrian Army was too feeble and ill equipped to fulfil his offensive plans. In 1917 he was dismissed because he strongly opposed Emperor Charles I's peace overtures, but later held a command on the Italian Front.
Grand Duke Nicholas (1865–1929), second cousin of Tsar Nicholas II, was Commander-in-Chief of the Russian Army, directing operations against the Central Powers until September 1915, when the Tsar took over command. He later campaigned in the Caucasus, and after the revolution went first to Italy in 1919, then to France.

GRAND DUKE NICHOLAS

Galicia's great fortress

Przemysl, the principal Austrian fortress in Galicia, was also a beautiful town with a poulation in 1914 of some 50,000, mainly Poles and Ruthenes. The fortress was rebuilt in 1896 and by the outbreak of war had been further improved to accord with its new function as the Austrian Army's forward base against the Russians. It guarded the gap between the San River in the west and the upper Dniester in the east.

Standing on hills rising to a height of 420m/1,378ft, the fortress was a large, enclosed camp, mainly of earthworks strengthened by armoured cupolas. The heavy armament comprised 1,000 artillery pieces, but many were obsolete or short range. The main weapons were the 10 and 15cm cupola guns, dating from 1898, the 24cm mortars, and four of the new 30.5cm mortars. The defences were increased by a million metres of barbed wire and extensive minefields in 1912.

Russian forces invested Przemysl in the third week of September 1914, but it was only on 22 March 1915 that it fell, soon to be recaptured.

extricating his army from encirclement.

Conrad now conceived a new and even more grandiose strategy. With Plehve far from the field, Auffenberg, rather than going in pursuit, should change direction and strike the advancing armies of Ruzski and Brusilov from the north, while the Second Army, from Serbia, at last in position, struck from the south.

These manoeuvres were doomed to failure, for both Ruzski and Brusilov had been ordered to turn northwest, with the object of taking in rear all Austrian forces engaged with, or pursuing, Plehve. Furthermore, the Russian right wing had recently been reinforced by a new army, the Ninth, which had been raised for a drive on Berlin but was instead deployed against Austria. The Russian Fourth and Ninth armies were charged with thrusting around the Austrian left wing and then encircling their left-flank armies.

Despite numerous orders and changes in strategy, Conrad's position was now rapidly becoming untenable. To the northwest, Dankl's army was at bay before the combined might of the Russian Fourth and Ninth armies, and on 9 September it was obliged to retreat to the River San. Meanwhile Plehve's undefeated Fifth Army had turned about and was threatening to engulf Dankl's now unprotected right flank.

Conrad, faced with the crisis of the defeat of his plans, and with the destruction of his armies, on the 11th gave the order for overall retreat. Russian generalship was bold, sound and greatly superior to that of the Austrians and after Lemberg there was no halt in their pursuit.

In the fight for Lemberg itself, the Austrians lost, at a conservative estimate, 130,000 killed, wounded or taken prisoner. It is certain, however, that some 64,000 prisoners were taken. Most of these are thought to have been Slavs, whom the retreating Austrians had stationed in the rear to sustain the impact of Russian cavalry attacks. The Russians are believed to have detected this deployment and fired their shells at a high angle over the heads of the Slavs to hit the Austrians ahead.

Germany's ailing ally

As a result of the campaign, Austria lost Lemberg, the gateway to eastern Galicia and centre of all its rail and road networks. And shortly, in her armies' unremitting retreat, the great fortress of Przemysl was abandoned to siege. It finally fell, together with its garrison of 120,000 men, on 22 March 1915.

Just on two-thirds of the retreating Austrians reached the temporary sanctuary of the River San; then, on 16 September, Conrad was obliged to order a further retreat to the River Dunajec, 129km/80mls farther west. Soon all Galicia was abandoned. The Russians lost some 250,000 men, 40,000 of whom were taken prisoner, and 100 guns. But from an original total of about one million Austrian soldiers, more than 350,000 were lost, as were 300 guns.

This was grievous enough, but there was worse: the confidence and coherence of the Austrian Army had been broken in these first weeks of the war, and it was never again to comprise an efficient military weapon. Moreover, Germany was obliged to hurry from the west troops that could ill be spared, in order to succour her enfeebled and demoralized ally.

For Germany, the military situation was transformed by the end of 1914: in the west, stalemate; in the east, danger. During 1915, Germany and her bolstered ally, Austria, were to achieve great successes in the east and make large conquests of territory, but any prospect of a quick victory for the Central Powers, upon which all had been so confidently staked, were now forfeited beyond redemption.

Austrian hussars, *far left*, moving through Przemysl after its recapture on 3 June 1915. Newly arrived German infantry reserves march 'at ease' in the foreground. A supply column has been halted to allow their passage.

A casemate wall of a courtyard in the fortress, *left*. The casemates were used to store ammunition, each being separated from its neighbour by strong brickwork in case of an explosion. The armoured pillbox, for machine-guns and a cannon, could provide sweeping fire on any enemy intruder.

Battle of First Ypres *October–November 1914*

World War I was characterized by lack of invention and stubborn adherence to discredited strategy in the higher staff ranks; occasionally, however, the rival staffs produced manoeuvres of brilliance. Among these must rank the transference of the BEF from the Aisne to Flanders.

In the closing days of September 1914, following the Battle of the Marne, stalemate ensued on the line of the Aisne. Sir John French, Commander-in-Chief of the BEF, proposed to General Joseph Joffre, French Commander-in-Chief, that the British Army should be moved northward. He had two persuasive arguments to support this: not only would the BEF's line of communications to their bases in England be shortened, but the British troops, constantly being ferried across the Channel, could be concentrated in one area. Joffre was convinced, and the BEF reached its positions in Flanders between 16 and 18 October.

To remove an entire army in this way, secretly while within sight of the enemy, was a remarkable achievement of staff work. The complex procedures were executed without a hitch: artillery positions were abandoned by the British and smoothly taken over by French units; as British battalions moved out at night, their French replacements moved in—and all the while without any sign that the Germans recognized what they were about.

As General Joffre ordered his troops northward, the Germans followed suit. As they did so, their southern line became depleted, allowing more Allied units to be taken north from that sector. The BEF now comprised six divisions, an infantry brigade and two cavalry divisions.

Meanwhile, the siege of Antwerp was entered upon. Mindful of the manner in which the fortresses of Liège and Namur had been taken prior to the Battle of the Marne, at relatively little cost, by the use of the new and highly effective howitzer, General Erich von Falkenhayn ordered up a 42cm version of this formidable weapon and commenced the bombardment of the city's outer fortifications on the night of 27/28 September.

Belgium's allies were unable to offer any real assistance, but at least Winston Churchill, then First Lord of the Admiralty, understood the immense strategic importance of Antwerp. With passionate argument, he finally wrung permission from the British War Cabinet for three naval brigades to be dispatched to fortify the city, with himself in attendance. This was no more than a gesture but it helped sustain the morale of the Belgians.

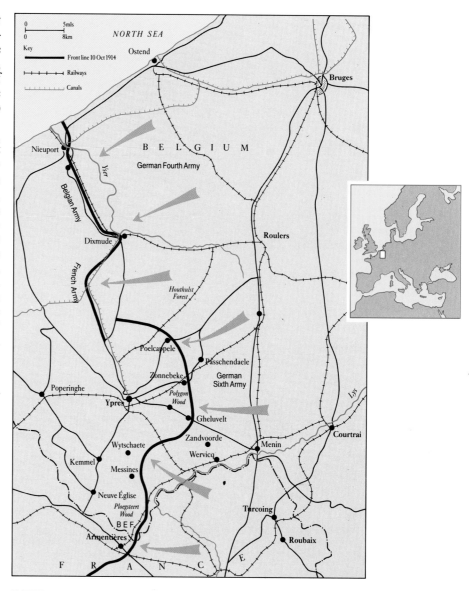

The 'race to the sea'

It was only after their defeat on the Marne and enforced retreat to the River Aisne that the Germans came to appreciate the importance of the Channel ports, ignored in the Schlieffen Plan. Dunkirk, Boulogne and Calais, through which British munitions and troops could pass in growing numbers, might have been taken at little cost during the Germans' initial advance, now they would have to be fought for.

General Erich von Falkenhayn, who had replaced the discredited Moltke as Chief of Staff on 14 September 1914, determined as a first measure to reduce the fortress of Antwerp, where King Albert, with the tenacious Belgian Field Army of six divisions, had taken refuge in August. In accordance with Schlieffen's plan, the Germans had brushed it aside during their thrust into northern France, but Antwerp had now become of crucial importance. If not taken, it would pose a grievous threat to the Germans' right when they made—as Falkenhayn planned—a second attempt to outflank the Allied left.

Large numbers of troops on both sides were moved from the south to the north of the front, following the deadlock on the River Aisne. These manoeuvres, expedited by good lateral railway systems in both France and Germany, became misleadingly known as 'the race to the sea'. In fact, neither side was at first attempting to reach the defensive flank of the North Sea; rather, each was hastening to get around the enemy's northern flank in the only area where mobile warfare was still possible on the Western Front.

The **repulse** of the German 3rd Reserve Corps on the Flooded River Yser is vividly conveyed by this coloured lithograph.

King Albert of the Belgians, in a desperate attempt to hold up the enemy advance, had ordered the lock gates on the canalized river at Nieuport to be opened, and thousands of German soldiers were caught by the rising waters and drowned.

The rifle: weapon of the infantryman

The firearm of the infantry soldier of World War I was the bolt-action rifle, and the rifles of all the armies were fundamentally much the same. Some had certain advantages, or were more reliable, but none was markedly superior.

Since the rifle was the infantryman's main weapon for both defence and attack, he took great care of it. Indeed, in Slav armies, the formal ceremony during which the rifle was presented to the soldier marked his transition from raw recruit to warrior.

The difference in attitudes to musketry between British and European armies was pronounced. The British, with experience gained in the Boer War, had designed a standard rifle, light and holding the maximum number of rounds for fast, aimed fire at a specific target. The Lee-Enfield had a magazine which held 10 rounds and a rapid-action bolt which turned down; this gave the rifleman a rate of fire of 15 aimed rounds or more a minute.

The European powers produced heavier rifles, which held fewer rounds. They were used for unaimed shots, fired from the hip by men advancing in mass, while a British infantryman was trained to shoot from a prone position at a target.

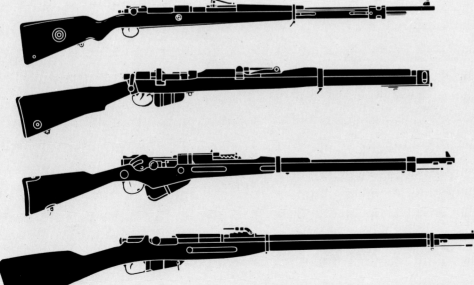

German Mauser M1898
Calibre: 7.2mm. Length: 125cm/49¼in. Weight: 4.3kg/9½lb. Magazine: 5 rounds. Muzzle velocity: 762m/2,500ft per second.

British Short Magazine Lee-Enfield MkIII
Calibre: .303in. Length: 113cm/44¼. Weight: 4kg/8⅞lb. Magazine: 10 rounds. Muzzle velocity: 628m/2,050ft per second.

French Lebel M1916
Calibre: 8mm. Length: 130cm/51¼in. Weight: 4.25kg/9 3/8lb. Magazine 8 rounds. Muzzle velocity: 725m/2.380ft per second.

Russian Moisin-Nagant M1891
Calibre: 7.62mm. Length: 130.5cm/51 2/5in. Weight 4.4kg/9 5/8lb. Magazine: 5 rounds. Muzzle velocity: 811m/2,660ft per second.

Partly because of this British presence, the Belgian Army was able to begin evacuating Antwerp on 8 October and to make an orderly retreat along the coast. It was covered by Lieutenant-General Sir Henry Rawlinson's 4th Corps, which two days before had landed at Ostend and Zeebruge. The inhabitants of Antwerp surrendered on 10 October.

By the second week of October, the Allied line, runing almost 800km/500mls from the North Sea to Switzerland, comprised, first, the retreating Belgian Army, then the French Eighth Army with, farther to their right and south, the British Expeditionary Force (BEF). Beyond this the line became the responsibility of the French Tenth Army. During that week, the BEF advanced eastward: the 2nd Corps toward La Bassée, the 3rd in the general direction of Armentières and the 1st Corps to the north, past Ypres.

Neither Marshal Joffre, General Foch (his deputy in the north) nor Sir John French had expected a German attack in Flanders. Indeed, they had reckoned German strength in the area to be at most one corps although British Intelligence had estimated it at three and a half corps—and even this, in the event, proved an underestimate. Thus, while the Allies thought they were embarking on an outflanking movement, they were in fact about to be attacked themselves.

The British 2nd Corps encountered the enemy on 10 October west of La Bassée, but, in face of heavy fighting, the German thrust petered out 10 days later with the British still about 1.6km/1ml west of the town. The 3rd Corps, meanwhile, though at great cost, had pushed eastward and reached Armentières. From here they hoped to command the bridges over the River Lys while the Cavalry Corps, under Major-General Sir Edmund Allenby, came up on their left; they could then, so they assumed, take the Germans in their right flank. The Germans were temporarily secure behind the bridges, however, and remained poised while they awaited the arrival of a new army of volunteers.

The advance of 1st Corps, commanded by General Sir Douglas Haig, to the north through Ypres had created an eastward-facing bulge in the line. When, on 21 October, their left wing became imperilled, the troops dug in and the line of the salient was formed.

The First Battle of Ypres fell into three distinct phases: the manoeuvres that brought the four Allied armies into position by about 20 October; the German attacks on the River Yser and at La Bassée and Arras; and the blows on the British

The city of Ypres, 'Wipers' to British soldiers since Marlborough's day, was renowned for the weaving of cloth in medieval times.

These two views, taken from the same spot, six years apart, show the ancient Cloth Hall. The hall as it had become by 1918, *bottom*, makes an awesome contrast with the view taken in 1912, *right*.

In 1914, Ypres was an important regional communications centre, but although it was flattened by constant artillery bombardment, the Germans did not manage to take it. What remained of the Cloth Hall and St Martin's Cathedral behind it, *centre*, by 1918 stood in a wilderness of rubble. The road on the right leads to the Menin Gate memorial.

After failing to overrun the Belgian defences along the North Sea coast, the chief object of the Germans' attack in Flanders in autumn 1918 became the capture of Ypres.

The town stood on the Flanders coastal plain, with a ridge of low hills lying between 4km/2½mls to 6.4km/4mls from it. These hills sloped down from Wytschaete (46m/150ft), through Verbrandenmolen and Gheluveldt, to Passchendaele (21m/70ft) in the northwest.

Ypres was a busy communications centre, with roads and railways radiating from it in all directions. It was also served by an extension of the Yser canal that ran to Comines on the French border.

It was evident that if the Germans could gain possession of both the high ground and the town, they could drive a wedge between the Allied armies. And, taking advantage of Ypres' position, they would be able to seize the coastal plain and ports with little difficulty.

German efforts to break through at Ypres began in the third week of October and, as the month progressed, they became much stronger. In the north, Fourth Army hammered at the French under de Mitry, while south of the Ypres-Roulers railway line they encountered the British. Below the Menin Road, Sixth Army, too, found itself in action against the BEF.

Despite renewed onslaughts in early November, German troops were still not able to break through.

Their last effort was made on 10 and 11 November. The right wing gained only 1.6km/1ml, the left no ground at all; and in the centre of the bulge, astride the Menin Road, the newly formed Army Group Linsingen met dogged opposition.

Any hope of pinching out the salient and encircling the town faded, and they ceased their efforts. From now on, the war in the west would be fought in the trenches.

1 Ypres
2 Bixschoote
3 Langemarck
4 Passchendaele
5 Ypres-Roulers railway
6 Zonnebeke
7 Gheluveldt
8 Menin Road
9 Zillebeke
10 Verbrandenmolen
11 Voormezeele

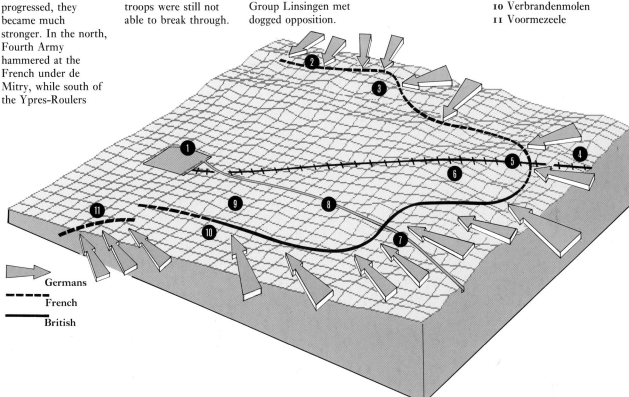

Germans →
French - - - -
British ———

salient that was forming east of Ypres.

Throughout the early days of October the Allies blithely assumed that Antwerp could withstand investiture. And Joffre, planning to extend his left flank, prior to eveloping the German right, appealed to King Albert of the Belgians to abandon the North Sea coast and thrust inland with the Belgian Army to join his swinging manoeuvre. With supreme strategical insight, King Albert declined to accede to the French commander's plea. Most fortunately for the Allies as it turned out, since within days Falkenhayn was to unleash all his troops from the area of fallen Antwerp, together with supplementary formations of volunteers, stiffened by regulars, in a massive stroke down the coastline, with the object of encircling the sanguine Joffre's left flank.

Through King Albert's foresight, the Belgian Army, though retreating, remained intact on the coast. Nevertheless, the Belgians were hard pressed and contrived to halt the German advance only on the River Yser and near Dixmude. On 24 October, the Belgians opened the locks on the canalized river at Nieuport, southwest of Ostend, allowing the sea gradually to flood great areas of the low-lying fenland in the enemy's path of advance. By 28 October the Germans were forced back by the rising waters, many were drowned and masses of weapons were lost.

This watery bulwark gave the Germans no option but to turn the mass of their force against the British salient, north, east and south of Ypres. From 29 October onward, fighting was continuous, both night and day, in conditions dominated by mud and wintery cold. At first, the Germans succeeded in penetrating a single point in the British line to the north. Then the southern British flank was broken open by a new German army of six divisions and massed artillery moving toward the Zandvoorde and Messines ridges. Here German numerical superiority of 2:1 made a hole in the line that could be only inadequately plugged.

The blow fell on the 7th Division and on Allenby's cavalry, which connected Haig's Corps with the 3rd Corps to its south. On 31 October—the third day of unremitting German attack—Haig's centre caved in at Gheluvelt and he ordered a withdrawal to a line just covering Ypres. Shortly afterward, however, a British counter-attack took the victorious and complacent Germans by surprise and ferreted them out of Gheluvelt, restoring the situation. Later the troops were again withdrawn to straighten the line.

French, it would seem, was no longer in touch with events, but German ineptitude came to his aid, for his enemy failed to exploit the penetrations they had achieved. On 1 November, the Germans again attacked the salient's belly, but this time at night, a ruse that enabled them to capture the Messines Ridge. The following morning, French forces arrived to succour the battered British line.

Then, on 10 November, the Germans launched a massive attack against the

FIRST YPRES/3

The flooding of the fenland near the mouth of the River Yser by the Belgians in October 1914 forced the main German assault south. They launched a fierce attack against the BEF in the salient that had formed around Ypres, with the object of seizing the ridge of high ground running from Passchendaele to beyond Menin.

Astride the Ypres-Menin road, at almost the highest spot, lay Gheluvelt, blocking the easiest approach to Ypres and providing good observation over a wide area.

On 29 October, wave after wave of German troops fell on the British defending the village, gradually driving them back.

By mid-morning on 31 October, the Germans had broken into the village itself. Men of the 2/Welch and 1/South Wales Borderers and 1/Scots Guards, in trenches north of the Menin Road, came under heavy artillery fire and were driven back into the grounds and stables of the château.

50

To prevent the line giving way, it was now essential to make a counter-attack. And soon after 12.00, Brigadier-General C. FitzClarence, in command of the front on the Menin Road, called upon almost his last reserves, the 2nd Battalion of the Worcestershire Regiment.

The men were resting in the hazy sunshine on the fringe of Polygon Wood, after almost 10 days in the front line, when the order came.

At 12.45, A Company advanced to a point on the embankment of the light railway (6) to prevent the Germans from moving out of Gheluvelt (5).

Scouts were sent out at about 13.45 to cut any wire fences, and extra ammunition was issued to B, C, and D companies. At 14.00, 370 men, including 7 officers, led by Major E.B. Hankey, filed with bayonets fixed along the edge of the wood to Black Watch Corner and across the shallow Reutelbeek.

In the shelter of a small wood, the companies extended into two lines, then advanced at the double over the rough open fields to the top of the Polderhoek ridge. Here they came under German artillery fire and more than 100 men fell dead or wounded.

The ragged lines of men (1) burst into the château grounds. With swords drawn (3) the officers ran forward, urging their men on.

The Germans, young Bavarians from the 16th Reserve Regiment, had been busy trying to round up troops of the South Wales Borderers who had occupied outhouses earlier in the day and were still holding out. They were taken by surprise; many were shot (2), and others crowded among the trees for cover.

The men of C Company rushed forward (4) and close fighting developed, but the Germans put up little resistance and soon retreated.

The Worcestershires were joined on the château lawn by the South Wales Borderers who greeted them with relief and gratitude.

B, C and D companies then took station along the sunken road, which they held under fierce bombardment.

A Company drove most of the Germans out of the burning village during the afternoon; but soon after 18.00 all British troops were withdrawn under cover of darkness to less exposed positions at Veldhoek.

Gheluvelt remained in German hands until 27 September 1918, but the Worcestershire's gallant counter-attack, during which 187 men were killed or wounded, helped save Ypres from almost certain capture.

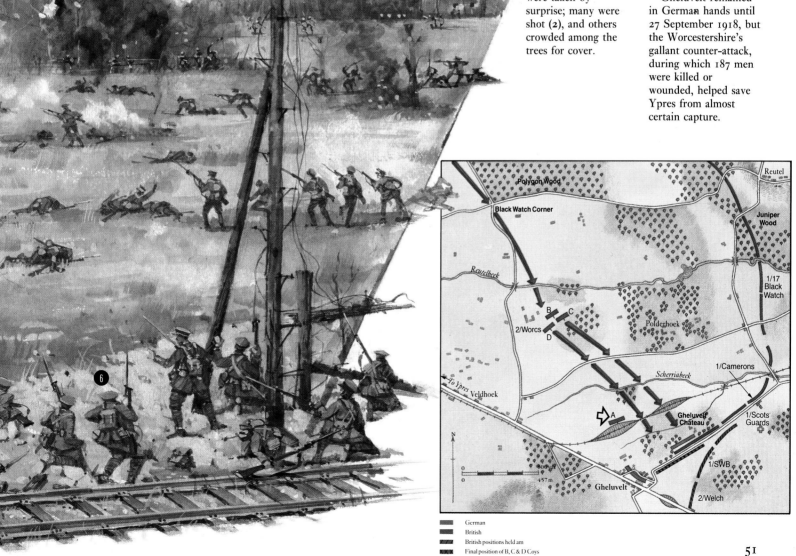

German
British
British positions held am
Final position of B, C & D Coys

In 1914, the strength of the BEF lay in the fact that its soldiers, like those, *left*, in a makeshift trench in Ploegsteert Wood near Ypres, were skilled marksmen. But the little army was almost wiped out in the battles of Mons, Marne and First Ypres, so Lord Kitchener, Secretary of State for War, set out to raise a huge volunteer army to replace the BEF.

He made great use of recruiting posters, of which the one with his portrait was the most celebrated. Others played on mens' consciences, at the same time showing an updated image of the army, with big guns and aircraft.

Kitchener's efforts increased Britain's strength from 20 divisions in 1914 to 70 in 1916, when conscription was introduced.

Field Marshal Sir John French (1852–1925) had had a long military career before the war, culminating in his appointment as Chief of the General Staff in 1912. He led the BEF from 1914 until December 1915, when he was replaced by Haig and was deputed to reorganize home defences.

FRENCH

His chief failing was a volatile nature, which caused him to swing from wild optimism to needless despair. At Ypres, when he finally perceived the danger of the German advance, he plunged from complacency to advocating the establishment of a camp at Boulogne from which the BEF might shortly be evacuated. But he was also susceptible to flattery, and it was Foch's blandishments that eventually induced French to stand firm at Ypres.

Albert I, King of the Belgians, (r1909–34) led his country's army throughout the war, and Belgium's brave resistance contributed greatly to Allied success. On 24 August 1914, to relieve the French and British fighting on the Sambre and at Mons, Albert ordered a sortie against the German right flank that tied up four reserve divisions and three Landwehr brigades. A second Belgian sortie reduced German strength on the Marne.

KING ALBERT

His tenacious defence of Antwerp and later decision to open the locks on the Yser were crucial to the successful outcome at Ypres. In 1918 Albert led the offensive to regain the Belgian coast.

After the war he did much to improve social conditions at home and in the Congo. He was killed in a climbing accident in 1934.

French in the north of the salient toward Dixmude. This was arrested, but the following day—11 November—a renewed German attack by the 4th Guards Division was launched in the southern sector against the British 1st Guards Brigade: the two crack units of the opposing armies. The Germans broke through the British line, but seemed unable, once again, to follow up their success, and were driven back by the last Allied reserves.

With that German failure the Allied crisis at Ypres ended, for more and more French troops had been brought up to sustain the salient's southern flank. German attacks wavered, then virtually ceased; though spasmodic fighting continued until 22 November, intense cold brought large-scale activities to an end.

A truth of modern warfare, which was first disclosed in the Russo–Japanese War (1904–5), had been underscored though leaders on neither side fully comprehended it as yet; defensive weaponry was more than a match for charging infantry. The Germans, indeed, had been so confused by British musketry that they had assumed the enemy was equipped with a plethora of machine-guns. In fact, the British had hardly any (often fewer than two to a battalion) but their infantrymen had mastered rapid rifleshooting. Fifteen aimed rounds a minute was usual, but many experienced marksmen would be able to discharge 30.

But, the British paid an inordinately high price for their prolonged, stubborn and ultimately triumphal resistance. Between 14 October and 30 November losses amounted to some 58,000 men. In all, from the war's outbreak to 30 November, the total was nearly 90,000; of these a disproportionate number were young officers and long-serving regular soldiers. The 7th Divison alone lost all but 44 of its 400 officers and 2,336 of its 12,000 men.

German losses in the fighting at Ypres are not precisely known, but their total losses on the Western Front from mid-October to 30 November appear to have been not far short of 150,000.

The beginning of stalemate

The First Battle of Ypres ranks as one of the great Allied, principally British, victories of the war. Between Armentières and the North Sea the Germans had massed 402 battalions, against which the Allies had only 267. Moreover, the Germans were twice as strong in cavalry.

The consequences of the battle and campaign were momentous. The Germans were denied the Channel ports, but the small, victorious British professional army was almost destroyed.

The battle was also a landmark in the conduct of the war, for henceforth both sides dug in and a complex line of trenches soon stretched from the North Sea to the Swiss frontier. For three and a half years these lines would be advanced less than 16km/10mls in either direction, and Allied strategy would be devoted to penetrating this formidable barrier.

The Germans, halted at Ypres, now adopted a defensive stance in the west while trying to reach a victorious conclusion in the east, where much of the military activity of 1915 was to take place.

The Gallipoli Campaign *March 1915—January 1916*

The Dardanelles, a strait some 60km/40mls long and varying from 1.6–6.4km/1–4mls wide, connect the Aegean Sea with the Sea of Marmara. The strait separates the Gallipoli Peninsula of European Turkey from Turkey in Asia and, with the Bosporus, is strategically of the utmost importance, since it is the only naval route from the Mediterranean to the Black Sea. The Dardanelles were, in 1915, also crucial to the defence of Constantinople (Istanbul).

The first phases of the campaign were exclusively naval operations, since it had been assumed by the British War Cabinet and the French that a naval force could not only bombard and destroy the Turkish forts on the peninsula but in some way occupy Constantinople. Winston Churchill repeatedly urged the Russians to cooperate by mounting a local offensive, but they declined.

The outer forts on the Dardanelles were bombarded on 19 February 1915, and the Greek island of Lemnos occupied as a base. Treacherous weather held up operations, but Marines were landed on the tip of the peninsula to demolish Turkish guns, which they achieved unmolested. Bombardment of the inner forts followed, and for some three weeks attempts—desultory at best—were made by trawlers to sweep the first line of mines. At this point Vice-Admiral Carden, commanding the squadron, fell ill and was replaced on 16 March by Vice-Admiral de Robeck, his second in command.

When the attempt to force the passage with naval craft on 18 March went disastrously wrong, de Robeck soon persuaded not only himself but many of the senior Allied commanders that the passage could not be forced by ships alone; a military expedition was also required. Thus the naval bombardment, which had, in fact, opened the way to Constantinople were the attack pressed home, served only to alert the Turks and their German ally to their peril in this area.

As a result of de Robeck's change of mind, on 26 March Lord Kitchener dispatched the Mediterranean Expeditionary Force from Egypt to make landings on the peninsula. This force of some 70,000 men, mainly Australians and New Zealanders, or 'Anzacs', with little battle experience, was commanded by Lieutenant-General Sir Ian Hamilton. He was reluctant to exercise authority over his subordinate generals, in direct contrast to the German General Liman von Sanders, in overall command of the Turkish forces. This was to have decisive consequences in the ensuing campaign.

Matters went awry for the Allies from the start. It was belatedly discovered at Lemnos that the transport ships had been incorrectly loaded so that crucial material, required immediately on landing, had been packed at the bottom of the holds. The ships were obliged to return to Alexandria for their contents to be restowed, causing a delay of almost a month.

The chance of surprise had already been forfeited. At the time of the preliminary naval bombardment the Turks had only two divisions at the Dardanelles; these had been raised to four when the naval attack began and six by the time Hamilton made his first landings, giving the defenders a numerical superiority of six to five divisions. Moreover, the north

Charles Dixon's painting, *right*, shows the *River Clyde*, an old collier, which had been converted to carrying troops, disembarking men on 'V' Beach, Cape Helles, during the British landings on 25 April.

Despite the speed with which troops were put ashore, 1,200 of the 1,500 men landed were brought down by Turkish machine-gunners on cliffs above the beach.

By the end of 1914, in the west, both the Germans and the Allies were digging trenches; and in the east, the advent of winter had also temporarily brought the war of movement to a halt. In October, however, Turkey, hoping to gain territory from Russia and to reinforce her flagging influence in the Balkans, had entered the war on the side of the Central Powers.

The bulk of her army was speedily dispatched to attack Russia in the Caucasus; the result, for Turkey, was disastrous. By January 1915, when the Turks were thrown back, they had lost some 70,000 men of an original total of 100,000, either killed or frozen to death.

The Commander-in-Chief of the Russian Army, Grand Duke Nicholas, then appealed to Field Marshal Lord Kitchener, British Secretary of State for War, to provide some relief from enemy pressure. When a British and, to a lesser extent, French landing in Turkey was resolved upon, the site was obvious: the Gallipoli Peninsula.

If the assault proved successful, Egypt would no longer be vulnerable to attack (the Turks had already sent a force to attempt to seize the Suez Canal) and Turkey's traditional enemies in the Balkans might be won over to the Allies. In addition, once Constantinople (Istanbul) was taken, Russia would have a year-round, ice-free sea passage, allowing her to export much-needed wheat to the western Allies and to receive arms and ammunition.

The strategic concept had everything in its favour; for success it required efficient planning and ruthless aggression. In the event, neither was to be forthcoming.

A CALL FROM THE DARDANELLES

"Coo—ee—
Won't YOU
come?"

GULF OF SAROS

GALLIPOLI

SEA OF
MARMORA

ENLIST NOW

1915'de
Çanakkale'de
TÜRK

shore of the strait consisted mainly of steep sandy cliffs, rising from the sea to a height of 30–90m/100–300ft, terrain that provided ideal cover and artillery sites for the Turks, while leaving the invaders perilously exposed.

Preparations for the landings were mostly inept and inadequate. Although a Turkish Army handbook existed, the command structure of the Turkish Army had not been studied, nor its dispositions and strength verified. No thorough reconnaissance of the landing sites had been possible and maps had largely been taken from tourist guide books.

Remarkably similar propaganda posters were produced by both sides. The Turkish one extols their successful defence of Çanakkale; the Australian recruiting poster paints a sanguine picture of conditions and prospects.

Naval action in the strait

The Allied attempt to force the passage of the Dardanelles with capital ships on 18 March could well have succeeded, had it not been for a seemingly insignificant event. The main lines of Turkish mines were laid in the Narrows, but on 8 March a small Turkish vessel had laid another line of 20 mines close to the shore of Eren Keui Bay. Three of these were cleared on 16 March but, believing them to be floating mines, the Allies did not completely sweep the area.

By about 13.30 on 18 March, the guns of the main Turkish batteries had almost all been put out of action by long-range bombardment by Allied ships. The mine-sweepers were, therefore, sent even farther into the Dardanelles to complete their work, while the French warships, hitherto in the van of the fleet, were withdrawn. As they passed back through Eren Keui Bay, at 13.55 *Bouvet* struck a mine and went to the bottom with her crew within two minutes.

Some two hours later, shortly after 16.00, the British vessels *Irresistible* and *Inflexible* were holed; *Gaulois*, too, was holed. *Ocean*, ordered to the aid of *Irresistible*, was struck in turn, and later both sank.

Vice-Admiral de Robeck, unaware of the true cause of the disaster and fearing the presence of land-based torpedoes, seems either to have lost his nerve or simply to have resolved on caution. He ordered a general retirement of the flotilla, not realizing that the Turkish guns were mostly destroyed and the surviving gunners exhausted. The opportunity to press home the naval attack was thus lost and with it the possibility of the overthrow of Turkey.

Despite being outnumbered, unaware of the enemy's dispositions and ignorant of the terrain, Hamilton was ordered to make the first British landings on 25 April at the southern tip of the peninsula near Cape Helles, while Anzac troops went ashore about 24km/15mls farther up the Aegean coast near Gaba Tepe. At about the same time, French units made a diversionary landing at Kum Kale on the Asiatic side of the strait to confuse the Turks as to the Allies' true intentions.

The invading force left Mudros on the island of Lemnos on the morning of 23 April and moved toward its stations off the landing beaches. Some 200 ships were involved and by midnight on 24 April they were in position off the Gallipoli coast. All engines were stopped, the troops given a meal and then, in orderly fashion, embarked on lighters and later transferred to rowing boats, which put them ashore. That part of the operation—and almost solely that part—went according to plan.

British submarines waged a highly effective campaign against Turkish ships, coastal installations and even railways. Here the crew of HMS *Grampus* cheers one of the most daring and successful submarines, E11, as she surfaces after an exploit. Between May and August 1915, she sank five Turkish ships, including the merchant ship *Stambul*, lying actually in the Golden Horn at Constantinople, and the battleship *Barbarousse Haireddine*.

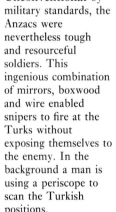

In the summer of 1915, in an effort to break the stalemate, Hamilton decided to make another landing, at Suvla Bay to the north.

At the same time, there was to be a major assault out of Anzac by the New Zealand infantry and Indian and Australian troops. The Suvla and Anzac forces were then to link up on the high ground overlooking the Narrows.

On the night of 6/7 August, Birdwood's forces moved up from the coast to try to gain the Sari Bair ridge, Chunuk Bair and Hill 971. Turkish resistance was fierce and a bloody battle, lasting until the 10th, took place. Many thousands of men on both sides died but the Anzacs could not gain their objectives. Stalemate persisted.

Plan of attack:
1 Hill 971; 2 Hill Q;
3 Chunuk Bair;
4 Existing Anzac line;
5 New Zealand
infantry; 6 Australian
and Indian troops.

This panorama, made up from photographs taken from No 1 Outpost, just above the beach about 0.4km/¼ml north of Ari Burnu, shows Table Top (1), Rhododendron Ridge (2), Chunuk Bair (3), Snipers' Nest (4), Battleship Hill (5) and Baby 700 (6).

The Anzacs had to fight in this wild, rugged terrain when they attacked in early August. The dry, eroded hillsides, which became churned clay when wet, were patchily covered in gorse, with here and there a scrub oak or olive tree.

Unconventional by military standards, the Anzacs were nevertheless tough and resourceful soldiers. This ingenious combination of mirrors, boxwood and wire enabled snipers to fire at the Turks without exposing themselves to the enemy. In the background a man is using a periscope to scan the Turkish positions.

Hamilton elected to station himself on the *Queen Elizabeth*, de Robeck's flagship. He would have done better to board a fast, independent ship with good signalling equipment, for on the *Queen Elizabeth*, which had been given tasks of her own, he became a virtual prisoner, unable to respond to events or give directions. Thus Hamilton cruised up and down the coast, out of touch with what was happening on the beaches.

All decisions had to be made by his two corps commanders. Lieutenant-General Hunter-Weston (whose pre-battle proclamation to his troops pessimistically stated that heavy losses were to be expected) commanded British 29th Division, which landed at Cape Helles, and Major-General Sir William Birdwood the Anzac forces. However, these two commanders also remained at sea throughout the landings and so had as little idea as Hamilton of what was going forward.

Each unit, once landed, had therefore to make its own decisions undirected by the higher command, with the result that one company, though separated by only a short distance from the next, could be unaware of what their comrades were attempting.

But there was worse. Shortly after 04.00 on 25 April, 1,500 men of the first Anzac assault wave got safely ashore—at the wrong place. Unknown to the insufficiently briefed navigators, a strong current had swept the boats about 1.6km/1ml north of the intended spot. Instead of landing on a sandy beach stretching some way inland, the men were trapped on a rocky shore north and south of the craggy headland of Ari Burnu. Nevertheless, because the Turks thought it inconceivable that their enemy would land in such an inhospitable situation the Anzacs met little opposition, and, four hours after the initial landing, some 8,000 men were safely ashore. They made good progress and some were soon scaling the dominating ridge leading to Chunuk Bair.

Now another misfortune befell the invaders. Mustafa Kemal, the one Turkish soldier of genius in the area, arrived on the scene. He immediately garrisoned the crucially important Chunuk Bair and Sari Bair ridges and halted the Anzac advance. Had the attack been properly organized and coordinated, these vital heights might have been taken with little loss and the successes consolidated. As it was, some 50,000 soldiers were to lose their lives during the next few months in fruitless attacks on Chunuk Bair.

Around Cape Helles, inefficiency and disorder likewise reigned. Shortly after

GALLIPOLI/3

On 8 December 1915, the order was given to evacuate the Anzac beachhead. In the fierce winter storm of November, hundreds of men had frozen to death, and casualties and illness were steadily mounting; the War Cabinet decided to cut its losses.

Major-General Birdwood's plan was to take off as much equipment and as many of the 97 guns as possible over a 10-day period. At the same time, about half the 36,000 men would be removed, the final 22,000 being taken off on the nights of 18/19 and 19/20 December. The whole scheme depended on secrecy and good weather.

So as not to arouse the Turks' suspicions, the work went on only at night. By day the pattern of artillery fire interspersed with days of quiet or fire from naval guns continued. As numbers of men dwindled, those left behind moved up and down the trenches, firing rifles from points all along the front, to maintain the illusion of a large, vigilant force.

All the Anzacs' subterfuges succeeded. The Turks interpreted the activity and the build-up of supply dumps by the shore as signs of a probable attack and at no time realized what was actually happening.

By the night of 19 December, only some 10,000 men were left at Anzac.

The troops had been divided into three parties. The first, A Party, of 4,000 men was to embark as soon as it got dark; B Party, also 4,000 men, was to withdraw between 19.00 and 23.00. After that, only 2,000 men would be left to guard the entire beachhead.

Each man had a card with written instructions as to the time he was to leave his post and the route he was to follow to the shore. Nothing was left to chance.

The night was fine, with a full moon, the sea dead calm. Paths not overlooked by the Turks had been dug over and marked with salt, sugar and flour. At junctions, signs such as coloured lights burning inside a tin showed the way. Boots were wrapped in sacking to muffle all sound.

By 03.00 on the 20th, the 275 men of the handpicked final garrison were clear of the hills, and the three huge mines laid at the Nek (1) were detonated. A red glare briefly lit up the undersides of great clouds of dust and smoke that rose above the spot.

At North Beach (2), hospital tents had been left standing, and there were huge dumps of supplies: ration boxes, old clothes, a motorbike or two, carts without wheels and a water distillation plant.

Existing piers had been strengthened and a new pier (3) and walkway built out to the *Milo* (5). This old steamer had been sunk at the end of October to act as a breakwater.

Silent as cats, lighters (4) loaded with men— 400 in a full load—had been plying between the piers and ships lying offshore all night. Now the last 600 or so men waited quietly to be taken off.

The operation went exactly to plan; only one man was wounded and nine guns left behind. As a German critic later wrote: 'So long as wars exist, the British evacuation . . . will stand before the eyes of all strategists of retreat as a hitherto quite unattained enterprise'.

the 29th Division began landing, officers walked unmolested to the village of Krithia some 3km/2mls inland and to the 180m/600ft high summit of Achi Baba, commanding positions from which it would have been easy to repel any Turkish counter-attack. But the officers had been given no orders to occupy these positions, so they simply returned to their lines to await instructions. By the time the order to push forward was given, Turkish forces had moved up; and here also thousands of lives were to be lost to gain positions which had, in effect, already been won.

Thus, almost immediately, the chief object of the campaign—a quick victory to restore mobile warfare in contrast to the stalemate on the Western Front—was forfeit. The troops began to dig trenches, as their comrades had in France.

For the next three months virtual deadlock ensued, troops dug in as best they could, and lives were lost through disease and fruitless assaults. In July, fearful of a disaster, the British Government dispatched a further five divisions to bolster the seven already deployed. But by the time of their landing the Turks had massed 15 divisions. Hamilton, faced with this inequality of manpower, resolved on a master stroke: a further landing, this time to the north at Suvla Bay. He hoped to sever the peninsula and, in company with the troops at Anzac Bay, to gain the high ground dominating the Narrows to the east.

The plan, although strategically sound, was doomed from the beginning, for the officer appointed to command the undertaking was Lieutenant-General Sir Frederick Stopford. He was an ailing man of 61 who had never commanded in the field, knew nothing of Gallipoli and was appointed solely because of seniority on the army list. The result was predictable.

The landings on the night of 6–7

Australian troops rest in a captured trench on 26 April, the day after the landings at Anzac Beach.

In December 1915, men of 5th Brigade at Steele's Post lived in conditions like those of a gold rush camp. The front trench was just 9m/10yds from the crest and, mindful of accurate Turkish artillery fire, they tucked their shacks into the hillside so they were vulnerable only to howitzers.

One of the many stratagems employed by the Anzacs during the evacuation, to hoodwink the Turks, was to leave rifles cocked and set in position along the front. Two cans were attached to each rifle, the top can being filled with water, which slowly dripped into the lower can. When this was full, the weight pulled a wire which had been attached to the trigger, and the gun went off.

HAMILTON

BIRDWOOD

SANDERS

KEMAL

General Sir Ian Hamilton (1853–1947) was a highly professional soldier who had served in many campaigns in Asia and Africa, and in 1904–5 was British military attaché with the Japanese in their war with Russia. He had no knowledge of the Turkish Army or of the terrain, nor was he given time to acquire any, since he left for the Dardanelles the day after becoming commander-in-chief.
He was a scholarly man and a gifted writer.

Major-General Sir William Birdwood (1865–1951) was born in India and, as a junior officer, saw action on the North West Frontier and later in the Boer War. He then again served in India until 1915, when he was selected to command the Anzacs. Birdwood planned and carried out their evacuation with consummate skill. He continued to lead the Anzacs on the Western Front until, in May 1918, he took command of the British Fifth Army.

General Otto Liman von Sanders (1855–1929) was appointed head of the German military mission to Turkey in 1913, and Inspector-General of her army. It was at his insistence that the defences of the Dardanelles and the Gallipoli Peninsula were strengthened and updated. When Turkey entered the war, he commanded her army and brought to the fore the gifted Mustafa Kemal. In 1918, Sanders was given supreme command in Palestine.

Colonel Mustafa Kemal (1881–1938) joined the Young Turks, a liberal movement, early in his career. Later (1911–12) he served in Libya and, in 1913, in the Second Balkan War. It was the Gallipoli campaign, however, that brought him to prominence. After the war, he established a rival government to that of the sultan and in 1922 became president of the new republic. During his 15-year rule he dramatically westernized Turkey.

August, though safely made, were not exploited. The troops, lacking adequate maps and orders, wandered about the shore in disarray; many had been landed indiscriminately (often in the wrong place) and stores and ammunition had been stockpiled without regard to their future use. Along the length of the coast the story was now everywhere the same: Allied troops hanging on to vulnerable footholds, saved from annihilation only by their dogged courage.

The British Government had, by late autumn, begun to sense that the situation was hopeless and was veering toward an immediate withdrawal. Hamilton, asked for his views, advocated continuing the struggle and, in consequence, was recalled on 15 October. His replacement, Lieutenant-General Sir Charles Monro, who did not even bother to land on the peninsula, declared for evacuation. Winston Churchill was to sum up his appraisal in a contemptuous phrase: 'He came, he saw, he capitulated.'

The withdrawal—the one successful feature of the entire campaign—began at Suvla Bay and Anzac Beach during the night of 18 December, and from Cape Helles on 8 January 1916. High-ranking officers, notably Hamilton himself, estimated that as many as 50,000 lives might be lost in the operations: in the event every surviving man was taken safely away. Nevertheless, the Allies had suffered 252,000 casualties out of a total commitment of 480,000. The Turks admitted similar losses, but the correct figure is generally believed by historians to be considerably higher.

The penalties of failure

The Gallipoli campaign was a daring, imaginative scheme, thrown away, as Field Marshal Montgomery was to write, 'because of every conceivable mistake in its execution by the commanders'. For the Allies the consequences were dire. Many lives had been lost, Turkey continued active on the side of the Central Powers, and the passage from the Black Sea remained closed to Russia, leaving her still separated from, and unsupplied by, her allies. This was to prove crucial to her collapse, revolution, and withdrawal from the war in 1917.

Although a signal failure, the campaign produced one benefit for the Allies: it destroyed some of the best Turkish units, facilitating Allenby's later victories in Palestine. This advantage was, however, more than offset by the fact that those senior Allied officers and statesmen who had advocated the invasion of Turkey, in order to step up the pressure on the Central Powers in the Middle East and so save lives in the war of attrition in France, had lost the argument. More years of trench warfare and carnage on the Western Front were now almost unavoidable.

Action & Stalemate *1915*

It was already clear by November 1914 that the war would not 'be over by Christmas', as so many had optimistically supposed. Deadlock, total and seemingly unbreakable, obtained both at sea and on the Western Front.

Lying idle in impregnable harbours, the German fleet could not be enticed to battle by the British, while on land the trench line—now being hastily dug and fortified—ran without interruption along the entire battlefront. Moreover, hitherto unexploited elements of warfare—defensive barbed wire and massed machineguns—were being deployed along the whole front of some 563 km/350 mls, manned for the first time in history by millions of men.

This produced a tactical problem as yet

'La Patrouille', a painting by Georges Scott, *right*, depicts a French infantry patrol crawling through barbed wire. Night patrols were of three types: standing patrols, when men kept station for some hours; fighting patrols, when the object was to kill the enemy, and patrols sent out to capture a prisoner and bring him in for questioning. The last was generally the most useful.

'Soldats Masques', by Zingg, *left*, creates a powerful image of the inhumanity and horror of gas warfare. When the first attacks were made in 1915, men's only protection was a damp cloth over nose and mouth; the grotesque box masks were introduced later.

Joseph Gray's painting, *right*, shows a ration party of the Black Watch bringing up provisions at night during the fighting at Neuve Chapelle on 10–12 March 1915.

unknown. Until 1915, there had always existed the possibility of making a short or wide turning movement of one or other of an enemy's flanks; that option no longer existed. But a frontal attack in the face of barbed wire and entrenched machineguns was unlikely to succeed, and it guaranteed heavy losses.

There was a further problem: to destroy the barbed-wire obstacles necessitated a prolonged artillery barrage, which in turn removed the crucial element of surprise. So on the Western Front a monstrous war of attrition developed in which hundreds of thousands of soldiers were thrown in repeated and hopeless assaults against their enemy.

The spring of 1915 thus found the Allies dug in opposite the German Army,

which had been halted on the Marne. The immediate victory on which Germany had counted had been denied her, though she had overrun Belgium and now occupied the industrial districts of northeastern France. In the east, despite Germany's great success at the Battle of Tannenberg, Russian mobilization of her limitless manpower enabled her again to threaten East Prussia and, in the south, Galicia.

Furthermore, the Central Powers were virtually besieged and cut off from their new ally, Turkey, which had entered the war in October 1914. Italy was to join the war on the Allied side on 23 May 1915, although at first her declaration of hostilities specified Austria-Hungary only. Moreover, the German Navy, blockaded in harbour, was unable to succour German

colonies in Africa and Asia, which by 1915 were being rapidly overrun. Japan, too, had joined the conflict on the Allied side on 23 August 1914 and had swiftly helped herself to German possessions in the east, including the Carolina group of islands on 7 October and Kiauchau on 7 November.

All the evidence seemed, at first glance, to indicate Allied victory during the course of 1915. However, there were other, potent factors involved. The Allied command was not unified. In Great Britain, Lord Kitchener was the commanding voice; in France, General Joffre; and in Russia, the Grand Duke Nicholas. Each was capable in his way but no overall strategy for 1915 was devised between them. Furthermore, Germany was making offensive preparations with Teutonic

thoroughness, producing munitions and enlisting soldiers at a far greater rate than the more sanguine Allies.

Hindenburg, following the triumph of Tannenberg in August 1914, was now a German hero and could, in effect, reverse Schlieffen's plan: that is, seek a decisive victory in the east while merely containing the Western Front. New tactics were to be used against the Russians in which the destructive power of artillery fire would be the principal weapon. Heavy guns would support the fire of the usual fieldpieces.

Before the Germans were ready to attack, however, the Russians renewed their thrusts westward in the spring, both into East Prussia and toward the Carpathians. During the latter offensive, they captured the great Austrian fortress of Przemysl on 22 March. But in the north they suffered a great defeat in the area of the Masurian Lakes ('The Winter Battle', 7–21 February) and retired behind their frontier, never again to mount an attack on East Prussia.

Russia's success against the Austrians on the southern front marked the high point of her advance, for she was doubly burdened. Her industries produced an inadequate supply of munitions and weaponry and, in 1915, with stalemate in the west, she had to bear the full offensive impact of the Central Powers.

With the Russian advance everywhere either stemmed or repulsed, the Central

On 7 May 1915, a German U-boat sank the unarmed British liner *Lusitania*; 1,195 people died, including 128 Americans. The Germans issued a medal to mark the event but, curiously, dated it '5 Mai'. The British seized on this, since it appeared to damn the sinking as premeditated, and they issued 300,000, medals like the one above, to arouse anti-German feeling in America. The Germans hurriedly withdrew their medals and later reissued them; this time inscribed with the correct date.

Powers (or rather Germany, who was now obliged to sustain her flagging ally) implemented earlier plans for massive drives eastward. The main blow, under General August von Mackensen, was to be delivered in Galicia, with a subsidiary thrust in the north, through Courland toward Riga, by General Otto von Below.

The German attack in Galicia, centred on Gorlice, began on 28 April and, by the concentrated deployment of great quantities of artillery, swept the Russians east in disarray. And by the first days of May,

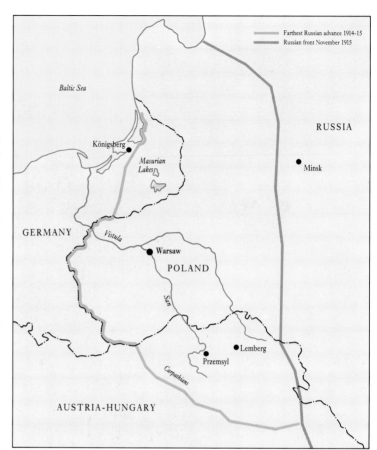

This German vivat band celebrates the surrender of the British garrison at Kut-el-Amara, in Mesopotamia, to the Turks in April 1916.

the entire Russian line in the area was in flight. This, in turn, exposed the flank of Russian troops in the Carpathians under General Brusilov, and they, too, were obliged to withdraw. On 3 June, the fortress of Przemysl was retaken as the Germans thrust east toward Lemberg.

In the north, the German advance from East Prussia had taken them as far as Windau, near the Gulf of Riga. But now a more menacing threat was posed for Russia: massed German units were attacking the Polish salient from the north, while Austro-German armies thrust up from the southeast—precisely the strategy that the Austrian commander General Conrad von Hötzendorff had advocated in 1914. The great German superiority in artillery made the outcome inevitable: the Russians abandoned Warsaw and the city was occupied by the Germans on 5 August.

The Austro-German advance became an irresistible tide, forcing the Russians to retreat to a line running almost straight, north to south, from Riga to Czernowitz. Russian losses were massive—General Falkenhayn estimated human loss at about 'three-quarters of a million men in prisoners alone'—and artillery and weaponry of all kinds had been taken in great quantity. For Russia, for the Allies, the brief campaign had proved a disaster of unsurpassed magnitude and marked the beginning of the disintegration of the Russian Army.

As a result, Mackensen was freed to attack the northern region of Serbia; and Bulgaria, which had been watching the fortunes of war, anxious to identify the winning side, joined the Central Powers on 6 September 1915. She, too, invaded Serbia, which was overrun and virtually ceased to exist as a nation. Thus the Central Powers had conquered the neutral region that separated them from their ally in the east, Turkey.

The gloom was equally profound for the Allies elsewhere. Stalemate prevailed on the Italian Front and all their offensives on the Western Front had been frustrated with heavy loss—at Neuve Chapelle (March), at Ypres (April) and in Champagne and at Loos (September). The Gallipoli campaign ended in dismal and costly failure, with withdrawal from the peninsula commencing on 19 December.

After the Central Powers' invasion of Serbia, a British and French force was landed at Salonika. But the Bulgarians swept around the Serbian Army, cutting it off from any Allied aid. However, troops and guns, such as this 60-pounder, remained in Salonika until 1918. The gun had a long recoil of 1.5m/56in, so the wheels gouged deep ruts, and it needed frequent realigning.

Austrian infantry, *left*, have been temporarily taken off the road to allow the passage of German infantry units in the advance on Przemysl, which was recaptured by their joint forces on 3 June 1915.

Italians hauling a heavy gun, *above*, through a pass on the Isonzo. This area was the most heavily fought over in the Italian theatre.

Germany and Austria had begun the year of 1915 besieged in central Europe; now the strategic situation was transformed in their favour. As 1916 dawned, the Allies were unable to plan any immediate offensive, since the new British armies were not yet ready; but the Central Powers could plan two: one at Verdun and an Austrian attack on Italy.

Battle of *Verdun* *February–December 1916*

Verdun was the longest battle of World War I, among the most costly in life, and militarily the most pointless. In February 1916, when the battle opened, the Western Front ran south from the Ostend area, east to Verdun and then roughly southeast to the Swiss frontier. Verdun itself was situated on the River Meuse in the middle of a horseshoe-shaped salient. Even a glance at the map shows that the French would at this time have been strategically much better placed without

Verdun, for withdrawal would have straightened and shortened their line, thus strengthening it.

Another factor also should have brought the French staff to this conclusion: the great fortress, and its double defensive ring of 21 smaller forts, had recently been shorn of many guns for service elsewhere on the Western Front. General Joseph Joffre, the French Commander-in-Chief, following Germany's easy capture of Liège and Namur early in the war, had lost all confidence in the defensive capability of fortresses. In reality, though this was not generally known, Verdun was now guarded by a single line of trenches—and a single line could be penetrated by the enemy with relative ease, whereas two could not.

A certain Lieutenant-Colonel Driant, the Deputy (parliamentary representative) for Nancy, who in 1916 was serving in the Verdun sector, took the opportunity, when on leave in Paris, to inform the Army Commission and his brother deputies of the true state of affairs. This was duly reported to General Joseph Galliéni, now Minister of War, who had heard similar disquieting news from other

---

Falkenhayn's fateful scheme

By 1916, bereft of most of its heavy guns for service elsewhere, the fortress of Verdun was of little strategic importance to France, still less to Germany. To the French, however, it was a symbol of national pride.

Verdun had a long history: it was an important city in Roman times; Vauban, the great fortress builder of Louis XIV's reign, had fortified it with ditches and bastions; in the Franco–Prussian War of 1870–1 Verdun had withstood a siege of 10 weeks, falling only through lack of supplies. Most important of all, Verdun was the principal eastern bulwark of France, standing opposite the enemy's citadel of Metz.

Verdun epitomised France's grandeur, in some measure her history, and above all her proud independence. The fortress and city could be ceded without great military

significance, but the blow to the national spirit of France would be calamitous.

Therein lay the cunning intention of the German Chief of the General Staff, General Erich von Falkenhayn. This enigmatic man—one reluctant to disclose his plans even to his closest associates and so often the military miscalculator—in this instance judged the French national character correctly: if the Germans attacked Verdun, the French would resist.

Once it was shown that Verdun was deemed worth capturing, it must be worth defending; if worth defending, then worth taking. In this way, the bulk of the French Army would be drawn into the battle, bled white, and its spirit broken. Thus the two powers became locked in a struggle for a citadel of no military value to either.

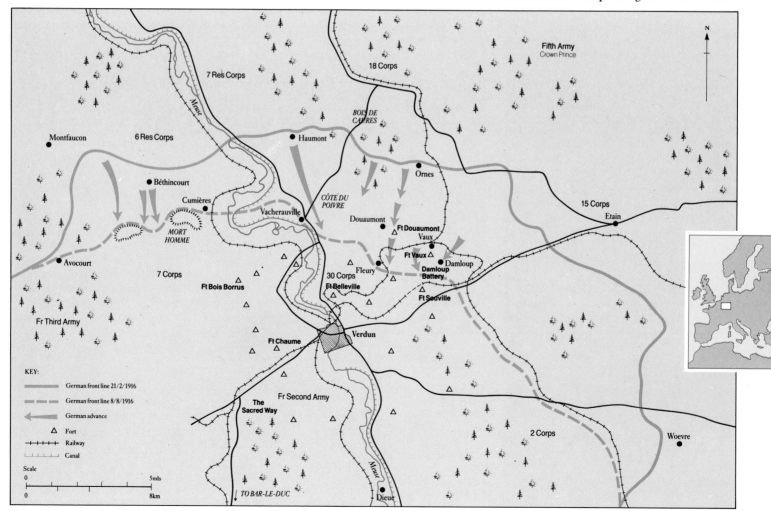

KEY:
— German front line 21/2/1916
-- German front line 8/8/1916
← German advance
△ Fort
+++ Railway
⊥⊥⊥ Canal

Scale
0 — 5mls
0 — 8km

French private, *left*, of the 22nd Regiment of Infantry, 1914. From 1915, soldiers wore steel skull caps under their képis. By the time of Verdun, they had horizon-blue field uniforms and steel helmets, like this private, *right*, of the 56th Regiment. Both men carry an 8mm Lebel rifle M1886–93, with a sword bayonet.

Falkenhayn tried to defeat the French at Verdun by constant bombardment with heavy guns such as the 42cm 'Big Bertha', *below*. The resulting devastation can be seen in the aerial view, *right*: shell holes and a network of ruined trenches and communications trenches zigzagging across a hillside. Three French *poilus*, *below right*, take cover in a shell hole in the midst of the desolation.

The French replied with equally savage gunfire, as the piles of shell cases being removed for melting and re-use, *opposite*, testify. In 10 months, 37 million shells, German and French, were fired.

sources. Gallièni at once wrote to Joffre, calling for a full report.

Joffre was outraged. He replied that there was no substance in the allegation of French unpreparedness in the Verdun sector and asked for the names of those who had given Gallièni the information so that they might be admonished. 'I cannot', he wrote, 'be party to soldiers placed under my command bringing before the Government, by channels other than the hierarchic channel, complaints or protests concerning the execution of my orders.' This petulant and bureaucratic state of mind did not bode well for the conduct of a battle that was now plainly imminent.

Falkenhayn gave Crown Prince Wilhelm, commanding the Fifth Army, a clear assurance that the object of Operation 'Gericht' was to seize the fortress. Yet, if that were so, why did his plan entail an attack from the east bank of the Meuse only, and not from the west bank also, to achieve a successful pincer operation? Some have argued that the first attack was intended to lure the French forces to the east bank, so leaving a German attack on the west bank relatively unopposed.

Indeed, Falkenhayn never attempted to break through the enemy lines—so far the sole tactic attempted by both sides—but planned rather to bleed France white by attacking that which the French nation would not tolerate being taken.

To this end he had devised a new strategy: the assault was not to be made by men but by guns. By massing overwhelming artillery strength on a short front, and replacing prolonged duration of fire (which had hitherto given ample warning of attack to the defenders) by the number of guns employed, he hoped so to disrupt French trench lines that, when the bombardment ceased, a relatively small German force could advance with little loss. Then the depth of the massed artillery fire could be extended and the process repeated.

More than 1,200 guns of every type—including 42 cm mortars, known as 'Big Berthas'—were brought forward and closely packed on a front only some 13km/ 8mls long. Opposed to this formidable array of artillery, the most powerful in history, were a mere 270 guns, mostly with insignificant stocks of ammunition. All depended on the French falling into the trap; this, as Falkenhayn had predicted, they immediately did.

Had the German attack been mounted on 12 February, as planned, the French, caught as it were in transit—for though now aware of the impending peril they were only beginning to bring up reinforcements—must have been overcome in a total and horrible manner. But at that precise moment Nature intervened.

The great bulk of German artillery and manpower had been assembled in the area due north of Verdun between the River Meuse and the Woevre, a boggy plain. Ammunition, provender, railway lines—all had been provided with Teutonic thoroughness. During the night preceding the planned offensive, however, the weather suddenly deteriorated: the temperature dropped, snow soon covered the ground and a blizzard reduced visibility to

The 'Sacred Way'

All rail links with Verdun were soon destroyed by the German bombardment, so Pétain ordered the improvement and widening of the sole remaining road to the fortress—that from Bar-le-Duc, 48km/ 30mls to the south. This route, the 'Sacred

Way' as it came to be called, saved Verdun.

For the first time in warfare, motorized trucks were the sole means of transport, for to have used horses would have choked up the whole movement of supplies. Along this road, which was nowhere wider than 6m/

20ft, some 3,000 French trucks passed night and day for seven months, at the rate of one every 14 seconds. Each week, an average of 50,000 tons of food and material was brought up and some 90,000 men transported in one direction or the other, for Pétain's policy was to rotate his troops so that none should be in the 'cauldron of fire' for long.

One American war correspondent wrote of this incessant traffic; 'The one sight of the battle of Verdun that will always live in my memory is that of the snow-covered and ice-coated road . . . constantly filled with two columns of trucks. . . . For long hours at night, I have watched the dim lights of all these trucks winding their way from north to south like the coils of some gigantic snake which had no end to it.'

Impassable potholes rapidly developed in the iron-hard, frosted road once the spring thaw set in. So vast quantities of stone were stockpiled along the way, and gangs of territorials, perhaps 1,000 in all, were set to work around the clock filling in and levelling the holes as they formed. By this and other stratagems, the Sacred Way was kept open throughout the battle.

Pétain rotated his troops at Verdun; at a terminus on the Sacred Way, *above*, some are going to rest camps, others up to the front. The road was kept in constant repair by Algerian territorials, *left*.

General Nivelle's brilliant attack at Verdun on 2 April 1916 led to his appointment as C-in-C of the French armies.

He devised a bold plan to win the war and his confidence won him political support. While the British attacked at Arras, he launched a sudden punch between Rheims and Soissons on 16 April 1917.

The blow was initially successful but then little was gained and the French lost 100,000 men. A crisis ensued in France, troops mutinied, and on 15 May Nivelle was dismissed and replaced by Pétain.

an arm's length. The German plan of attack was delayed by 24 hours. Then, as the fog, rain and snow persisted, it was futher delayed; then again and again, until at dawn on 21 February the weather and visibility improved sufficiently for the bombardment to be opened.

During those nine days, the concealed German troops remained, like hibernating animals, in the reinforced, underground galleries that they had methodically constructed. The French meanwhile, now belatedly alert to the impending peril, were frenetically bringing up reinforcements and more armament. It is perhaps no exaggeration to suggest that the weather saved France from a catastrophic defeat, for by 21 February there were still only two French divisions in position, facing six German divisions and their massed arsenal.

The opening shot of the battle has often been described. A gigantic 38cm gun, a product of Krupp's munitions factory, disgorged a shell to a distance of 32km/ 20mls. The projectile was imperfectly aimed but exploded in Verdun, smashing down part of the Archbishop's palace. For a terrible nine hours, the bombardment continued, constantly intensifying in its ferocious impact.

Tree branches, whole trunks, were blasted into the air, then fell to the ground, only to be interred or repeatedly thrown upward by further explosions; likewise mangled machinery and dismembered human bodies and those of horses. Soon the landscape was one of lunar bleakness. Nothing stirred, save involuntarily from

the impact of unremitting bombardment. The entire scene was overcast with clouds of débris and pock-marked by shell holes.

Severed human limbs, heads and trunks lay scattered over a wide area; other human remains, accompanied by tattered shreds of uniform, hung grotesquely from the remaining tree branches. The dead and dying lay either interred or where they fell. Many soldiers, still manning their guns, were bespattered with the bowels, blood and brains of their stricken comrades. The bombardment continued unabated until, at 16.00, it reached its maximum intensity, inflicting such destruction that the Germans supposed nothing—man, horse, even rodent—could have survived.

Then, at about 16.45, the deluge of shells suddenly ceased. French troops, deafened by the thunderous roar, felt

French infantry, *top left*, resting by the roadside on their way up to the front.

Above, a dramatized painting by Paul Thiriot of a French counter-attack on the village of Vaux during a snowstorm on 15 December, when the German lines at Verdun were broken.

Germans, *left*, attacking Fort Vaux from their trenches in March 1916. Each trench was occupied by three men. By this time, German troops had dispensed with their helmet spikes, which could be an impediment in battle.

yet more deaf with the unexpected, but long-prayed-for, silence. Tranquillity, however, they knew to be the harbinger of attack. Soon, the grey-clad German infantry, equipped with a new and revolting weapon—the flame thrower—advanced in small formations on the French, along a 3.3km/4ml front between Bois de Haumont and Herbevois on the east bank

THE COMMANDERS

FALKENHAYN	PRINCE WILHELM	PÉTAIN

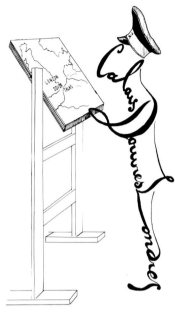

Field Marshal Erich von Falkenhayn (1861–1922), cold, introvert and uncommunicative, was the most enigmatic military figure to emerge during the war. Initially his career was unremarkable, but in the early 1900s he won the Kaiser's favour, and promotion came rapidly. In 1906 he became Minister for War and in 1914 succeeded Moltke as Chief of the General Great Staff.

The Battle of Verdun was entirely of his making, and after its disastrous outcome he was replaced in August 1916 by Hindenburg and Ludendorff and transferred to the Eastern Front. He commanded the German troops in the invasion of Romania and, in 1917, those sent to Palestine.

Crown Prince Wilhelm of Germany (1882–1951), although a professional soldier, had had no practical experience of war. But he grasped early on, as the Kaiser and general staff did not, that the conflict would be prolonged. After the war he went into exile in Holland, as did his father.

General Henri Pétain (1856–1951) became Commander-in-Chief of the French Army in 1917 and was made a marshal in 1918. Before Verdun, promotion had been slow, largely due to his undisguised contempt for the French politicians and his rejection of the doctrine of *attaque á l'outrance*, which he rightly claimed courted disaster if met by heavy firepower.

Pétain emerged from the war a hero and, during Hitler's war, when France was on the point of collapse in 1940, he was made vice-premier, in the hope that he could rally the country. But Pétain was unable to face the prospect of losses like those of the 1914–18 war and, when he became prime minister on 16 June, agreed to an armistice and headed the Vichy government in unoccupied France.

He was tried by a French court after the war for his collaboration with the Nazis and condemned to death; his sentence was, however, commuted to life imprisonment because of his distinguished service in World War I. He was held in a fortress on the Ile d'Yeu off the French Atlantic coast.

The cartoon 'Quite a simple thing by the map', by Alick Ritchie, appeared on the cover of the *Bystander* on 5 May 1915. Allied propaganda usually showed the Crown Prince, 'Little Willie', as feckless and a fop. In fact, he was quite astute militarily and had the acumen to oppose the attack on Verdun. But if it were to be made, he thought it should be simultaneously from both banks of the Meuse. As casualties mounted, he did all in his power to have the attack called off.

of the Meuse. Driant's men in the Bois de Caures bore the brunt of the attack and he himself was killed.

The French line was destroyed and its troops nearly annihilated, but a few remained and, farther back, still more. Their minds concentrated by the proximity of the detested enemy, the French soldiers resisted with the utmost stubbornness and, to German surprise and dismay, began to inflict heavy casualties. Fighting ceased only with the advent of darkness—but the respite was to be brief. The following morning, the bombardment was resumed as a preliminary to a stronger infantry attack by the German 3rd, 7th Reserve and 18th corps in the general direction of Fort Douaumont, the largest in Verdun's defensive ring.

The procedure was repeated the next day, 24 February, the Germans suffering unexpectedly high casualties but remorselessly, if slowly, pushing the French back. On 25 February, the Germans gained their greatest triumph of the battle when advance units penetrated the great fort of Douaumont and, finding many of the ill-armed French soldiers asleep through exhaustion, seized the citadel without loss of life.

By now all was confusion: the streets of Verdun presented a scene of total disorder, not unlike a disturbed ant heap, for troops and transport (all civilians had earlier been evacuated) milled about in congested and seemingly pointless movement. At the front, orders and conflicting counter-orders were adding to the general

chaos, as was the badly damaged, and anyway inadequate, telephone system.

The horror of the battle and the danger to France of those first days had, however, at last become imprinted on Joffre's sanguine and complacent mind. General de Castelnau, Joffre's right-hand man and chief of staff, extracted from him permission to move General Henri Pétain's Second Army to join the Third at Verdun, with Pétain in command of the entire sector's defence.

Whatever judgement is ultimately made of Pétain's conduct during World War II, nothing can detract from his achievement at Verdun. 'They shall not pass!' was not just a battle cry; it was a national cry that all of France echoed. Not only did he immediately assume overall direction of the battle, organizing his forces and ever-increasing artillery power, but he at once ordered the reoccupation and rearming of the outlying forts, to each of which two weeks' supply of food and water for every man was dispatched. Most importantly, since the rail links to Verdun had been severed by artillery fire, he enlarged the road for trucks between Bar-le-Duc and Verdun—the 'Sacred Way'—the only supply line to the front.

By the end of February, a week or so after the battle opened, the German advance had been stemmed. However, it was a temporary hold, for on 6 March the three

original German corps were reinforced by the three flanking corps: the 6th Reserve on the German right, the 15th and 5th Reserve on their left. They mounted a bloody attack throughout that month and the next, directed mainly at the ironically aptly named hill of Mort Homme—the dead man—on the river's left bank, and at the Côte du Poivre. But now troop numbers and artillery were more nearly matched, and the renewed German attack gained little ground.

Men on both sides were dying in scores of thousands all the same, and the casualty trains homeward-bound became both more frequent and more crowded. The Germans inevitably lost heavily in attack, the French through their stubborn but misguided determination to fight for every metre of ground. As Winston Churchill put it: 'The French suffered more than the defence need suffer by their valiant and obstinate retention of particular positions. Meeting an artillery attack is like

French troops seen in the squalor of their trenches in the Fort Vaux sector, 1916. The view is typical of conditions prevailing in the battle area.

Lucien Jonas's painting, *The Ramparts of Verdun, far left*, depicts the monstrous losses that the Germans, too, suffered in the battle. Jonas was a French artist who painted many moving pictures of the war's horrors, as well as portraits of commanders and some propaganda posters.

German attacks at Verdun

The first infantry attacks toward Verdun were made on 21 February. Near Beaumont the Germans used flamethrowers for the first time. Their uncoordinated attacks were made first on one side of the Meuse, then on the other. This gave the French time to bring up reserves. After months of fighting, the Germans made a fierce attack toward Fort Douaumont, the biggest fort in Verdun's ring of defences. When this fell, they thrust southward to Fleury and Fort Vaux. At the same time, other formations drove down from the northeast, to converge on Vaux.

This also fell but the Germans were held on a line from Vacherauville, running north of Bras and Fort Souville (which they never manged to take) to Damloup.

1 Vacherauville
2 Bras-sur-Meuse
3 Beaumont
4 Damloup
5 Fort Vaux
6 Fort Douaumont
7 Thiaumont
8 Fleury
9 Fort Souville

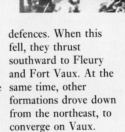

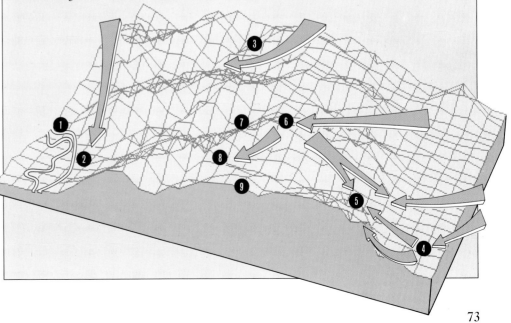

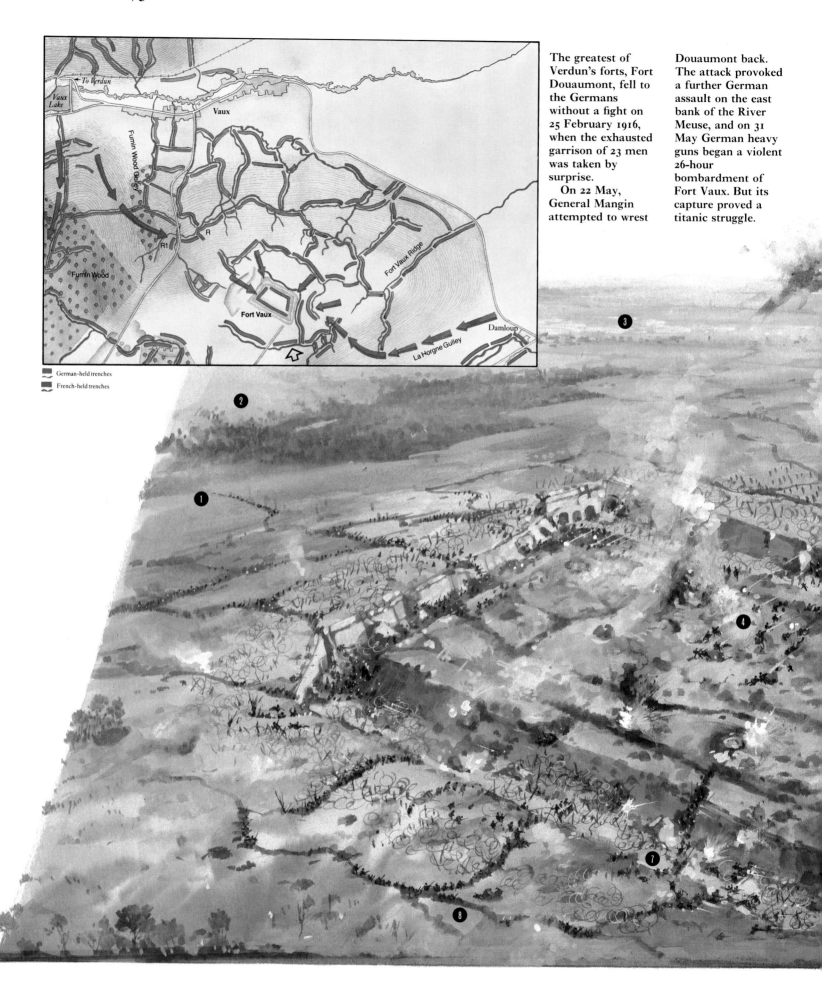

German-held trenches
French-held trenches

The greatest of Verdun's forts, Fort Douaumont, fell to the Germans without a fight on 25 February 1916, when the exhausted garrison of 23 men was taken by surprise.

On 22 May, General Mangin attempted to wrest Douaumont back. The attack provoked a further German assault on the east bank of the River Meuse, and on 31 May German heavy guns began a violent 26-hour bombardment of Fort Vaux. But its capture proved a titanic struggle.

At about 04.00 on 4 June, three days after the direct assault on Fort Vaux began, a French Nieuport 17C (5) flew low over the fort on reconnaissance. Below him the pilot saw a scene of utter desolation.

The chalk plateau was pitted with shellholes, and shells had smashed the fort's thick walls and concrete roof, domed like a tortoise's back. The roof swarmed with German soldiers (4), who turned their machine-guns on the aircraft.

Waves of Bavarian infantry had fought their way up La Horgne Gulley (6) and up Fumin Wood Gulley (2) from the village of Vaux (3). The French trenches had all been overrun, except on the ridge above Damloup, due south of the fort, and the redoubt R1.

Here, every attack was repulsed by 8th Company of 1/101st Regiment, led by Captain Delvert. Under constant shell-fire, attacks with grenades, gas, and flame throwers, these few men raked their enemy with machine-gun and rifle fire and, 'like a fishingboat' at anchor in a hostile sea, R1 held out until the night of 8/9 June.

Inside the fort, by 4 June, conditions were grim. The small garrison had been swollen to 600 by men seeking refuge. Crowds of wounded and dying men lay huddled together in the half-dark in the barracks and main corridor, and there was a desperate shortage of water.

The only contact with the outside world was by signals or by brave messengers who crept out through the south moat (8) at night. When this became impossible, the commander, Major Sylvain Raynal, used his six carrier pigeons to appeal, vainly, for relief of the fort's terrible plight.

Relentlessly the Germans forced their way into the fort, using grenades and flame throwers, but the defenders had sandbagged the passages and they fired machine-guns through these barricades.

Major Raynal surrendered on 7 June, and then only because his men, in the stifling heat and darkness, the air full of gas and smoke, had had no water for two days.
     Truly, the real victor at Fort Vaux was thirst.

The defender of Fort Vaux

Major Sylvain Raynal was a man of great courage who had risen from the ranks. He had twice been badly wounded and was still hobbling around with a stick when he was given command of Fort Vaux, the smallest of the forts ringing Verdun but crucial to the defence of the important Fort Souville.

Raynal's task was daunting. The fort had been subjected to ceaseless bombardment from the start of the German offensive and had been almost flattened, *bottom*. The garrison of some 250 had been more than doubled by soldiers seeking refuge, and the corridors were crowded with dead and wounded. The men were tormented by fleas and suffered agonies of thirst; by the end they were forced to drink their own urine. The picture, *below*, taken when the French recaptured the fort later, gives some idea of the conditions.

Raynal limped among his men, calm and kindly, organizing a fighting defence. But on 7 June, when all attempts to relieve the fort had failed, the exhausted survivors had no option but to surrender.

Shortly before the fort was captured, Major Raynal was appointed commander in the Legion of Honour; he learned of the award from his admiring German captors. Later, in a special review at Les Invalides in Paris, the insignia was bestowed upon his wife. Raynal's gallant defence so impressed Crown Prince Wilhelm that he personally returned Raynal's officer's sword to him as a mark of respect.

Plan of Fort Vaux: 1 Dry Moat. 2 Observation turrets. 3 West corridor. 4 75mm gun turret. 5 Latrines. 6 Magazines. 7 Barracks.

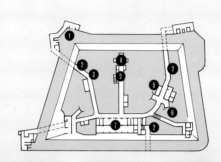

catching a cricket ball. Shock is dissipated by drawing back the hands. A little "give", a little suppleness, and the violence of impact is vastly reduced.' This the French did not grasp.

Mort Homme was ultimately taken by the Germans, though at terrible cost. More and more men were thrown into the struggle on both sides; even so, it was May before the French were completely cleared from the left bank of the Meuse. By now German commanders were beginning to lose their nerve. The Crown Prince, who had never favoured Falkenhayn's plans, was adamant in his belief that the offensive should be called off; Falkenhayn himself wavered—as well he might, for his reputation and professional future depended on success at Verdun. Only General Schmidt von Knobelsdorf, Chief of Staff to the Crown Prince's army, was resolved to continue.

The French commanders also were in an indecisive state of shock. Pétain, a general considerate of his men, was promoted to command of the Army Group and two lesser generals assumed immediate responsibility—Nivelle, who was to bring the French Army to the point of mutiny in the following year, and Mangin, dubbed 'the heroic defender of Verdun' by some, 'the butcher' by others. By making repeated attacks, Nivelle and Mangin played into Falkenhayn's hands and incurred horrendous casualties.

On 7 June, after a week's resistance by Major Sylvain Raynal and 600 men, with a heroism hardly equalled in the war, Fort Vaux finally fell. Then, on 20 June, the Germans for the first time employed a new type of diphosgene gas shell. The effect was dramatic, paralysing French artillery support and enabling the Germans to make deep advances that brought them to within striking distance of Verdun itself. In reality, however, the German advance was losing momentum.

As early as 11 June, Pétain had asked Joffre to bring forward the Allied attack in the Somme area. This had been scheduled to open earlier in the year but had been pre-empted and postponed by Falkenhayn's attack at Verdun. Since French troops had been removed from their positions on the Somme to bolster their imperilled comrades at Verdun, this offensive was to be undertaken largely by British troops. The objectives had also been changed; now it was designed to take pressure off Verdun.

In this—though in nothing else—it was to prove successful. The British bombardment on the Somme began on 24 June (the infantry attack went in on 1 July) and on that same day Falkenhayn stopped the massive flow of ammunition to Verdun and cancelled all reinforcements. The German advance came to a halt, and during the autumn months the French were able to retake all the ground that they had earlier lost. It is a cruel irony of the Battle of Verdun that the outlying forts that Joffre, deeming them useless, had stripped of their guns, were found to have withstood constant bombardment by both sides for many months almost unscathed.

Verdun was saved for the French by the British Somme offensive. A reasonable estimate is that the French lost some 377,200, the Germans 337,000, the only occasion in the war when the defenders lost more than the attackers.

Moreover, the French Army's spirit was broken, its men on the verge of mutiny. Germany, too, had lost the best of her young manhood. It was a high price to pay for anything; it was an intolerable price to pay for nothing.

German soldiers near Douaumont rescue a Frenchman who has become embedded up to his waist in a muddy shell hole. Despite the terrible bloodshed, there was little personal enmity between fighting men and incidents such as this were common.

This plaque on the wall at Fort Vaux is dedicated to all the carrier pigeons that died for France, and especially the last one to leave the fort on 4 June bearing Major Raynal's request for support. 'We are still holding out, but are subjected to a very dangerous smoke and gas attack. It is urgent that we should be extricated; let us have immediate communication by visual signals from Souville, which does not answer our appeals. This is my last pigeon.' The bird accomplished her mission, but was wounded and later died, asphyxiated during a gas attack in the headquarters pigeon loft.

'Unity of front'

After the bitter Allied reverses in 1915, a new effort was made at Chantilly, Joffre's headquarters, to devise a coherent military strategy—'Unity of front', in the phrase of the new French prime minister, Aristide Briand. And, as 1915 drew to its close, some overall plan could be formulated.

A joint British and French attack on the Somme was part of this coordinated strategy, designed to hammer the Central Powers simultaneously from all sides. Once the great armies had become locked in senseless slaughter at Verdun, however, the plan had to be revised. Sir Douglas Haig, British Commander-in-Chief, reluctantly agreed to bring forward from 1 August to 1 July 1916 the Somme offensive. This was to achieve little save loss, but it was at least a factor in bringing the German attack at Verdun to an end.

Meanwhile Russia had re-equipped and enlarged her army to an astonishing degree, considering her antiquated and corrupt administrative system. She was now ready to launch a major attack. An Italian attack on Austria–Hungary was also planned.

It was not only strategy that was affected by Verdun; personalities, too, were involved. Falkenhayn was relieved of his command by the Kaiser in August and replaced by Hindenburg and Ludendorff. In France, Joffre, though discredited, was appointed Chief Military Adviser to the Government, a titular post that gave his incompetence less scope.

Verdun was a watershed in World War I: before it, all were confident that victory was attainable, albeit with great sacrifice; after it there was a ghastly realization that no one had the solution to the war.

Battle of Jutland *31 May 1916*

At the outbreak of World War I, both informed and common opinion held that a major, probably decisive, naval action would soon take place between the British and German fleets. At first appraisal, Great Britain was, in 1914, undisputed mistress of the seas, as she had been since 1805 when Admiral Lord Nelson destroyed the combined Franco–Spanish fleet at the Battle of Trafalgar. But many of her ships, though more numerous than Germany's, were obsolescent and lacked new, virtually impenetrable armoured plating. By contrast, the German Navy, created under the compulsive ambition of the Kaiser, had newer and better-armed and armoured ships.

In the event, the two great fleets—the British Grand Fleet under Admiral Sir John Jellicoe, and the German High Seas Fleet, commanded by Admiral Reinhard Scheer—were not to engage until 31 May 1916. The origins of the battle, however, can be traced to 29 July 1914, before the outbreak of war, when the British Fleet was prudently dispatched by Winston Churchill, First Lord of the Admiralty, to

its war station at Scapa Flow, off the northeastern tip of Scotland. The British Navy thus became the dominant force between northern Britain and Norway, so poised as to frustrate any German sortie into the North Sea. The German High Seas Fleet was locked into its harbours; nevertheless two questions remained. Would the Germans put to sea and, if so, when?

As on land, new weapons developed prior to the war played an important part in future operations. Mines and submarines now posed a potent peril to an enemy's ships, and the Germans, conscious of their numerical inferiority at sea, at first resolved to deploy these rather than risk a major naval battle. However, they made various sorties to test Great Britain's coastal defences: as early as 1914, German squadrons had bombarded the Norfolk coast and, farther north, Scarborough and Whitby in Yorkshire. To protect Britain's east coast, a new battle-cruiser squadron, under Vice-Admiral Sir David Beatty, moved south on 7 May 1916 to Rosyth.

The German submarine offensive in

the first 18 months of the war was largely contained. Indeed, the torpedoing of the liner *Lusitania*, also on 7 May, in which some 1,100 people, including a number of Americans, perished, outraged world opinion. It brought a virtual ultimatum from US President Woodrow Wilson, so strong that Germany temporarily gave up unrestricted submarine warfare.

Admiral Scheer's flagship, *Friedrich der Grosse* and, ahead of her, the 3rd Battle Squadron of the High Seas Fleet, were photographed from beneath the huge guns on the afterdeck of *Ostfriesland* at about 19.10 on 31 May 1914, just before the formation fetched up opposite the centre of Jellicoe's Grand Fleet.

Early naval battles

In 1914 there were several German warships scattered throughout the Atlantic and Pacific oceans. The most powerful flotilla was the East Asiatic Squadron based on the China coast. It was commanded by Vice-Admiral Maximilian von Spee.

By the late autumn Spee's flotilla of five ships had moved to the Juan Fernandez Islands some 644km/400mls west of Chile. His approximate area of operation then became known to Rear-Admiral Sir Christopher Cradock, whose responsibility it was to guard the southern tip of South America.

Cradock's force, based in the Falkland Islands, comprised two obsolescent armoured cruisers, *Good Hope* and *Monmouth*, which were heavily out-gunned by Spee's formation; a modern cruiser the *Glasgow*; and the armed merchantman *Otranto*. The out-of-date battleship *Canopus* was yet to join him.

On 14 October, Cradock left the Falklands and steamed around Cape Horn to intercept the Germans. Spee, meanwhile, moved south along the coast to Chile, and the two formations met, in heavy seas, on the evening of 1 November not far from the port of Coronel. The result was inevitable: *Good Hope* was sunk, as later was *Monmouth*; *Glasgow* and *Otranto* fled

south, seeking the protection of the fast approaching *Canopus*. The British lost 1,654 officers and men, including Cradock; the Germans a mere two men wounded.

Retribution, however, was at hand. The Admiralty had dispatched two battle-cruisers—*Invincible* and *Inflexible*—to the south Atlantic, where they were joined by six light cruisers. This flotilla reached the Falkland Islands on 7 December; the following morning, the victorious Spee also arrived. His flotilla was taken wholly by surprise when fired upon by the British warships and turned tail.

The weather was bright, providing the British guns, now superior in range and number, with clear targets. Spee, knowing he was doomed, ordered his light cruisers to escape southward while his flagship, *Scharnhorst*, and *Gneisenau* delayed the enemy in hopeless contest. At about 16.15 the *Scharnhorst* succumbed to ceaseless bombardment and sank; and at 17.45, having fired all her ammunition and riven by shell bursts, *Gneisenau's* captain ordered her to be scuttled. These gallant efforts failed to save the light cruisers. British ships overtook and sank two of them, the third, the *Dresden*, escaped but was sunk in March 1915.

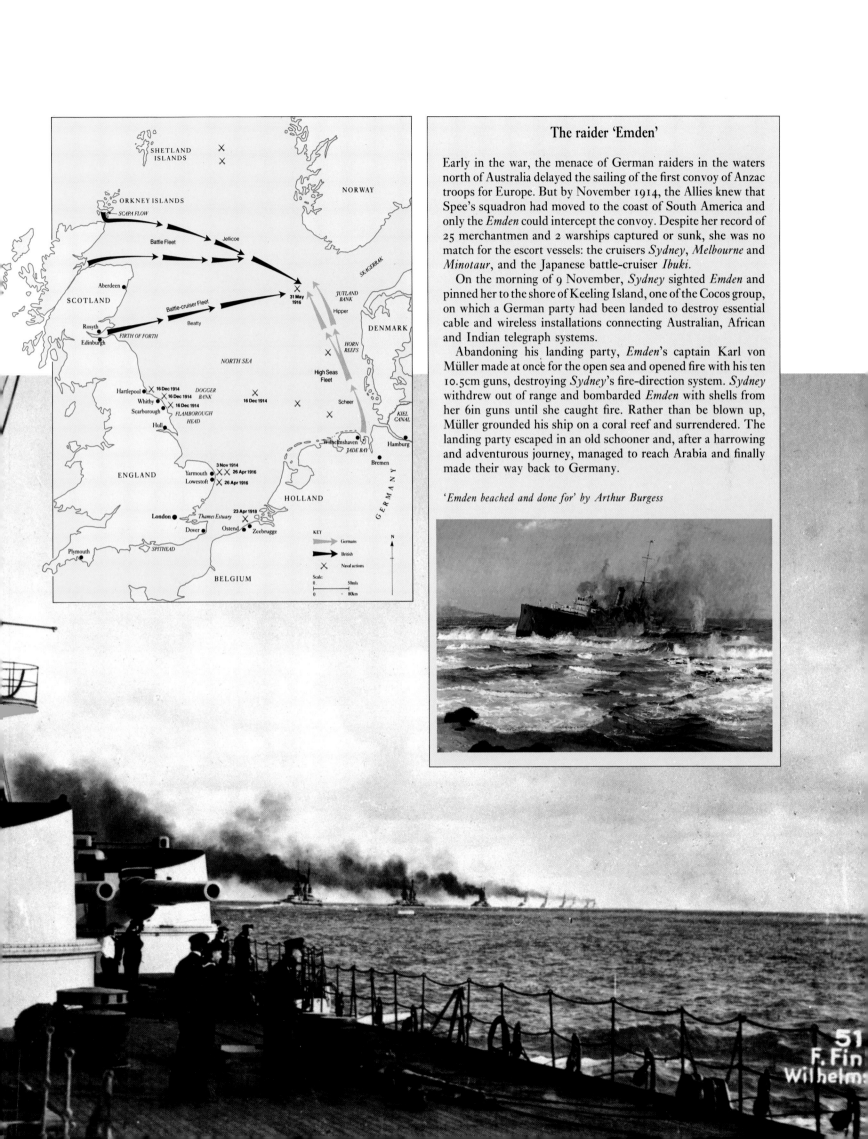

The raider 'Emden'

Early in the war, the menace of German raiders in the waters north of Australia delayed the sailing of the first convoy of Anzac troops for Europe. But by November 1914, the Allies knew that Spee's squadron had moved to the coast of South America and only the *Emden* could intercept the convoy. Despite her record of 25 merchantmen and 2 warships captured or sunk, she was no match for the escort vessels: the cruisers *Sydney*, *Melbourne* and *Minotaur*, and the Japanese battle-cruiser *Ibuki*.

On the morning of 9 November, *Sydney* sighted *Emden* and pinned her to the shore of Keeling Island, one of the Cocos group, on which a German party had been landed to destroy essential cable and wireless installations connecting Australian, African and Indian telegraph systems.

Abandoning his landing party, *Emden*'s captain Karl von Müller made at once for the open sea and opened fire with his ten 10.5cm guns, destroying *Sydney*'s fire-direction system. *Sydney* withdrew out of range and bombarded *Emden* with shells from her 6in guns until she caught fire. Rather than be blown up, Müller grounded his ship on a coral reef and surrendered. The landing party escaped in an old schooner and, after a harrowing and adventurous journey, managed to reach Arabia and finally made their way back to Germany.

'Emden beached and done for' by Arthur Burgess

Map labels

SHETLAND ISLANDS
NORWAY
ORKNEY ISLANDS
SCAPA FLOW
Jellicoe
Battle Fleet
Aberdeen
SCOTLAND
SKAGERRAK
31 May 1916
JUTLAND BANK
Battle-cruiser Fleet
Beatty
Hipper
Rosyth
FIRTH OF FORTH
Edinburgh
DENMARK
NORTH SEA
HORN REEFS
High Seas Fleet
Hartlepool 16 Dec 1914
DOGGER BANK
Whitby 16 Dec 1914
16 Dec 1914
Scarborough 16 Dec 1914
Scheer
FLAMBOROUGH HEAD
Hull
KIEL CANAL
Wilhelmshaven
Hamburg
JADE BAY
Bremen
ENGLAND
3 Nov 1914
Yarmouth 26 Apr 1916
Lowestoft 26 Apr 1916
GERMANY
London
Thames Estuary
23 Apr 1918
Dover
Ostend Zeebrugge
Plymouth
SPITHEAD
HOLLAND
BELGIUM

KEY
Germans
British
Naval actions
N
Scale:
0   50mls
0   80km

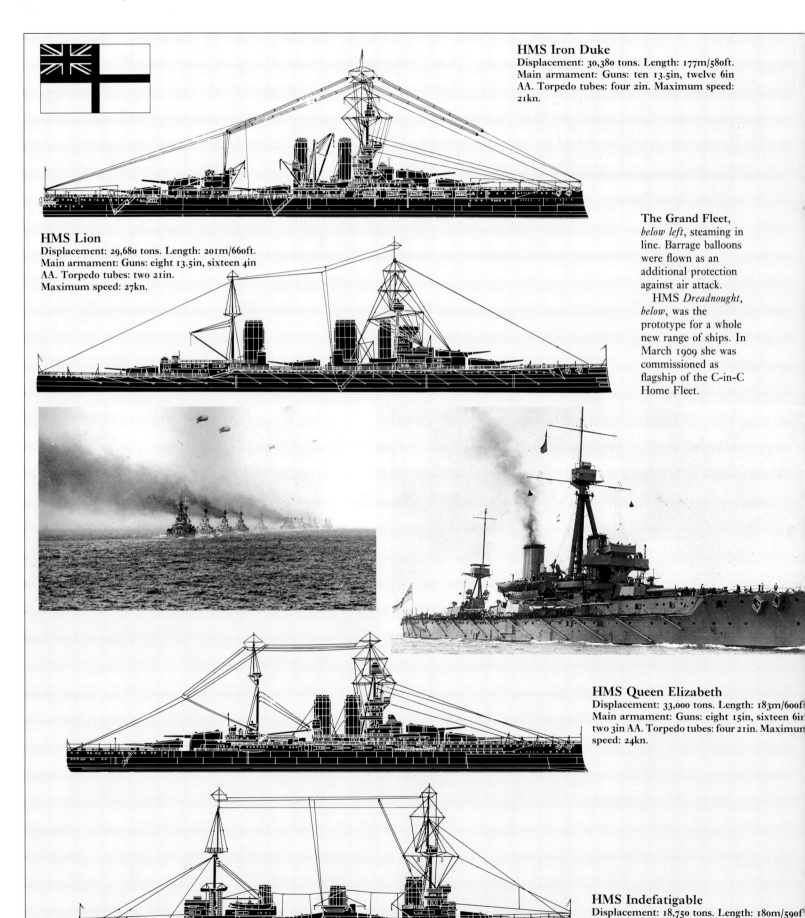

HMS Iron Duke
Displacement: 30,380 tons. Length: 177m/580ft.
Main armament: Guns: ten 13.5in, twelve 6in
AA. Torpedo tubes: four 2in. Maximum speed:
21kn.

The Grand Fleet,
below left, steaming in
line. Barrage balloons
were flown as an
additional protection
against air attack.
    HMS *Dreadnought,*
below, was the
prototype for a whole
new range of ships. In
March 1909 she was
commissioned as
flagship of the C-in-C
Home Fleet.

HMS Lion
Displacement: 29,680 tons. Length: 201m/660ft.
Main armament: Guns: eight 13.5in, sixteen 4in
AA. Torpedo tubes: two 21in.
Maximum speed: 27kn.

HMS Queen Elizabeth
Displacement: 33,000 tons. Length: 183m/600ft.
Main armament: Guns: eight 15in, sixteen 6in,
two 3in AA. Torpedo tubes: four 21in. Maximum
speed: 24kn.

HMS Indefatigable
Displacement: 18,750 tons. Length: 180m/590ft.
Main armament: Guns: eight 12in, sixteen 4in,
four 3-pounder. Torpedo tubes: two 18in. Maximum speed: 26.89kn.

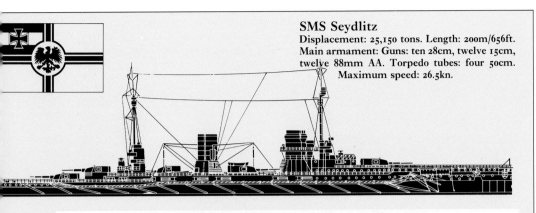

SMS Seydlitz
Displacement: 25,150 tons. Length: 200m/656ft.
Main armament: Guns: ten 28cm, twelve 15cm,
twelve 88mm AA. Torpedo tubes: four 50cm.
Maximum speed: 26.5kn.

SMS König
Displacement: 28,150 tons. Length: 175m/574ft.
Main armament: Guns: ten 30cm, fourteen
15cm, two 88mm AA.
Torpedo tubes: five 50cm.
Maximum speed: 21kn.

SMS 'Seydlitz',
above, sustained more
hits during the Battle
of Jutland than any
other ship that was not
sunk, but still
managed to limp home
to Germany.

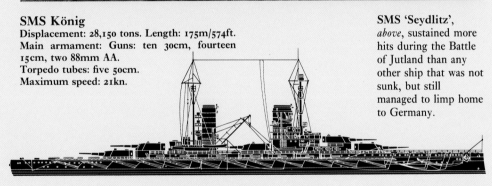

Development of the dreadnoughts

For many decades Great Britain had undisputed mastery of the seas. Then, toward the end of the nineteenth century, Germany emerged as a rival, increasing the size of her navy to support her expansionist policy. This was made possible by her great industrial centres, which by 1910 were producing twice as much steel as the British and three times that of the French.

Sir John Fisher, the First Sea Lord, was determined to maintain Great Britain's supremacy and quickly grasped the potential of the design of a new warship, to be named *Dreadnought*. A great advantage was that her four-shaft Parsons steam engines were both more reliable and cheaper to run than earlier engines, and she was at least

three knots faster than any other warship. As well as increased speed, her design gave her ten 12-in guns in five twin turrets, without any reduction in armour.

The drawback to *Dreadnought*, which gave her name to a whole era of warships, was her cost—£1,783,883. Fisher to some extent solved this problem by scrapping many older ships of doubtful value.

The launching of *Dreadnought* on 10 February 1906 both infuriated and dismayed the Germans, who at once deepened the Kiel Canal and widened its locks to accommodate larger, more powerful vessels. A massively expanded naval programme was inaugurated. The race for naval domination accelerated.

What could Germany now do, and achieve, at sea? The German plan was simple yet subtle. Scheer resolved to use Vice-Admiral Franz von Hipper's battle-cruisers again to bombard towns on the east coast of England; this, he judged, would bring Beatty and his battle-cruisers down from their anchorage at Rosyth. Scheer himself, steaming some 80–90km/50–60mls behind Hipper, would then fall upon Beatty before Jellicoe and his Grand Fleet could reach the fateful scene from Scapa Flow, far to the north.

Unfortunately for Scheer, however, an earlier provocative raid by Hipper's ships had resulted in the *Seydlitz* being struck by a mine. Though she reached harbour safely, considerable repairs were necessary and Scheer's projected sortie had to be postponed.

This event had two consequences: the German submarines stationed off Scapa Flow, with the task of harassing Jellicoe when he put to sea, were running out of fuel; and, on the new date set for sailing—31 May—strong winds prevented Zeppelins from reconnoitring ahead of the High Seas Fleet. Scheer, therefore, reverted to an earlier, alternative plan.

Late on Tuesday, 30 May 1916, the British Grand Fleet left its bases for one of its occasional reconnaissance sweeps across the North Sea. Early on the following morning—31 May—the German High Seas Fleet also left harbour in Jade Bay. Hipper's battle-cruisers, light cruisers and destroyers steamed northward parallel to the Danish coast with the intention of attacking merchantmen off Norway. Their objective was to lure Beatty to the scene so that they might trap and destroy some small portion of the British Fleet before retiring to sanctuary in their harbours on the German mainland. Meanwhile Scheer, who had now decided to reduce the gap between the two German fleets to a mere 32km/20mls, would be close behind and in position also to strike at the outnumbered Beatty.

Again unfortunately for Scheer, the British possessed a copy of Germany's naval code and were aware, minute by minute, of her ships' movements. Thus Jellicoe, on his flagship, the dreadnought *Iron Duke*, and Beatty, on his battle-cruiser *Lion*, were fully aware of developments and accordingly prepared their courses to intercept the German fleet.

Beatty, whose force comprised 52 ships, including four of the most powerful and sophisticated super-dreadnoughts of the day—*Barham*, *Malaya*, *Valiant* and *Warspite*—sailed from Rosyth shortly after 21.30. At about the same time,

JUTLAND/3

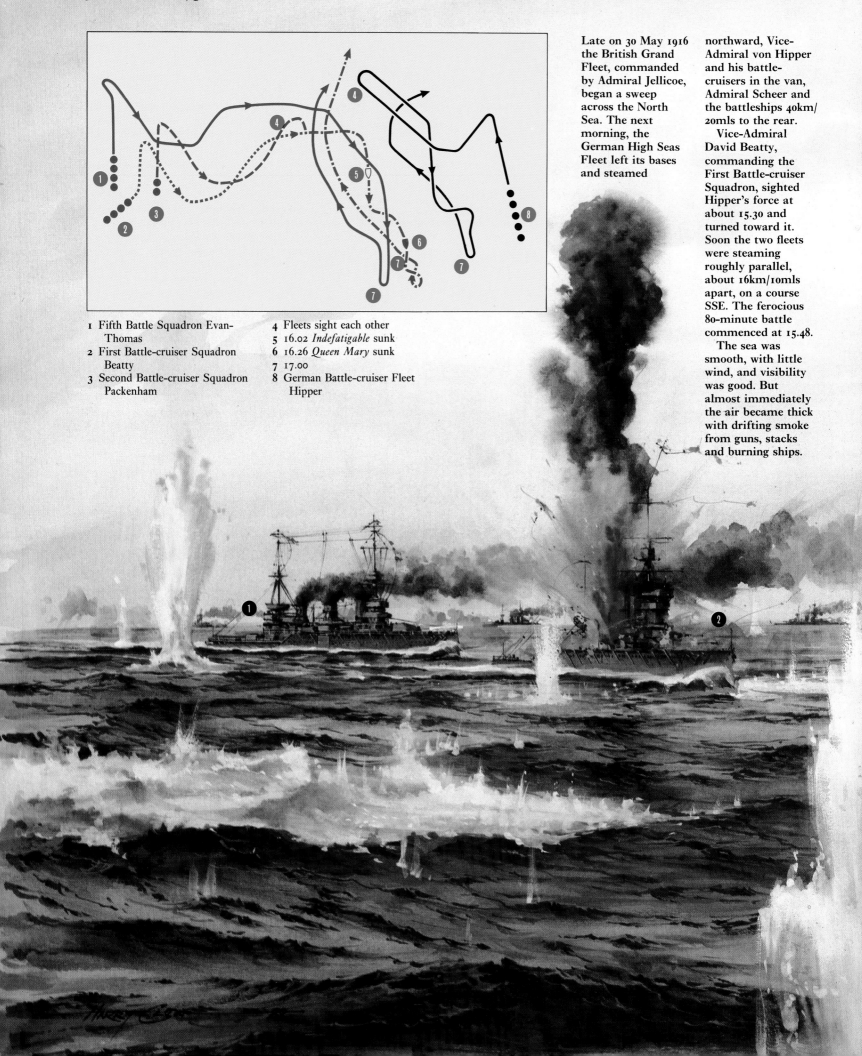

1 Fifth Battle Squadron Evan-Thomas
2 First Battle-cruiser Squadron Beatty
3 Second Battle-cruiser Squadron Packenham

4 Fleets sight each other
5 16.02 *Indefatigable* sunk
6 16.26 *Queen Mary* sunk
7 17.00
8 German Battle-cruiser Fleet Hipper

Late on 30 May 1916 the British Grand Fleet, commanded by Admiral Jellicoe, began a sweep across the North Sea. The next morning, the German High Seas Fleet left its bases and steamed northward, Vice-Admiral von Hipper and his battle-cruisers in the van, Admiral Scheer and the battleships 40km/20mls to the rear.

Vice-Admiral David Beatty, commanding the First Battle-cruiser Squadron, sighted Hipper's force at about 15.30 and turned toward it. Soon the two fleets were steaming roughly parallel, about 16km/10mls apart, on a course SSE. The ferocious 80-minute battle commenced at 15.48.

The sea was smooth, with little wind, and visibility was good. But almost immediately the air became thick with drifting smoke from guns, stacks and burning ships.

BRITISH GRAND FLEET

24 Dreadnoughts

1st Battle Squadron:	*Marlborough Revenge Hercules Agincourt*
	Colossus Collingwood Neptune St Vincent
2nd Battle Squadron:	*King George V Ajax Centurion Erin*
	Orion Monarch Conqueror Thunderer
4th Battle Squardon:	*Iron Duke Royal Oak Superb Canada*
	Benbow Bellerophon Téméraire Vanguard

9 Battle-cruisers *Lion Princess Royal Queen Mary Tiger New Zealand Indefatigable Invincible Indomitable Inflexible*

4 Fast Battleships *Barham Valiant Warspite Malaya*

8 Cruisers

23 Light Cruisers

81 Destroyers

1 Seaplane Carrier *Engadine*   **1 Minelayer**

GERMAN HIGH SEAS FLEET

22 Dreadnoughts

1st Squadron:	*Oldenburg Helgoland Thüringen*
	Ostfriesland Westfalen Nassau
	Rheinland Posen
2nd Squadron:	*Pommern Hessen Deutschland*
	Schleswig Holstein Schlesien Hannover
3rd Squadron:	*Markgraf Krönpinz Wilhelm König*
	Grosser Kurfürst Friedrich der Grosse
	Prinzregent Luitpold Kaiserin Kaiser

5 Battle Cruisers: *Derfflinger Lützow Von der Tann Moltke Seydlitz*

9 Light Cruisers

63 Destroyers and Torpedoboats

given by flags, which for a time went undetected by the 5th Battle Squadron, commanded by Rear-Admiral Sir Hugh Evan-Thomas. It was only a good six minutes later that this squadron of battleships, which had been steaming some 8km/5mls behind Beatty in his flagship *Lion*, turned; this delay left the squadron about 16km/10mls behind Beatty's battlecruisers. Beatty consequently had a momentous task: to entice the Germans north toward Jellicoe, then hurrying south, without himself being overwhelmed by the superior enemy forces that he at present faced.

At about 15.20, Hipper sighted Beatty and turned south, hoping to lure the British toward Scheer's advancing fleet. Then, 10 minutes later, Beatty in his turn detected Hipper, and the action between the opposing battle-cruiser fleets, which lasted some 80 minutes, shortly began. The two fleets were steaming roughly

abreast, about 13.3–16.6km/8¼–10¼mls apart, on a course SSE—that is, directly toward Scheer. Jellicoe and his battle fleet were still well to the north. Beatty's aim was to keep Hipper so closely engaged that the Germans could not break off the action until Jellicoe arrived; Hipper's task was to lure Beatty to destruction at the hands of Scheer.

The two fleets were vigorously engaged when suddenly disaster befell the British. The *Indefatigable*, the last ship in the line, sustained a hit and sank with the loss of all but two of her crew of 900 officers and men. Fortunately, Evan-Thomas in *Barham*, steaming at maximum speed with his four battleships, had come within firing range. Nevertheless, the Germans had the advantage, for the British ships, silhouetted against the western sky, made ideal targets and, shortly after 16.20, the battle-cruiser *Queen Mary* was hit by a salvo and also sank.

Beatty, who had begun the engagement with a numerical superiority in battlecruisers of six to five, was now inferior by a margin of five to four. Nevertheless, the crisis had passed with the timely appearance of Evan-Thomas. This changed the entire tactical situation, for Scheer, steaming toward the scene, had no option but to go to Hipper's assistance.

Beatty sighted Scheer's fleet shortly before 16.40 and, being greatly outnumbered, turned north to join Jellicoe. The signal to turn about was, like Beatty's earlier order, missed by Evan-Thomas, who continued on his original southward course until he ran into Scheer's battleships and came under heavy fire.

By now the two great flotillas—Jellicoe's and Scheer's—were rapidly closing with each other and the second major engagement of the action was about to open. The problem for the British was that they had seriously miscalculated their

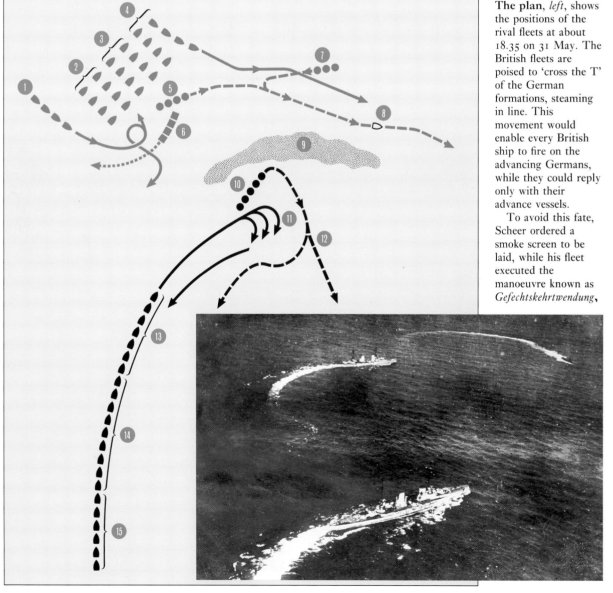

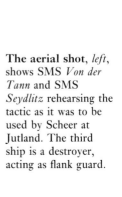

The plan, *left*, shows the positions of the rival fleets at about 18.35 on 31 May. The British fleets are poised to 'cross the T' of the German formations, steaming in line. This movement would enable every British ship to fire on the advancing Germans, while they could reply only with their advance vessels.

To avoid this fate, Scheer ordered a smoke screen to be laid, while his fleet executed the manoeuvre known as *Gefechtskehrtwendung*,

turning away in battle. This entails all ships of the line reversing to port or starboard to change direction; once they move forward again, the van has become the rear and vice versa.
1,2,3,4 5th, 1st, 4th and 2nd Battle Squadrons (Evan-Thomas, Burney, Sturdee, Jerram). **5** Beatty's battle-cruisers. **6** 1st Cruiser Squadron (Arbuthnot). **7** Hood's battle-cruisers. **8** *Invincible* sunk 18.35. **9** German smoke screen. **10** Hipper's battle-cruisers. **11** German fleet turns about 18.35, **12** Damaged *Lützow* makes for home. **13** 3rd, 1st and 2nd German Battle Squadrons (Behncke, Schmidt, Mauve).

The aerial shot, *left*, shows SMS *Von der Tann* and SMS *Seydlitz* rehearsing the tactic as it was to be used by Scheer at Jutland. The third ship is a destroyer, acting as flank guard.

At the first rival salvoes, ships of both sides were engulfed by great spouts of water from shells as gunners gauged the range. The German ships, painted pale grey, were difficult targets because they merged into the haze on the horizon, while the British ships, with their dark grey colouring, stood out clearly against the sunlight to the west.

German guns quickly found the range. At 16.05 *Indefatigable* was hit, her magazine blew up and she sank; only two of her crew survived. Soon most of Beatty's ships had been hit. At 16.26, having been hit by five shells, *Queen Mary* (2) exploded. A tremendous dark red flame burst from her, a pillar of smoke rose 244m/800ft into the air, and debris crashed on the decks of nearby ships. She and her crew of 1,266 vanished.

Beatty's flagship *Lion* (6) had been severely damaged by five shells and the wireless room was out of action, so signals had to be made by flags. Then another shell struck Q turret amidships, but the flash was prevented from reaching the magazine below the gun by the heroic action of Major Francis Harvey of the Marines. Despite being fatally wounded, he ordered the magazine to be flooded, so saving the ship from certain disaster.

After three hits, the forward and after gun turrets of *Princess Royal* (5) were out of action, while *Tiger* (4) had been hit four times and was firing only intermittently. Only *New Zealand* (1), pulling out of line to avoid the stricken *Queen Mary*, remained undamaged at this time.

The German battle-cruisers, led by Hipper's flagship *Lützow* (7), had also taken punishment. *Lützow* herself had been hit once by *Lion*. Behind her, *Derfflinger* and *Seydlitz* were hit, and *Von der Tann*, the last in line, holed in the stern and difficult to steer, had only two guns still firing.

HMS Tiger, *above*, making dense smoke as she steams into action at full speed, had eight 13.5in guns. During the battle she was hit 14 times and badly damaged, with 24 men killed and 37 wounded. Later she was refitted at Rosyth and continued in service until 1931.

Two of the 28cm guns on the battle-cruiser *Seydlitz* delivering a broadside during the battle; though badly mauled, the ship survived Jutland. In 1918, after the German surrender, she was taken into custody at Scapa Flow, where she was among the 51 ships successfully scuttled.

Submarine warfare and the convoy system

On 1 February 1917, Germany declared unrestricted submarine warfare, with the object of starving the British into surrender; the prescribed areas encircled the British Isles and covered large areas of the Mediterranean. And some 200 U-boats, capable of remaining at sea for up to four weeks and armed with torpedoes and guns, were deployed in the Atlantic, covering the approaches from North America along which most merchantmen passed. Sinkings by U-boats rose steadily, from around 100 merchant vessels in January 1916 to about 800 a month in the spring of 1917.

In reply, the British equipped a number of merchantmen, called Q-ships, with torpedo tubes and concealed guns. They acted as bait and, once a U-boat surfaced, could out-gun her. But Allied and neutral losses continued to mount so steeply that the Germans supposed a further five months would see Great Britain subdued.

The final remedy was found in the convoy system. Each convoy comprised 40 or more merchantmen, with escort ships, mostly destroyers equipped with depth charges, stationed on either side. On sighting a U-boat, they would at once break away in pursuit. Advance patrols acted as look-outs and another ship took station in rear to rescue survivors from any stricken vessel. To the end of October 1917, of more than 1,500 vessels in homeward-bound convoys, only 24 were lost. So successful was the system that it was reintroduced at the beginning of World War II.

Below left, a British destroyer laying a convoy smoke screen cover; *insert*, view from a U-boat as its target explodes; *below*, interior of a U-boat's oil-engine room.

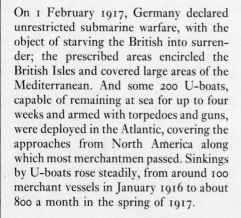

Beatty had begun the action with an advantage of six to five battle-cruisers; now he was inferior by four to five. But his dangerous situation was redeemed by the arrival from the northwest of the Fifth Battle Squadron (3), commanded by Vice-Admiral Evan-Thomas.

The fast battleships *Barham*, *Valiant*, *Warspite* and *Malaya* at once pounded the rear ships in Hipper's line, and *Moltke* was hit. At this moment, too, Beatty ordered 12 destroyers into the fray so that *Lion* and her followers could turn away to starboard to open the range and give time for fires to be extinguished.

At 16.42 Beatty sighted Scheer and his battleships to the southeast. From being the hunters, the British had become the prey. Beatty swung round to a northerly course, both to escape his more numerous foe and to lure Hipper toward Jellicoe's battle fleet, now hastening southward.

Jellicoe left Scapa Flow with a massive fleet of dreadnoughts, 3 battle-cruisers, 19 other cruisers and an armada of 51 destroyers. Thus two vast British fleets set sail to cut off and destroy the German navy. But there was more. Less than an hour after Beatty had sailed from Rosyth, the 2nd Battle Squadron of eight dreadnoughts, under Vice-Admiral Sir Thomas Jerram, left Cromarty to join Jellicoe's fleet, then steaming southeastward.

At the same time, Hipper and his battle-cruisers were moving north, followed by Scheer, and his battleships. The two opposing commanders—Jellicoe and Scheer—both believed that their opponent's dreadnoughts were too far behind their battle-cruisers to join in the imminent battle. But, in the event, an engagement of the utmost complexity ensued. Put at its most simple, and ignoring numerous small, subsidiary engagements, the battle fell into two parts, a fight between Beatty's and Hipper's battle-cruisers, followed by a monstrous and confused clash of dreadnoughts.

The crucial role of each battle-cruiser fleet was to engage the other in a manoeuvre that would seduce its opponent, and its battle fleet to the rear, into a conflict with its own battle fleet. At 14.20, one of Beatty's scouting cruisers, *Galatea*, reported the likelihood of enemy vessels in the vicinity. Beatty, who was steaming north toward Jellicoe, altered course to the SSE, in the direction of the Horn Reefs off the coast of Denmark. His intention was to place himself between the enemy battle-cruisers, now to his north, and their havens on the German coast. Beatty's lookouts sighted Hipper's force at about 15.30 and reported the German strength as five battle-cruisers, while Beatty himself had six.

The first sighting of the rival ships provided an unusual, and in the view of the military historian Sir Basil Liddell Hart, decisive element in the following battle. The *Galatea* had first seen an unidentified merchantman and steamed toward her to investigate; at almost the same moment, one of Hipper's ships also sighted the vessel and likewise made to examine her. The two vessels—*Galatea* and the German light cruiser—came into view of each other, and both immediately reported the fact to their superiors. Thus, Liddell Hart speculates, the British were probably denied an outright victory, for battle was at once joined. Without this chance double sighting, the opening shots would probably not have been exchanged until later, when the Germans would have been farther north and farther from their home bases, offering the numerically superior British the possibility of a victory on the scale of Trafalgar.

Beatty made his order to turn SSE toward Hipper at 14.32. The order was

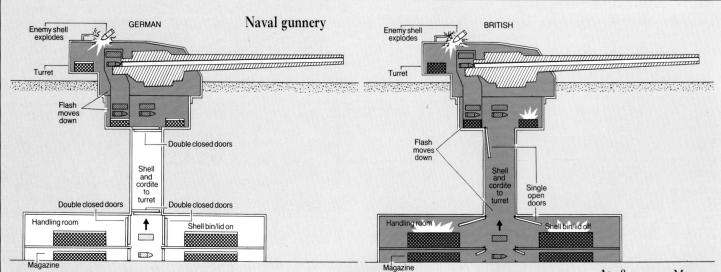

Naval gunnery

The increasingly destructive power of ships' guns compelled navies to fight at ever greater distances. Gunnery, therefore, was of crucial importance, and the advantage lay entirely with the fleet whose guns outranged their opponent's, and whose fire was more rapid and accurate.

In all three respects the German Navy outclassed the British. They relied upon accuracy achieved by constant practice and by directing fire from a central point high above the smoke from the stacks and guns. The Royal Navy, in contrast, hoped to achieve accuracy but was prepared to gain a hit by putting a great weight of shells into the air with each salvo.

The vulnerability of British ships was exacerbated by the great ease, *diagram above*, with which a shell could penetrate the magazine, causing a massive explosion.

At 18.34 on 31 May, when in close action with the enemy, a shell hit the starboard amidships 12in gun turret of *Invincible*. Flames rose 122m/400ft into the air as the flash ignited two magazines containing 50 tons of cordite. The ship exploded and broke in half in 15 seconds, but both bow and stern sections stuck vertically out of the shallow water for some time before sinking. All but six of her complement of 1,031 were lost. This photograph was taken from HMS *Inflexible*.

own positions. Thus, Beatty, when he
came within sight of Jellicoe, was more
than 8km/5mls west of the spot at which
his Commander-in-Chief had been led to
expect him; moreover, the German fleet
was to Jellicoe's starboard rather than, as
he had thought, straight ahead.

Jellicoe had sent Rear-Admiral Sir
Horace Hood and his 3rd Battle-cruiser
Squadron to aid Beatty but, because of the
misreckonings of position, this force
moved too far eastward. Paradoxically, the
error was to assist the British fleet.
Hipper, steaming northward parallel to
Beatty, again sighted his enemy to the west
at about 17.40; he immediately turned east
but was then bombarded by Hood, who
had inadvertently taken up a wrong station. Hipper, by now apprehensive,
turned away, first to the southeast, then to
the southwest, in order to avoid what he
thought was the vanguard of Admiral
Jellicoe's battle squadrons.

Jellicoe's fleet was coming southward
in six columns, running parallel and
stretching 6.4km/4mls from side to side.
At 18.15 he deployed his port wing column, while his starboard wing, presently
manoeuvring to the left, or port side,
opened fire. His decision to turn east
enabled him to steam across the head of
the German line, a manoeuvre, potentially
lethal, known as 'crossing the T'. Scheer,
observing this, at once turned about: he
had no intention of engaging the greater
firepower of the British Grand Fleet in its
entirety and was by now thoroughly
alarmed for the safety of his ships.

But Scheer turned westward, away
from the sanctuary of his harbours in

northern Germany, so Jellicoe then deployed his fleet in a curving line between
the Germans, now again out of sight, and
their bases. This was a skilful manoeuvre
but it risked frustration because the combination of fog, dense smoke from guns
and funnels, and failing light, was making
visibility increasingly poor.

Scheer continued steaming westward
for a further 20 minutes; and then, for
reasons never adequately explained,
turned east again. In any event, this move,
made in ignorance of Jellicoe's true position, brought him shortly after 19.00
opposite the centre of Jellicoe's fleet. The
distance between the fleets was no more
than 8km/5mls and soon most of the ships
in both flotillas were engaged. Scheer
quickly decided to attempt escape from
what was potentially a disastrous situation
by executing the manoeuvre known as the

The young lion

The Victoria Cross, the highest British accolade for bravery in action, was awarded posthumously to 16-year-old John Travers Cornwell, serving at Jutland on the light cruiser HMS *Chester*. He held the rank of Boy First Class, and his duty was to help sight *Chester*'s forward 5.5in gun.

At about 17.30, *Chester* came under heavy fire and all the gun crew except Cornwell were killed. Although severely wounded in the chest and under continuous fire, with the greatest fortitude, he stood by his gun for more than 15 minutes. Cornwell died in hospital on 2 June.

In his battle dispatch, Beatty described Cornwell's bravery and recommended him for 'special recognition . . . as an acknowledgement of the high example set by him.' The poster below, commemorating Cornwell's courage was signed by Edward Carson, First Lord of the Admiralty, Jellicoe and Beatty.

a '*Gefechtskehrtwendung*', a 'battle turn-about' in which all his ships turned 180° to starboard, reversing his line.

As he steamed off southeast, he came intermittently under heavy fire from ships in Beatty's and Hood's squadrons. At about 21.00, nightfall came to his aid, giving him nearly six hours of darkness, and he slipped away from his enemies. Scheer had three possible routes through German minefields to his harbours and safety; he elected to take the shortest, via the Horn Reefs, since most of his ships were slower than those of the British.

During the hours of darkness, Jellicoe was bedevilled by conflicting and often inaccurate messages, both from his scout ships and the Admiralty. Thus, when the first flicker of daylight broke on the horizon at about 02.30 on 1 June, Jellicoe found the sea empty: Scheer had eluded him and was even then reaching sanctuary. The British Commander-in-Chief, having searched for stragglers and stricken seamen in lifeboats until 13.15, ordered his ships to return to their harbours.

Who won Jutland?

The Battle of Jutland has often been judged a 'draw'; but in warfare there is really no such thing. Although losses may be equal, the side that is the better able to sustain them will derive most benefit from any encounter. Certainly the British suffered the more serious loss: three battle-cruisers, three armoured cruisers and eight destroyers against Germany's one battleship, five cruisers of various types and five destroyers. Moreover, the British had lost 6,097 sailors to Germany's 2,545.

Yet those British ships that reached harbour undamaged on 2 June were refuelled and made ready for sea within five hours, whereas the Germans took nearly four months to prepare their fleet to sail. The Germans made further, but limited assaults on the British coast, but the High Seas Fleet never again put to sea with the intention of engaging the Grand Fleet.

The lesson of Jutland for Britain was that it should never have been fought. As long as the British had numerical superiority in ships, as long as Nelson's unbroken string of victories remained unblemished by subsequent defeats, the authority of the Royal Navy was a generally accepted truth.

Although after Jutland Britain still had more ships than Germany, as the Kaiser remarked, 'The spell of Trafalgar has been broken.' Uncertainties in the minds of Britain's allies were increased by Jellicoe's delay in making a report, and the German version of the battle, couched in biased terms, became widely accepted.

Claus Bergen's painting of *Seydlitz* captures the awesome reality of the battle. Two of her starboard guns are out of action, but she is still firing to port. Her shell-torn deck is littered with spent shell cases and hoses for dousing fires.

Recruiting posters proliferated. That for the Women's Royal Naval Service shows a 'Wren' in dramatic pose on the white cliffs of Dover, calling young women to their duty; while, *right*, the image of Nelson, Britain's greatest sailor, is used to evoke a patriotic response from men.

1805 "ENGLAND EXPECTS" 1915

ARE YOU DOING YOUR DUTY TO-DAY ?

The Brusilov Offensive *June–September 1916*

Russian offensive strategy for 1916 had been designed to coincide with Anglo-French assaults in the west. The plan called for a main attack by 26 divisions in July on a 40-km/25-ml front running north and south of the village of Krevo, west of Molodetchno. Meanwhile, to ensure that the Germans did not rush reinforcements by rail to the threatened area, General Alexei Alexeievich Brusilov, commanding the South West Front, was ordered to make menacing probes in his area. In effect, these were intended to be little more than reconnaissance raids on a large scale.

Brusilov's extensive command, which stretched from east of Kovel in the north to Czernowitz on the Romanian border, comprised four armies under generals of proven worth. North to south, these were the Eighth Army (Kaledin), Eleventh (Sakharov), Seventh (Scherbachev) and the Ninth (Lechitski). Brusilov, who had directed Russia's southern thrust during the Battle of Lemberg, had already proved himself a redoubtable commander of troops in mass.

The Russians were opposed by the Fourth Austro-Hungarian Army (Archduke Joseph Ferdinand) just south of the Pripet Marshes with, on its right, the First Army (von Brlog). Into these was merged in an undefined manner the army of the German General von Linsingen, whose forces consisted of both Austrian and German formations. The Second Austro-Hungarian Army (Böhm-Ermolli) held the front between Dubno and a point a little north of the Tarnopol-Lemberg railway. The rest of the line was held by the Prussian Count Felix von Bothmer and General von Pflanzer-Baltin's Seventh Army, which had a strong Hungarian contingent among the Austrian troops.

Although the Austrian and Hungarian armies were ethnically very mixed and contained Germans, Magyars, Poles and even Italians, there were very few Czech, Slovene and Ruthenian regiments on the Russian Front. Since at heart these men were friendly to the Slav cause, Allied propaganda claimed that those who were posted to the east were always stationed in the most exposed positions, and at the slightest sign of wavering, or what might be termed 'treason', were shot at from the rear.

Near the end of May, Italy, suffering reverses at the hands of the Austrians, besought her Russian Ally for assistance. Indeed, the King of Italy telegraphed the request personally to the Tsar. The Stavka, Russia's supreme war council, asked Brusilov what he could do to take

Russian resurgence

Russia had been mauled in 1915 and forced into general retreat, but she had not been destroyed. To the Germans, however, it seemed she was incapable of further immediate offensives; so, late in 1915, General Erich von Falkenhayn felt secure enough to transfer troops and artillery to the Western Front. At the same time, General Conrad von Hötzendorff syphoned off large numbers of Austrian troops to pursue his offensive in Italy.

Given this period of respite during the winter of 1915–16 and the following spring, Russia had, in fact, made an astonishing recovery. She was producing some 100,000 rifles a month; many more were received from her allies; and hundreds of thousands of recruits had been enlisted and partly trained. But she was still seriously underarmed and undersupplied. Nevertheless, the Russians planned a new offensive for the summer of 1916, to be mounted in unison with Anglo-French attacks on the Somme and Italian thrusts against Austria.

But Falkenhayn's assault on Verdun disrupted the Allied plans. The offensive on the Somme was in jeopardy, and the Italians were suffering in Austrian attacks in the Trentino, where they lost some 300 guns and 150,000 men.

Both France and Italy implored Russia to attack to relieve their distress. Although the appeals came when Russia was not yet ready to advance, for the second time she went immediately and unhesitatingly to the aid of her allies.

Officers and men of a Russian heavy fieldgun regiment, *above*. Dust goggles were needed when the thousands of men and horses involved were on the move.

An Austrian dog-drawn light ration train for a machine-gun unit, *right*. Dogs were also used to draw the machine-guns. Since rabies was prevalent, all army dogs wore muzzles.

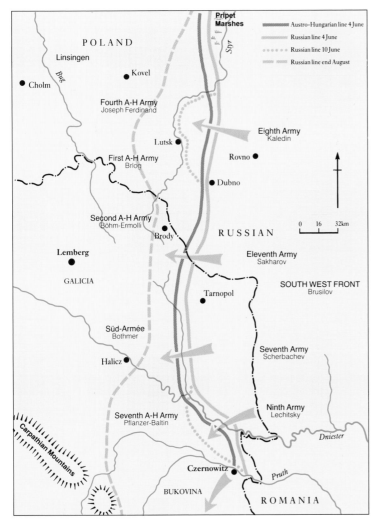

Corporals of the Tiroler Kaiserjaeger on the Eastern Front in 1916. The five green woollen balls attached to their uniforms indicate that they are marksmen. The Jaeger battalions were specially trained and equipped to act as infantry support to the cavalry.

pressure off the Italians by preventing even more Austrian troops being taken from the Eastern Front to the Trentino. Brusilov, a thrusting and optimistic commander, replied that he was as well placed to advance against Austria now as he would be in July. Nothing, he was informed by his superiors, was to affect the main blow to be delivered in the area of Krevo; but apart from that Brusilov was virtually empowered to do whatever he thought fit.

Brusilov's response was, typically, unconventional. He had bare parity of strength with the Austrians—38 divisions to 37—a wholly inadequate number with which to mount an attack, since all evidence had shown that a ratio of 3:1 was the least that could reasonably be expected to ensure success. However, he had one potentially decisive factor in his favour: the element of surprise.

The Russian field bakery, *left*, was photographed by Florence Farnborough. This intrepid Englishwoman had been working as a governess in Moscow, and when war broke out she enlisted as a nurse, serving with the Russian Army.

BRUSILOV OFFENSIVE/2

The Russian Eighth Army, under General Kaledin, lay on Brusilov's right wing in Volhynia. The three centre corps—the 8th, 39th and 40th—with almost 100 battalions, were drawn up on a front 42km/30mls long in the region of Lutsk, where the main blow of Brusilov's four-pronged attack was planned to fall.

Opposite them lay the Fourth Austrian Army of Archduke Joseph Ferdinand, with an almost comparable number of men and guns.

Kaledin's offensive opened at 04.00 on 4 June 1916 with a five-hour barrage by some 420 heavy guns and howitzers. The main thrust was made by 102nd Reserve Infantry Division and 2nd Rifle Division on Austrian positions south of the Stavok to Lutsk road (6).

Austrian defences were extremely strong, with a belt of barbed wire 12m/40ft deep in front of three lines of heavily fortified trenches close together (3). But the Austrians had become lax and overconfident, and the bombardment took them unawares.

Surprise was absolute when at about 09.00 Russian troops began to pour out of vast underground bunkers (1), which they had spent the past few weeks constructing.

These bunkers held up to 1,000 men and from them, under the Austrians' noses, the Russians had driven saps that in some places came within 50 paces of their lines.

Priests (8) with icons and banners blessed the Russians as they came up out of their dug-outs, boosting their morale. Within minutes, a wave of troops overran the first trench, crammed with men. Then, as they had been taught, the Russians went straight on to take the second, lightly defended trench before stopping to consolidate.

The bombardment had stirred up the dry sandy soil and the air was full of fine dust that clogged up the breaches of Austrian artillery and machine-guns. The gunners began to limber up and flee to the heights around Krupy (2).

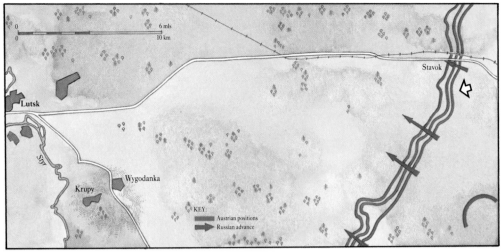

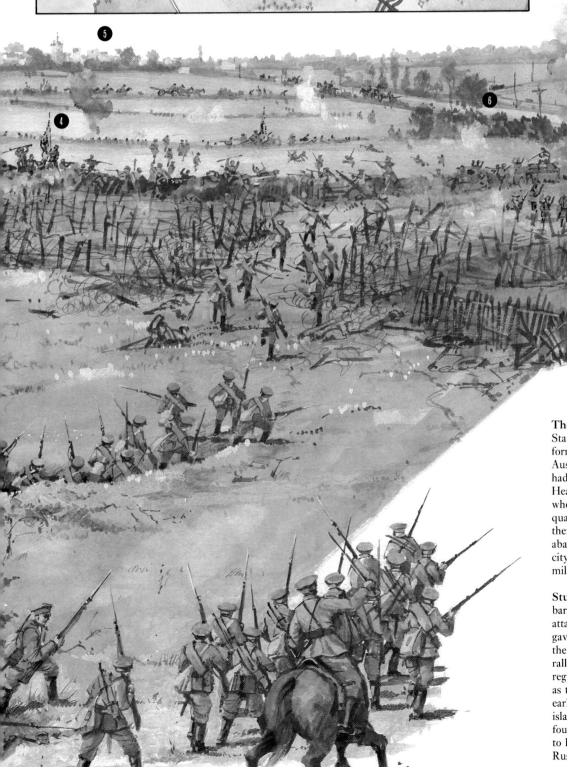

The little town of Stavok (7), which formed part of the Austrian front line, had been set alight. Headquarters staff who had been quartered there took to their cars and abandoned it for the city of Lutsk (5) a few miles off.

Stunned by the barrage and the swift attack, many Austrians gave up. But here and there, bands of men rallied around the regimental colours (4) as they had done in earlier wars. These islands of soldiers fought fiercely, hand to hand, with the Russian troops who surged around them.

By nightfall, the Russians had overrun almost all the enemy positions. In the first two trenches, more than three-quarters of the casualties were the result of gun or rifle-fire; but in the third, troops simply surrendered—there were even tales of officers fleeing ahead of their men. The demoralization of the Austrian Fourth Army was complete.

By 6 June, they had been driven back behind the Styr River and Lutsk had fallen. In two days the Russians captured 77 guns and 50,000 men.

To utilize this to the full, Brusilov resolved to launch all four of his armies at once over a wide front, rather than concentrating them as dictated by contemporary military thinking. The timing of these concerted attacks to the same day, along the entire front, made it impossible for the Austro-Hungarian forces to be switched back and forth behind their line, with the result that they had to fight each battle with the support of no more than local reserves.

In addition, Brusilov eschewed the current strategy of first pounding the enemy with prolonged artillery fire. On his instructions, the bombardment was intense but lasted less than a day, its object

being to take out selected points in the enemy's defence, rather than to destroy the Austrian trenches.

The effect was dramatic. Since Brusilov had not concentrated his troops in any one area, nor made tactical probes, and since the artillery bombardment lasted so short a time, the Austrians had no inkling of his intentions. As General Erich von Falkenhayn, in overall command of the German forces on the front, was later to comment: 'After a relatively short artillery preparation they [the Russian troops] had got up from their trenches and simply marched forward.'

Both officers and men of the Austro-Hungarian Army had, too, a handicap of

their own making: complacency, for they thought their positions impregnable. Indeed, on the eve of Brusilov's offensive, General Conrad von Hötzendorff, the Austrian supreme commander, told a Swedish journalist: 'We are not to be conquered again.'

The only justification for Austria's

Young Russian women, incensed that so many soldiers were surrendering in 1917, enlisted and formed the Battalion of Death, vowing to win or die. They went through the same training as men and carried the same Nagant rifle. Here, three of them take the oath.

The Bolsheviks, who hated them for wanting to fight to the end, raped, mutilated and killed any who fell into their hands.

The Austrian prisoners, *below*, were taken early on in Brusilov's campaign.

The Romanian débâcle

Romania entered the war against Austria on 28 August 1916, when Brusilov's offensive seemed irresistible. For two years she had awaited the turn of events before deciding which side to join, while maintaining a mobilized army. Her objective was to acquire Transylvania, and she now at once invaded that country and quickly occupied the greater part of it. But seldom has a military miscalculation been so gross and retribution so immediate.

The German supreme command had long foreseen Romania's strategy, and two powerful armies had been quietly assembled to counter just this eventuality. The First Austrian Army, under General von Falkenhayn, attacked Romania's left wing, while a second army group, under General von Mackensen, invaded her Black Sea province of Dobrudja from Bulgaria.

The Romanians, trapped in the pincers, were swiftly thrown out of Transylvania. Then, with Falkenhayn invading northern Romania, Mackensen's reinforced army was free to cross the Danube and assault her from the south. During November, Romania was occupied by the Central Powers, and on 6 December the capital, Bucharest, fell. Her remaining troops fled into the northern province of Moldavia, where they were in some measure protected by their Russian ally.

Within the space of some three months, Romania's ambitions had been frustrated and her territory overrun. Most significantly, her great reserves of wheat and oil had been lost to the Central Powers, who now also had direct access to their eastern satellites Bulgaria and Turkey.

misplaced sense of security was the strong front-line defences. In most sectors there were five lines of trenches, one behind the other, many as much as 6m/2oft deep, with dug-outs similar to those on the Western Front. These were all covered over with baulks of timber secured with concrete and well stocked with food and weapons.

Convinced of the impossibility of ever again having to retreat, the Austrian Army had settled into a comfortable, almost rural, existence. There were bakeries, sausage factories, and plants for pickling and smoking meat just behind the front, and cold stores had been established. Large numbers of men were employed, too, in growing vegetables and grain for the army; but it was not they who were to reap the harvest, for their crops and granaries were either captured by the Russians or burned.

The very suddenness of Brusilov's attack, on 4 June, caught Austria militarily off balance. As the Russians neared the enemy lines, their artillery used curtain fire to trap the Austrian forces in their deep trenches, which now became prisons from which the could not escape. Death or surrender became the only options.

Brusilov's attack broke through his enemy's line on a front of nearly 320km/ 200mls, throwing the Austro-Hungarian Army into bewildered retreat, and they began to surrender in large numbers. On the first day alone, the Russians captured 13,000 men; by noon on 6 June, the third day, the tally had risen to 900 officers and 40,000 other ranks, together with 77 guns and 134 machine-guns.

Although the Eleventh and Seventh armies in the Russian centre made only little immediate headway, in the north General Kaledin's Eighth Army advanced farther than 16km/10mls along a 48-km/ 30-ml front. And in the south General Lechitski's Ninth Army had even more spectacular successes in the region of Czernowitz.

The situation was transformed. The advance gathered momentum and within the month, Brusilov had penetrated nearly 96km/6omls along the entire front. He captured almost the whole of the Bukovina, and the important towns of Lutsk, Dubno and Czernowitz fell to his troops. In addition, he took 350,000 prisoners, some 400 artillery pieces and 1,300 machine-guns.

The Stavka, though astonished, were quick to reinforce Brusilov. The proposed and prepared offensive in the Krevo area now became of secondary importance; all reinforcements, weaponry and supplies must be hastened to Brusilov's support. Here, however, the inadequate Russian railway system was yet again to play its inhibiting part. Although from about 10 June, troops were transferred southward to Brusilov's aid, they could not be carried in sufficient numbers to provide the necessary support to maintain his attack or greatly to affect its outcome.

Reinforcements entering Czernowitz, in the Bukovina. They are marching past assorted Russian units which had earlier captured the town, an important rail junction.

THE COMMANDERS

KALEDIN	BRUSILOV	BOTHMER

General Alexei Brusilov (1853–1926) was the only man to give his name to a campaign. A celebrated horseman, in 1906 he was given command of the Second Guards Cavalry Division. Later, being a gifted administrator, he served as military assistant to the Governor-General of Warsaw.

In 1914, at the head of Eighth Army, he led the Russian invasion of Galicia and fought successfully in the Carpathians. Brusilov took over command of the South West Front from General Ivanov in April 1916. After the Russian Revolution, Brusilov served in the Red Army under Trotsky, and helped to plan the campaign against Poland in 1920.

General Kaledin (?) succeeded Brusilov as commander of Eighth Army. Although a competent cavalry general, who distinguished himself during the fighting in June 1916, he was a gloomy, neurotic man who had to be inspired by Brusilov.

General Felix von Bothmer (1852–1919) came to prominence when his German infantry had some marked success in opposing Brusilov's offensive. He is thought to have been shot by Communists in Munich in April 1919.

The sale of Vivat bands, designed by celebrated artists and skilfully printed on silk, was one means of raising money for Austrian war charities. The band, *above,* showing the 30.5cm mortar, with the words 'Our strength is their ruin', was sold in aid of the Red Cross and other war funds.

Early in July, it also became evident that while the Austrian troops were falling back in collapse, German formations on the front fought stubbornly and retreated with discipline. General von Bothmer's Südarmée, sited roughly between the Russian Eleventh and Seventh armies, delayed Brusilov's advance, as did General von Linsingen's troops opposite the extreme Russian right in the area of Kovel.

For the Central Powers, however, the situation remained perilous in the extreme. Falkenhayn was obliged to gather German reinforcements from wherever he could: three divisions from the north of the front, more from reserves, and four from the Western Front, where they were sorely needed. Conrad, too, had no option but to break off his offensive in the Trentino and, in an attempt to halt Brusilov's threatening advance, return to the Eastern Front the troops he had earlier withdrawn.

By mid-July, the situation had again changed. Austria was chastened and had to submit to Germany in all strategical decisions and Conrad was shortly relieved of his command. German railways, always more numerous and efficient than those of Russia, enabled reinforcements to be brought in rapidly, and the German line was now uninterrupted along the whole front. Some of the earliest reinforcements were used for a counter-attack by Linsingen and Böhm-Ermolli on the northern edge of Brusilov's offensive.

This propaganda postcard shows Austro-Hungarian horse artillery, with their 5cm gun, marching through the captured Polish village of Kazimierz, near Cholm.

This was the moment for Brusilov to call a halt. Instead, urged on by his military and political masters, he pressed on throughout July and into August, while at the same time fresh Russian attacks were made to the north of his armies. In the south, the Russian armies reached, and then foundered on, the great barrier of the Carpathian Mountains. By the end of August, Brusilov had advanced so far as to make replenishment of men and *matériel* difficult, often impossible. The impetus was spent.

The casual bravery of the Russian troops was no match for German massed artillery and machine-gun fire, and the Russians suffered nearly a million casualties; the Germans had relatively few. Romania's entry into the war against Austria at the end of August served only to lengthen Russia's frontier, laying her open to further attack when Romania collapsed in December 1916. But by this time, the great loss of life, and the increasing difficulties in obtaining weapons and supplies, had sapped the will of the Russian troops to attack, and the situation drifted into stagnation.

Victory heralds disaster

The Brusilov Offensive, at first so unexpectedly successful, in fact marked a fatal reverse. Few had realized that, despite Russia's remarkable recovery after 1915, her effort must be limited by inadequate weaponry and supplies. Fewer still realized that initial Russian successes were made possible mainly because the élite Austrian forces had been transferred to Italy. Nor did the Allies appreciate how great the loss of life would inevitably be, underequipped as Russia was.

But Brusilov understood this and was prepared to pay the price, for he later wrote: 'An offensive without casualties may be staged only during manoeuvres ... to defeat the enemy, or to beat him off, we must suffer losses, and they may be considerable.'

And so they were. Although Brusilov's achievements were great—he captured 350,000 prisoners, took the Bukovina and huge areas of Galicia—he sustained his offensive past the point of reason and in the process lost a million men. The blow to Russia was mortal. Such sacrifice, without significant lasting reward, was beyond human bearing, and the ingredients were now marinating for Russia's collapse into confusion, anarchy and, shortly, revolution.

Revolution in Russia

Russia's huge wartime losses in both life and material, culminating in those sustained during the Brusilov Offensive, were instrumental in bringing about the Russian Revolution in 1917. At the end of February, supported by many of the intelligentsia, workers in Petrograd and Moscow were incited to riot for better food rations.

Mutiny followed. The Tsar, Nicholas II, dissolved the Duma, or parliament, but was compelled to abdicate after the Duma appointed a moderate provisional government under Prince Lvov. This satisfied few but left the way open for the Bolsheviks who soon controlled the army and all communications and transport in Petrograd. They also set up 'soviets', or councils, in opposition to the liberal government.

In April, Lenin and other Bolsheviks abroad returned to Russia, aided by the Germans. The failure of the army's July offensive increased discontent, and on the night of 6/7 November the Bolsheviks staged an armed coup, and established a government under Lenin.

A symbolic painting by Kustodiev shows Revolution striding through Petrograd, while insignificant figures of soldiers, priests and capitalists mill around his feet.

Battle of The Somme *July–November 1916*

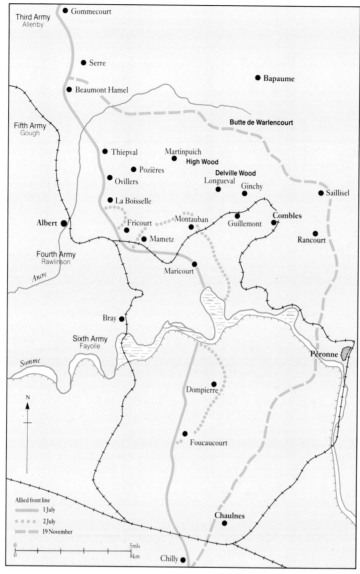

Allied front line
— 1 July
••••• 2 July
— — 19 November

In the early months of 1916, British troops in France, both the few remaining regulars from the old BEF and the eager recruits to Kitchener's New Army, were preparing for the 'Big Push'. There was a spirit of optimism and excitement among the men, for they felt, and had been led to believe, that this was the offensive—carefully planned and prepared for—that was going to smash the German Army and bring an early end to the war.

The formations designated to make the attack, on a front stretching from Gommecourt in the north to near Chilly in the south, were the British Third Army (Allenby), the Fifth (Gough), the Fourth (Rawlinson), and the French Sixth Army (Fayolle). They were opposed by Prince Rupprecht of Bavaria's First Army.

In accordance with current military methods, the new offensive was preceded by five days of intensive artillery bombardment, with the intention of obliterating German trenches and eliminating resistance. In this expectation the Allies were to be disappointed. Not only did the bombardment forewarn the Germans of the area of the attack, it was largely ineffectual. For in the words of General Sir Douglas Haig in his post-battle dispatch, the German defence's formed 'not merely a series of successive links, but one complete system of enormous depth and strength.'

The chalk soil had made excavation easy, and some of the German dug-outs were as much as 12m/40ft deep. In addition, the Allies' artillery fire had created myriad craters, which were to prove an obstruction to their advance while providing excellent cover for German machine-gunners and sharpshooters. To break through the German defences in this section was, therefore, on any rational assessment, extremely difficult.

Against these defences, eager young soldiers of Great Britain and France were thrown. Some British soldiers carried up to 30kg/66lb of equipment—half the weight of an average man—which, in addition to rifle and ammunition, included such items as field telephones, shovels and picks. As the military historian, Sir Basil Liddell Hart, observed: 'Even an army mule, the proverbial and natural beast of burden, is only expected to carry a third of his own weight!'

The troops had to struggle out of their trenches, and the wounded, once fallen, had difficulty in rising, like armoured knights of old. Moreover, Fourth Army's orders to the untried battalions was to advance across no man's land at a 'steady pace': they could hardly have achieved

An ill-chosen battleground

Allied strategy for 1916 had been agreed in outline on 5 December 1915. Russia was to mount an offensive in the east, while Anglo-French armies attacked on the Somme, and Italy assailed the Austrians. But General Erich von Falkenhayn's unexpected attack at Verdun in February 1916 overthrew these plans.

Though the Russian Brusilov Offensive achieved such spectacular temporary success, the sanguinary fighting at Verdun obliged the western Allies to redeploy their forces. The French Tenth Army was withdrawn to reinforce formations at Verdun, and the Somme offensive, intended as a concerted attack of 40 French and 25 British divisions along a 63-km/49-ml front, had to be reorganized. The British were now to play the major role.

Historians, informed by hindsight, still dispute the wisdom of the Somme attack. Few strategic benefits could be gained even if the German line were penetrated, which was improbable since their strong, deep defences were sited on high ground. Certainly, General Foch, who commanded the five French divisions available for the offensive, was sceptical of the enterprise, as at first was General Sir Henry Rawlinson, commander of the Fourth Army; while General Sir Douglas Haig would rather have attacked in Flanders.

But to draw off the Germans from Verdun, the political leaders ordered their commanders to attack. They hoped the offensive would, in addition, either destroy the enemy army in the field or at least bring back a war of movement.

more given their burdens. They advanced in close formation, the disposition most vulnerable to machine-gun fire.

Thus the scene was set for the worst disaster in the history of the British Army. Yet Haig was hugely confident; so confident, in fact, that his enthusiasm engulfed even those of his subordinate commanders who had been critical of the undertaking.

The one chance of Allied success lay in speed of advance; that is, for the troops to reach the German line of defence before those soldiers who might have survived the artillery bombardment had time to emerge from their dug-outs and man their guns. Haig had ordered the artillery to bombard not merely the enemy front-line trenches but those to the rear, to prevent German reinforcements coming up. Moreover, British and French cavalry had been stationed close behind the Allied line, with the object of quickly exploiting a breakthrough. But for the British infantryman, overburdened and attacking up

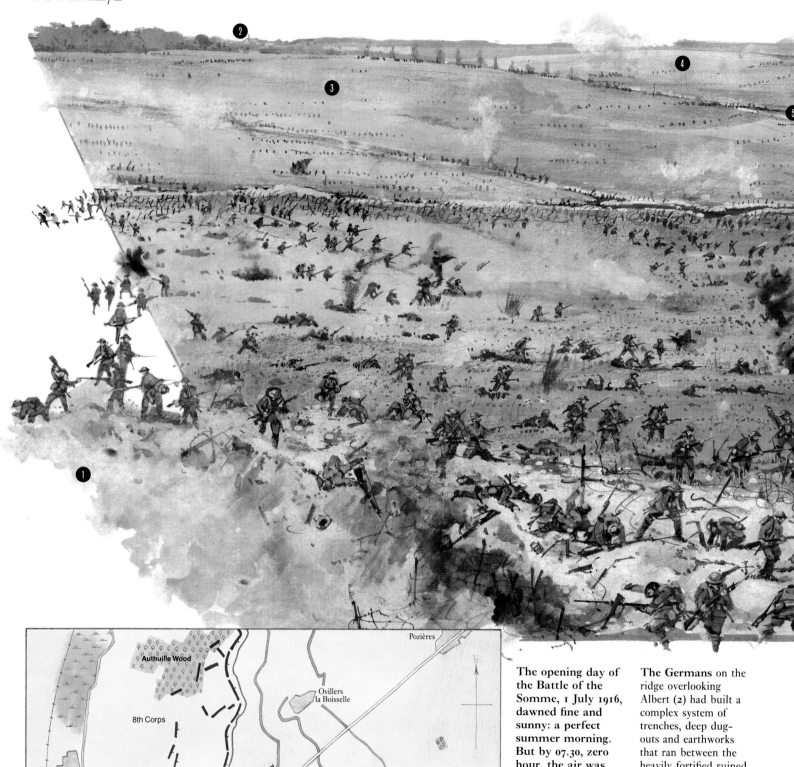

The opening day of the Battle of the Somme, 1 July 1916, dawned fine and sunny: a perfect summer morning. But by 07.30, zero hour, the air was full of smoke and dust from the intense shelling of the German trenches. And at La Boisselle, in the centre of the 34-km/21-ml line, where 12 battalions of 34th Division were poised to attack, two huge mines had just exploded, creating further confusion.

The Germans on the ridge overlooking Albert (2) had built a complex system of trenches, deep dug-outs and earthworks that ran between the heavily fortified ruined villages of Ovillers and La Boisselle. The British trenches lay up to 20m/66ft below the German positions, and no man's land—grassy and full of flowers—varied from some 732m/800yds wide north of La Boisselle to 457m/500yds near Sausage Redoubt.

Poziéres

Authuille Wood

8th Corps

Ovillers
la Boisselle

Contalmaison

Aveluy

Bailiff
Wood

Mash Valley

La Boisselle

Usna Hill

25th NF

Glory
Hole

Schwaben
Hohe

102nd Bde

Sausage Valley

Sausage
Redoubt

26th NF

3rd Corps

101st
Bde

Tara Hill

Shelter
Wood

24th NF

103rd Bde

Fricourt
Farm

Albert

27th NF

Becourt Wood

Bottom
Wood

0   1,000 yds
0   914m

German positions

British positions

Mine craters

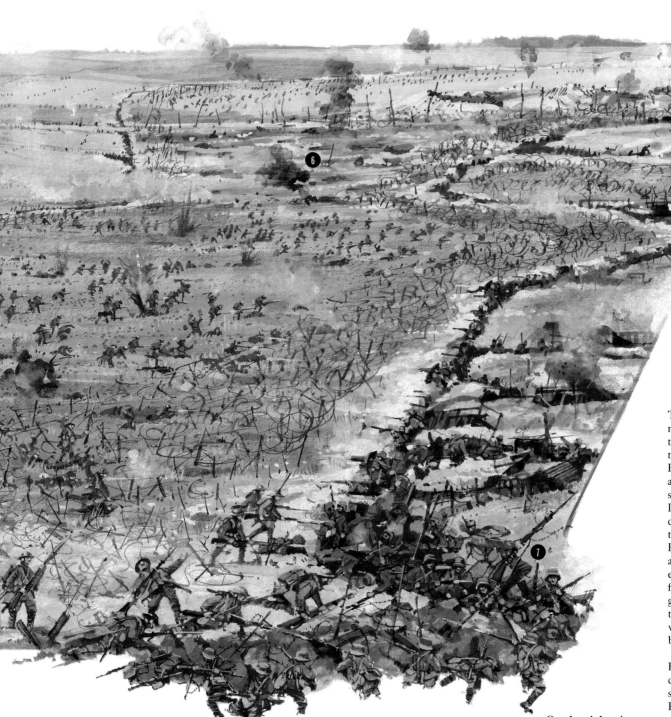

In the trenches at the foot of the La Boisselle spur, in the Glory Hole (6), an area of overlapping shell holes, lay a pioneer company of the 18th Northumberland Fusiliers. About 1.6km/1ml farther back, on either side of the Albert–Bapaume road (5) were two slight rises, called Tara and Usna hills (3,4) by the British troops.

From these positions, just after zero hour, four battalions of the Northumberland Fusiliers rose almost as one man, and advanced in columns at a steady pace across no man's land. There was no cover and, under raking fire from machine-guns of the German 110th Reserve Regiment on the high ground, they were soon in trouble.

As the leading men fell, those behind caught them up and bunches began to form, making an easy target for the German machine-gunners who had emerged unscathed from their deep dug-outs as soon as the barrage lifted at 07.43. Within 10 minutes, the British left had suffered 80 per cent casualties..

On the right, the 26th, 24th and 27th battalions tried to pass south of La Boisselle, but the 26th was largely mown down as it left Tara Hill. The earlier explosion of the mine containing 27,216kg/60,000lb of ammonal near the redoubt of Schwaben Höhe (7), left a crater (1) some 82m/90yds across and 21m/70ft deep. Despite this, the Germans rapidly mounted a fierce defence against 24th and 27th battalions.

These battalions nevertheless managed to overrun the trenches of Schwaben Höhe, and some men advanced up the west side of Sausage Valley. Detachments of troops carrying grenades tried to make raids on La Boisselle, but once again the Germans enfiladed them with fire from machine-guns hidden among the ruins of the village, driving them back with heavy losses.

The men of 101st Brigade, in trenches close to the front line, skirted Sausage Redoubt and made quite good progress up the Fricourt spur.

The 34th Division lost well over half of its total strength on 1 July. By the end of the day, only a small part of La Boisselle had been occupied, but by 3 July, by dogged, bloody fighting, both Fricourt and La Boisselle had been encircled and taken.

the slope, speed was the one thing of which he was incapable.

The British Fourth Army attacked with 13 divisions north of the River Somme on a front of some 24km/15mls; five divisions of the French Sixth Army attacked astride, but mostly south, of the river. Because German opposition was light in this sector, and because the Germans thought that, after their bleeding at Verdun, they were incapable of massed attack, the French made some gains. These were, however, insufficient to enable them to break through and then turn the German lines. The British did not fare so well.

Haig had hoped, on the first day, to penetrate the German lines opposite Albert from Serre in the north to Maricourt in the south. In the second phase, the British planned to take the high ground running between Bapaume and Ginchy, while the French took that in the region around and north of Rancourt.

Then the British were to turn left toward Arras and, in conjunction with a supportive attack southwest of the town, face the German flank and enlarge the penetration. Once all this was achieved, a general advance was to be made eastward in the direction of Cambrai. As Liddell Hart later observed: 'What a contrast between intention and achievement!'

Northwest from Péronne there runs a line of low hills, broken only by the valley of the River Ancre. German defences were sited in depth all along the ridge, giving them an uninterrupted view of British movements. Moreover, Allied artillery during the bombardment had been evenly spread along the whole front, not concentrated; in consequence, the fire was too thin to achieve the intended level of destruction.

The first day of the offensive broke with cynical summer loveliness on a scene shortly to be one of unmitigated horror. Rawlinson wished to attack at first light, or even earlier; the French insisted on waiting until daylight so that they might gauge the effect of their all-night artillery fire. The British reluctantly agreed.

At 07.30, the Allied artillery, which for the previous 65 minutes had been firing at its greatest intensity, lifted. Along the entire front the British and French struggled up out of their trenches and advanced in successive waves. The consequences were inevitable, immediate and annihilating.

Those Germans not knocked out by the week-long bombardment were given time to reach their gun positions, and they poured an unremitting enfilade of lead at the doomed British soldiers. Prime targets

Trench warfare

Although trenches had been constructed on a limited scale in the Russo-Japanese War of 1904–5, they became a significant factor in warfare only in World War I. By the end of 1914, the conflict had developed into what amounted to a siege and both Allied and German soldiers dug trenches to protect themselves from enemy small-arms and machine-gun fire.

At first the trenches were merely lines dug to the depth of an average man's height, with little attempt being made to shore them up, so even a little rain could cause the sides to collapse. The excavated earth was used to make a parapet in front of the trench and a reredos behind it; the front was further protected by barbed wire entanglements of varying depth and complexity.

As time passed and stalemate continued, trenches were more stoutly constructed, with sandbags, wooden—sometimes concrete—sides, and duckboards. Allied trenches and dug-outs, however, never had the same air of permanence that many German ones exhibited, with brass bedsteads, carpets and other comforts.

The slightest movement above trench level drew rifle fire. Initially the Germans were more proficient at this than the Allies, for they kept their snipers in the same sector for long periods so they became familiar with the enemy's trench systems there, while the Allies rotated their snipers with the units to which they belonged.

Chief among other trench weapons were grenades and trench mortars, which fired several types of shell, shrapnel, incendiary and gas among them. Gas was one of the most dreaded weapons, blinding men and

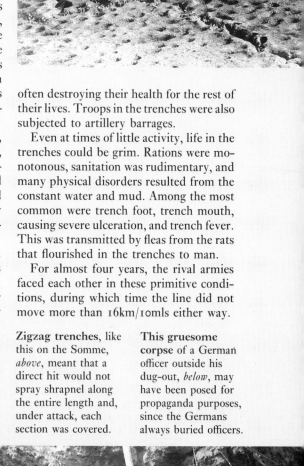

often destroying their health for the rest of their lives. Troops in the trenches were also subjected to artillery barrages.

Even at times of little activity, life in the trenches could be grim. Rations were monotonous, sanitation was rudimentary, and many physical disorders resulted from the constant water and mud. Among the most common were trench foot, trench mouth, causing severe ulceration, and trench fever. This was transmitted by fleas from the rats that flourished in the trenches to man.

For almost four years, the rival armies faced each other in these primitive conditions, during which time the line did not move more than 16km/10mls either way.

Zigzag trenches, like this on the Somme, *above*, meant that a direct hit would not spray shrapnel along the entire length and, under attack, each section was covered.

This gruesome corpse of a German officer outside his dug-out, *below*, may have been posed for propaganda purposes, since the Germans always buried officers.

Those Tubular Trenches
'Is this right for 'eadquarters?'
'Yes, change at Oxford Circus.'

Bruce Bairnsfather's cartoons, *above*, reflect the ordinary soldier's wry humour amid the miseries of trench warfare.

Men of the 1st Battalion, Lancashire Fusliers, *left*, in a communications trench near Beaumont-Hamel. They are fixing bayonets prior to going up to the front line and 'over the top' on 1 July.

Scrape holes in the side of a trench give some shelter to these men of the Border Regiment, *below left*, resting near Thiepval Wood.

This congested Australian dug-out, *below*, is 4.5m/15ft underground. Heavy timber support s, holding up a roof of steel girders, enabled the dug-out to stand up to heavy shelling.

'Every step in my plan has been taken with the Divine help'

General Sir Douglas Haig (1861–1928) took command of the British Expeditionary Force in succession to Sir John French on 10 December 1915. His appointment was not greeted with universal enthusiasm, for while his tenacity and methodical approach were respected, his mind was slow and he lacked any spark of technical brilliance.

Haig had seen action in the Sudan in 1898 and at the Battle of Omdurman, where he served with the Egyptian cavalry. During the Boer War he acted as chief of staff to French. His early rapid promotion was certainly due in some measure to his friendship with King Edward VII.

Silent, humourless and reserved, Haig was also shrewd and ambitious and had unbounded self-esteem. Perhaps his greatest failing was his eternal, often unfounded, optimism, which seemed to stem from his belief that he had been chosen by God to 'do much good and benefit' to his country. It was probably this inability to recognize defeat that led to his continuing attacks on the Somme and to the prolonged bloodbath at Passchendaele. Haig was made a field marshal on 1 January 1917.

Controversy continued to surround his tenure as Commander-in-Chief of the BEF. But, in his favour, Haig strongly advocated Foch's appointment as generalissimo in 1918, and he handled the last British actions of the war with resolution and thoroughness.

Haig was made an earl in 1919 and after the war devoted much of his time to organizing the British Legion and to work on behalf of disabled ex-servicemen.

The most devastating weapon of the war

All the combatant armies went to war with machine-guns. Initially there were only two to a battalion, but as the weapon's capabilities in defence and attack were realized, more and more were issued and soon whole units were armed with only these fast-firing automatic weapons.

There were two basic types of machine-gun. One was a tripod-mounted, water-cooled gun with a belt feed containing 250 rounds, of which the British Vickers and German and Russian Maxim were examples. The other was an air-cooled weapon, of which the French Hotchkiss and the American Lewis were representative. Both of these had magazines, that of the Hotchkiss held 30 rounds, of the Lewis 47. Most machine-guns had a cyclic rate of fire of 500–600rpm, which necessitated a great number of ammunition carriers.

The tripod-mounted weapons were heavy; indeed the Austrian *Schwarzlose* had, in addition to barrel and tripod, a third load, the metal shield. The *Schwarzlose* could also be fired from a monopod, turning it into a light machine-gun. The Russians towed their machine-guns on small wheeled carriages. Early German Maxims had their own gun carriages, while the British broke their guns into two loads—barrel and tripod—carried either by mule or the men themselves.

British soldiers wearing gas helmets, *left*, as they man a Vickers machine-gun near Ovillers.

The deadly fire of the German Maxim, *right*, caused 90% of the casualties on the Somme on 1 July.

in the bright light of a summer morning, they fell in their thousands. Many did not even get past their own wire defences. A single machine-gun, two at most, could bring down an entire battalion, as the men advanced, on Rawlinson's orders, at a steady 90m/100yds a minute.

Soon the ground was smothered with British dead and dying; by 08.30, an hour after the attack started, losses, at a conservative estimate, were in the region of 30,000. Rawlinson continued to throw in his troops and by midday some 100,000 men had been engulfed in the carnage.

The unexpected French attack on the right made good headway. So, too, did the British right wing, where two divisions of 13th Corps captured Montauban and Mametz, thereby isolating Fricourt— which nevertheless the Germans held until the following day.

The Hindenburg cult

One of the most interesting phenomena of the war was the growth of the Hindenburg cult. It arose after the victory of Tannenberg, as a deliberate attempt by the German General Staff to distract attention from the failure of the Schlieffen plan in the west, and to associate themselves with Hindenburg's triumph. Hindenburg, who had taken part in the victorious campaigns of the Franco-Prussian War of 1870-1, was now built up into a father figure: the old general who had again thrown back the invaders of the Fatherland.

Significantly, Hindenburg and not the Kaiser became the focus of the German will to resist. As the war progressed, and the civilian population became increasingly disillusioned, the more important it was to foster a belief in his invincibility, and his image was widely used in propaganda.

Most bizarre was the creation of great wooden statues into which people then drove nails to turn Hindenburg into an

WE ARE VICTORIOUS

'Iron Man', paying toward war funds for the privilege. The practice has its roots in the symbolic importance of iron in German culture. Bismarck, the creator of a unified Germany in the late 1800s, was known as the 'Iron Chancellor', and Germany's most frequent honour to valour was the Iron Cross.

The postcard of the 'Iron Man' of Berlin, *below*, was sold for 15 pfennig in aid of the next of kin of the fallen. British cartoonists, however, *left*, ridiculed the cult as an absurd Teutonic excess.

Schach! Schach!

In the propaganda postcard, *above*, Hindenburg, backed by Conrad, checkmates Grand Duke Nicholas, Cadorna, French and Joffre. But his idolization was also given a sentimental gloss as the postcards, *right*, of an adoring small girl show.

To the north, however, all reports were of failure. Repeated attempts to capture La Boiselle and Ovillers were repulsed, while farther north the three divisions of 10th Corps, designated to take the strongly fortified area around Thiepval, were beaten back with heavy loss. From the extreme British northern flank, the same dismal reports came in. The attack against Beaumont-Hamel proved abortive, and a thrust made by the Third Army against Gommecourt failed utterly.

By nightfall on this first day of the battle, about 60,000 British troops, nearly half the original attack force, had fallen or been taken prisoner. The medical services, not expecting such large losses, were incapable of caring for all the wounded and there were insufficient ambulance trains to take the thousands of serious cases to base hospitals.

The day belonged unquestionably to the Germans, for their six divisions had withstood the heroic, doomed assault of 18 Allied divisions and had relinquished only a small area of ground. Here for all to see was the great lesson of World War I: the machine-gun made direct attack too costly even to contemplate.

Yet Haig was unchastened, indeed remained supremely confident. It is curious, therefore, that he did not immediately exploit the worthwhile gains that had been made on the right. It was some days before he resolved on this, but he then met with strong opposition from both Joffre and Foch, who wanted him first to penetrate the centre ridge between Pozières and Thiepval. Haig wisely refused to do this until he was fully prepared.

The battle continued, but temporarily with less ferocity than on the terrible first day. On 20 July, however, a new offensive on a great scale was launched by 17 British and French divisions on the line Pozières-Foucaucourt. A few hundred metres were overrun but at heavy cost in life.

Winston Churchill was to write: 'The conflict sank once more to the bloody but local struggles of two or three divisions repeatedly renewed as fast as they were consumed, and consumed as fast as they were renewed. By the end of July an advance of about two and a half miles had been made on a front which at this depth did not exceed two miles.' Meanwhile, both sides were bringing up more and more artillery pieces and vast numbers of shells to feed them: the pattern of Verdun was repeating itself.

The struggle now became more equal, for the churned, blood-stained mud affected both sides; and both were short of food and ammunition, since their supply lines had been largely demolished by rival artillery fire. Shell holes made the scene one of pitted lunar desolation, with rotting corpses and mangled abandoned weapons littering the ground.

Great Britain's first conscript army

Conscription, the compulsory enlistment of civilians into the armed forces, was the standard form for recruiting servicemen in most European countries. Great Britain, however, relied for her defence on her naval supremacy, and in 1914 the army consisted wholly of volunteers in the regular and territorial forces. This small but experienced professional force, the BEF, was, however, largely destroyed in the first four months of the war.

If Great Britain were still to play a significant role in military operations in Europe, massed levies would be needed. The 'New Army' was comprised of volunteers only, who poured into recruiting stations in their thousands. By the end of 1915, the British Army in France, thus reinforced, had risen to 38 divisions, more than 3 million men having come forward to serve in 'Kitchener's Army'.

Even so, this did not provide sufficient manpower, together with that of France, to contain the German Army of millions of conscripted levies. The first British scheme for conscription entailed the limited enrolment of single men; those in essential work in industry and on the land were excused. This did not suffice, but the national mood had changed. There was no justice, so most people thought, now that the war was so costly in life and likely to be prolonged, in returning the middle-aged and wounded to the front while healthy, strong young men remained safely at home.

As a result, a Conscription Bill was introduced into the British parliament on 6 January 1916 and quickly passed with large majorities in both houses. In May, conscription was extended to married men. Thus, for the first time in recent history, Great Britain fielded a mass army in Europe, in contrast to her earlier, limited excursions, supported by her navy.

The new army had to hold the Western Front after the demoralization of the French, following General Nivelle's failed offensive of 16 April–21 May 1917 and did it with such success, that Allied victory became a possibility in 1918.

Conscientious objectors were allocated to other tasks, notably on the land. Some, such as the Quakers, volunteered for dangerous duty as stretcher bearers. But the category still carried a stigma and those legitimately excused often wore an official armband, *below right*, proving this fact.

The holocaust of Delville Wood

Delville Wood, lying on a ridge of high ground, was crucial to the Somme offensive, for its capture would allow the British to penetrate the second line of German defences. But first it was necessary to take the village of Longueval: the two positions were considered as one objective, since neither could be held without the other.

The Highlanders suffered such heavy losses in the assault on the village that the attack on Delville Wood was assigned to the South African Infantry Brigade, who had earlier been allotted merely mopping-up operations. They attacked at 05.00 on 15 July, making slow progress through the tangled undergrowth and dense trees of the 155-a/67-ha wood. But by midday they had taken most of it and had begun to dig in.

They came under rifle and machine-gun fire, strong counter-attacks and a three-hour bombardment with shells and tear gas, which also affected their rifles and machine-guns. On 16 and 17 July the South Africans resumed the offensive and strove to take the northwestern corner of the wood; both attacks failed for lack of artillery support.

On the night of the 17th and into the next day, the Germans mounted a massive bombardment; shells are said to have fallen at the rate of 400 a minute. Then at 03.00 on

19 July, nine crack German battalions attacked. They were repulsed by the South Africans, who, when they ran out of ammunition, charged with bayonets fixed. The dwindling band of men held on until they were relieved on 20 July.

Delville Wood in September 1916, with an ammunition limber going up to the front, lies devastated after the six-day battle in

July. Of the 121 South African officers and 3,032 men who fought their way into the wood, only 29 officers and 751 men survived.

The villages of Ovillers and La Boisselle formed part of the Germans' strongly fortified front line. They stood on spurs of high ground overlooking the British lines, enabling any attack along the old Roman road from Albert to Bapaume to be subjected to enfilade fire.

Between Ovillers and La Boisselle lay a shallow valley, called by British troops 'Mash Valley'; south of La Boisselle was another, known inevitably as 'Sausage Valley'. Just below La Boisselle the British and German trenches were, at places, within 46m/50yds of each other. The area, much fought over and scarred by shell holes,

became known in 'Tommy' parlance as 'The Glory Hole'.

The British needed to take both villages. Ovillers was first attacked on 1 July by 8th Division, but to do so the men had to advance up Mash Valley, which provided no cover. Here British troops were cut down in their hundreds by machine-gun fire. One battalion suffered 90 per cent casualties, others hardly less.

La Boisselle was attacked by 34th Division. Only a small part of the village was captured the first day, but the division's losses were the heaviest of all, some 80 per cent, most of whom fell within the first 15 minutes.

Successive attacks, notably on 3 July, all failed. Both villages were so strongly defended, and German resistance so stiff, that it was only when British troops fought their way around to the rear that they were captured.

The whole of La Boisselle was in British hands on the 6th; Ovillers did not fall until 16 July.

1 La Boisselle
2 Mash Valley
3 Attack that seized Ovillers on 16 July
4 Albert-Bapaume road
5 Later attack on La Boisselle, 6 July
6 Sausage Valley
7 The Glory Hole

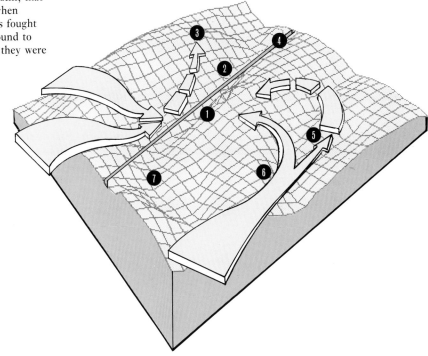

The battle, never dormant, again erupted on a great scale on 25 September, and then once more on 13 November, when a massed British attack was launched along the River Ancre and Beaumont-Hamel was stormed. Before that, however, the British High Command had made a decision of the utmost ineptitude.

By September Haig was desperate to achieve a significant breakthrough. Casualties were mounting by the minute; in the

United Kingdom more and more homes were receiving the brief and dreaded telegram, beginning, 'It is my painful duty to inform you. . .'. Hitherto, confident reports from senior commanders and censorship had between them created an impression of light losses, but great numbers of prisoners taken. Now the truth was emerging; the British, though pushing forward with undiminished tenacity and courage, were suffering a disaster of

gruesome proportions, with hundreds of thousands of men perishing for little territorial, and no strategic, gain.

It was in this month that Haig decided to play his trump card: a new British invention, the 'tank'. This was a potentially decisive arm in warfare, and some 50 of them had been transported to France in the greatest secrecy. Haig, once sceptical, now sought their immediate deployment on the Somme.

On 15 September the first tanks went into action on the Fourth Army's front between Combles and Martinpuich. Through mechanical defects, not all the tanks reached the battlefield and of those that did only 31 crossed the German lines. Nine of these broke down, five ended up, like beetles on their backs, immobilized in shell craters, and only nine managed to operate fully with the infantry.

Their appearance on the field was nonetheless dramatic. British infantry advanced in their protective wake with relative safety; German soldiers were

A Mark I tank equipped with two 6-pounder guns, on its way to attack Thiepval. These tanks were generally accompanied by a machine-gun tank to give covering fire. The wheels at the rear acted as steering fins.

THE COMMANDERS

BELOW

General Fritz von Below (1853–1918), (no relation of General Otto von Below), entered the German Army in 1873 as a lieutenant of the Guard. Promoted General in 1912, he commanded the Eighth Army during the early part of the war, when he was largely responsible for the victory at Lyck in the first campaigns in East Prussia. In 1917 he was moved to the Western Front and in the following year led the Seventeenth Army in the Third Battle of the Aisne (May–June). After failing in his attack on Rheims on 18 June, he was replaced.

SIXT VON ARMIN

General Friedrich Sixt von Armin (1841–1919) served during the Franco-Prussian War until being severely wounded at Metz. In 1914, Armin took part in the German invasion of Belgium and received the surrender of Brussels on 20 August.

He commanded the Sixth Army against the British at Ypres, and again on the Somme in 1916. He made a strenuous resistance at Passchendaele in 1917 and was prominent in the battles of the Lys (1918). In March 1919, he was murdered at his château at Asch by a mob infuriated by his treatment of some peasant trespassers.

RAWLINSON

General Sir Henry Rawlinson (1864–1925) served in numerous colonial campaigns, including that in Burma (1886–7), the Sudan (1898), and in the Boer War. He was in command of the British Fourth Army during the heavy fighting on the Somme in 1916, and in 1917 became a member of the Supreme War Council. Later Rawlinson returned to command in the field and, with Haig, is credited for the plans for the British breakthrough between Cambrai and St Quentin in August 1918. From 1920, he commanded British forces in India.

The death of idealism

'Idealism', the historian A.J.P. Taylor has written, 'perished on the Somme.' Before that sanguinary campaign, in which the British lost some 450,000 men for an advance nowhere more than 8km/5mls, volunteers had poured in their hundreds of thousands to the recruiting offices. Now the men in the trenches had lost faith in their leaders; many lost faith even in the cause for which they fought and all had but one overriding loyalty—to their comrades.

Before the Somme campaign, the spirit of patriotic young Britons was epitomised by the poetry of Rupert Brooke—a belief in the justice of their cause and their hope for a better world. After it the national mood was caught by such disillusioned poets as Siegfried Sassoon, Isaac Rosenberg and Wilfred Owen.

Ordinary soldiers, who had enlisted with equal patriotic fervour, took comfort in simple but pungent humour, typified by Bruce Barinsfather's cartoon showing 'Old Bill', a war veteran, taking refuge in a shell hole and remarking to a young recruit, 'Well, if you knows of a better 'ole, go to it.'

Although the men fought doggedly on, a sense of hopeless despair now engulfed soldiers and civilians alike all over Europe.

'Le bombardement, 1916', aquarelle by André Ducuing

Original manuscript of *Spring* by Isaac Rosenberg.

A battle with only losers

Thousands of young volunteers, who had abandoned civilian safety to enlist in Kitchener's great New Army, were cut down at the Somme, and their comrades disillusioned. Mankind, it seemed, had created a monstrous unending carnage.

It was the same for the Germans. The official history of the German 27th Division, which defended Guillemont, records: 'In the Somme fighting of 1916 there was a spirit of heroism which was never again found in the division . . . the men in 1918 had not the temper, the hard bitterness and spirit of sacrifice of their predecessors.'

German losses at Verdun and on the Somme were so severe they were driven to enlist the entire male population between the ages of 17 and 60 for service in the forces or for war work. But the fighting had left the British and French armies even weaker. In addition, as Winston Churchill wrote, '. . . the actual battle fronts were not appreciably altered . . . no strategic advantage of any kind had been gained.'

taken prisoner in their hundreds, while others, astonished and terrified, fled. But the gain hardly offset the premature revelation to the Germans of this promising new weapon.

Thus the Somme offensive dragged on until, with the advent of winter rains in mid-November, when the exhausted, hungry men could no longer drag themselves through the deepening mud, it died away in disappointment and despair. By then the BEF was astride the ridge originally occupied by the Germans. For this the British and French between them lost in the region of 600,000 men; the Germans more than 440,000. In the opinion of their High Command, 'The Somme was the bloody graveyard of the German Army.' A decision on the Western Front remained as elusive as ever.

The poppy legend

Genghis Khan, the Mongol war lord, is said to have brought seed of the white poppy with him on his advance on Europe during the thirteenth century. Legend has it that the flowers turned red, with the shape of a cross in the centre, when they sprang up after a battle. Certainly, on the Western Front, it was found that the scarlet poppy proliferated on devastated battlefields, particularly those of the Somme. For this reason, the poppy has been adopted as the flower of remembrance, and a shower of poppies, representing British and Commonwealth fighting men who have died since 1914, is released at the annual service of remembrance in the Albert Hall, London.

Battle of Messines *June 1917*

Nivelle's misplaced optimism

The military situation at the beginning of 1917 was unfavourable to the Allies. True, Germany was beginning to feel the strain of war, particularly after her heavy losses on the Somme and at Verdun, but her armies stood on foreign soil. Romania and Serbia had been subdued and the Central Powers now had direct access to their allies Bulgaria and Turkey. Moreover, Russia was tottering toward revolution and collapse. Despite that, Allied leaders were optimistic as the year opened.

In Great Britain, the high cost of the Battle of the Somme had led to the fall of Asquith on 11 December 1916 and to his replacement as prime minister by David Lloyd George, in whose leadership the British people placed high trust.

General Robert Nivelle, who had taken Joffre's place as French Commander-in-Chief at the end of 1916, was particularly confident, largely as a result of Great Britain's increased munitions output and her stronger military presence on the Western Front. Early in 1917, her army numbered some 1,200,000 men, and there were some 2,600,000 French troops, including her colonial levies.

So, taken in conjunction with the small but resolute Belgian Army, the western Allies fielded some 3,900,000 troops, against whom the Germans could deploy only about 2,500,000. Yet, as events had invariably shown, numerical superiority in attack was not necessarily the deciding factor in the face of modern artillery and machine-guns.

Nevertheless, Nivelle resolved to attack, certain that he could achieve a decisive breakthrough. His plan entailed preliminary distracting thrusts north and south of the River Somme, to be followed by the main French blow in Champagne, between Soissons and Rheims.

General Robert Nivelle's plan caused early friction between himself and General Sir Douglas Haig. To give it a chance of success, some French troops had to be withdrawn from south of the Somme and their lines taken over by Haig's men, disrupting his own long-planned attack in Flanders. In addition, although Haig was reinforced with eight divisions, he was placed under Nivelle's overall command; matters did not auger well for harmonious Anglo-French cooperation.

In the event, Nivelle's plan of attack became disjointed when Field Marshal Paul von Hindenburg and General Erich Ludendorff, now in supreme command of all German armies, resolved to eschew attack in the west. They waited to gauge the effect of unrestricted U-boat warfare, which had commenced on 1 February 1917 in the hope of starving the British into submission. The submarines' main areas of activity were in the waters around the British Isles and in much of the Mediterranean.

Ludendorff, rightly expecting that the Allies would attack again in the Somme region, began to withdraw his forces eastward from the bulge in the German line between Arras and Rheims to the heavily defended Siegfried Line, known to the Allies as the Hindenburg Line. The main withdrawal was accomplished on 16 March; the entire abandoned area was laid waste, strewn with mines and booby traps, and the water supplies poisoned.

The situation had altered dramatically,

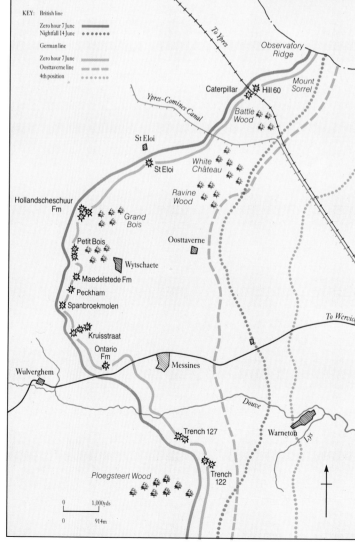

Naval guns were among the artillery pieces used in Flanders. Here a 6in gun is shown in action at night; the men stand with their backs to the glare so as not to be dazzled.

Ammunition was often taken up to the front by pack horses and mules. When it was hot, fringes of beads were attached to their brow bands to protect them from the swarms of flies found around derelict trenches.

At Messines, the British advance was so rapid, and the German troops so stunned by the mine explosions, that they abandoned their weapons; see the hand grenades in the foreground here. The New Zealanders cut the buttons off their prisoners' trousers so they had to hold them up with both hands, then sent them, dazed and compliant, to the rear unescorted.

A soldiers' general

General, later Field Marshal, Sir Herbert Plumer (1857–1932) was the embodiment of the traditional virtues of the British soldier. He was 60 years old at the time of Messines, with wide and varied military service behind him, including fighting in South Africa during the Boer War (1899–1902), when he played a distinguished part in the relief of Mafeking. In 1915 he replaced Sir Horace Smith-Dorrien as commander of the Second Army, and at the

Second Battle of Ypres displayed great decisiveness and coolness of mind.

Arguably, however, his most brilliant work was done during the many months of relative inactivity that followed, for it was then that he remoulded his demoralized command into a confident, compact fighting unit. There were no jealousies under his command; subordinates could contribute to his planning, yet every decision was, in the end, his alone.

Plumer's preparations for the action at Messines, 'methodical and patient', were in John Buchan's words 'carried to the pitch of genius'. Roads and railways were improved; frequent patrols were made to assess the enemy's strength and positions; and aircraft not only kept constant watch on the German lines but prevented their aircraft from taking off.

The regard Plumer had for his men's well-being was epitomised by his efforts to provide clean drinking water during the attack: crucial in midsummer. Lakes and ponds were tapped, water from the Lys sterilized and stored in barges, and cisterns built to trap rainwater. Pipelines, extended as the men advanced, took the water to the front; within 30 minutes of gaining an objective men could receive fresh water.

The reward for Plumer's dedication was the respect of all, and a totally successful action with minimum loss of life.

but Nivelle remained confident that he could break through German lines with little loss of life. He could not have been more misguided, for in the sector he had chosen to attack the Germans now had 43 divisions and the French only slightly more: a totally inadequate margin with which to launch an offensive.

On 9 April, the British Third Army, under Lieutenant-General Sir Edmund Allenby, attacked at Arras, while farther north the Canadian Corps stormed and took Vimy Ridge. Early gains, however, could not be exploited as German resistance stiffened. Nivelle's campaign in Champagne opened on 19 April and met with the same fate as most earlier attacks: some 120,000 Frenchmen fell before the German machine-guns and by the day's end an advance of only 550m/600yds had been made, in tragic contrast to Nivelle's expected 9.6km/6mls.

The bombastic, vainglorious Nivelle had virtually announced to the world his grandiose expectations, making the dreadful defeat doubly damaging. The next month—15 May—he was replaced in command by General Henri Pétain, the hero of Verdun; at the same time, General Ferdinand Foch was made chief of the French General Staff. Pétain resolved to stay on the defensive until American troops arrived and tanks were available in great number.

But Haig, ever the optimist, intent on winning the war with the BEF, now had the opportunity for his long-cherished

MESSINES/2

By June 1917, German troops had been dug in along the entire half-moon of high ground south of Ypres for more than two years. They overlooked all the British positions from their vantage points on the Wytschaete-Messines Ridge, so there was no way a conventional frontal attack against them could succeed.

But at 03.10 on 7 June, they were shaken from their complacency by the explosion of 19 huge mines, and overwhelmed by an immediate, well-planned attack on a 16-km/10-ml front by some 80,000 men of Sir Herbert Plumer's Second Army.

The sector opposite the key village of Messines was held by the 3rd New Zealand Rifle Brigade and the 2nd New Zealand Brigade. While the debris thrown into the air by the exploding mine at Ontario Farm was still falling, they surged across no man's land and the dry bed of the Steenbeek brook.

In most places the German lines had been destroyed. As the New Zealanders made their way up the slope through the tangle of metal, concrete and dismembered bodies, the few stunned men still alive offered no resistance. By about 05.00 the attackers had reached the edge of Messines itself.

The devastated village had been turned into a fortress by the Germans, with a strong trench system and massive barbed wire entanglements (2). German soldiers of the 18th Bavarian Regiment holding Messines sniped from windows and doorways, and threw grenades from behind walls.

Cellars had been converted into dug-outs and there were five concrete strongpoints of the pillbox type (3) and at least 10 machine-guns in the village (6), but they were rapidly put out of action.

Machine-gun fire from Swayne's Farm (1), north of Messines, was halted when a British tank smashed up the farmyard.

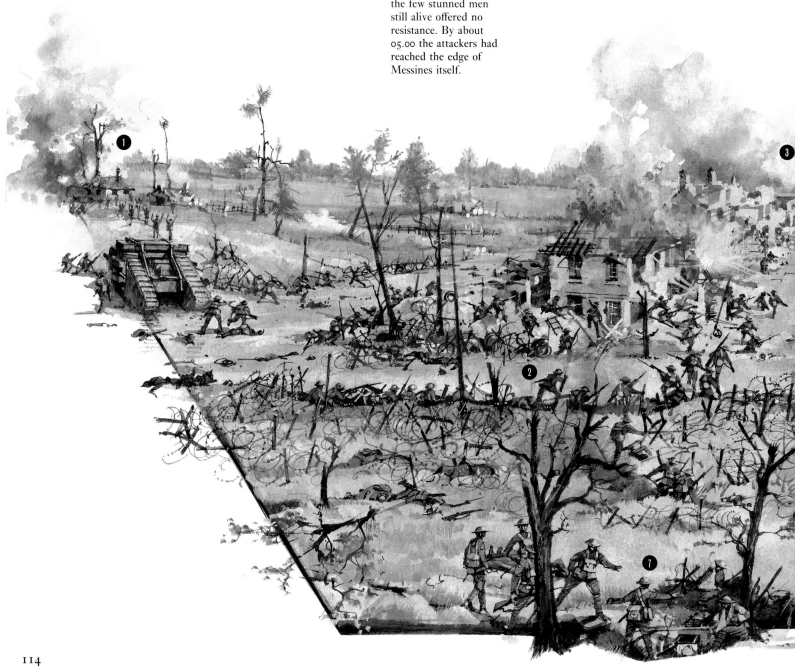

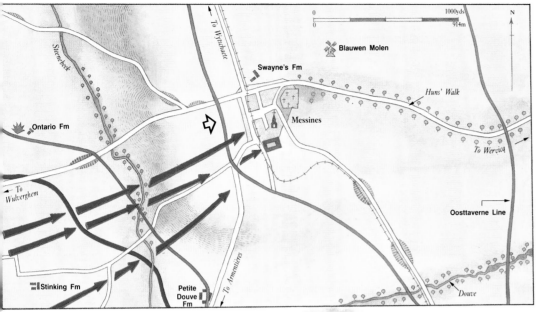

The following labels appear on the map:

To Wyschaete

Blauwen Molen

Swayne's Fm

Huns' Walk

Steenbeek

Ontario Fm

Messines

To Wervicq

To Wulverghem

Oosttaverne Line

Stinking Fm

Petite Douve Fm

To Armentières

Douve

German positions
New Zealanders' attack

1000yds
914m

N

The New Zealanders steadily worked their way through the village, taking the church and the local German HQ in the Institution Royale (5), formerly an orphanage.

Meanwhile, first-aid posts (7) were quickly set up to attend to the wounded and soon water carriers began to arrive so that the fighting men should not suffer from thirst. No detail had been overlooked in Plumer's careful preparations.

By 07.30, Messines was in the New Zealanders' hands, and they had moved on past the cemetery to Huns' Walk (4) the road leading to Wervicq, and Blauwen Molen, and by midday had reached their main objective, the Oosttaverne Line.

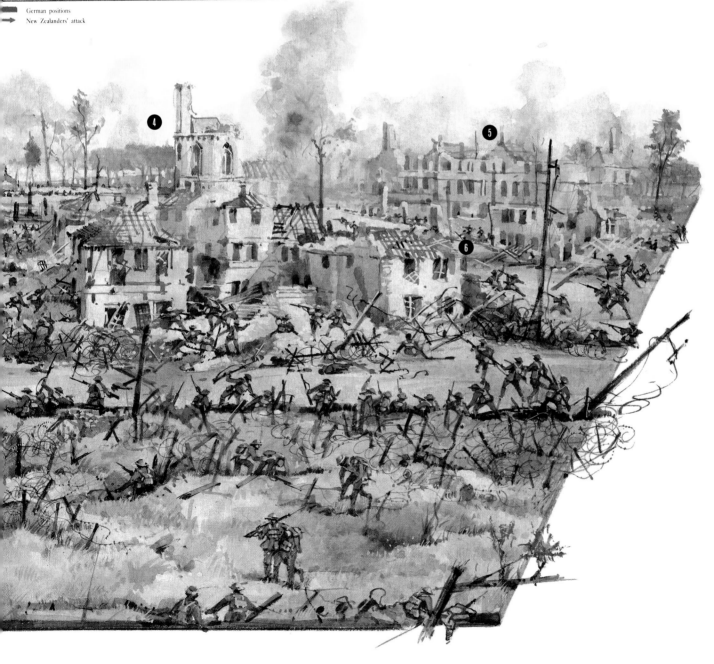

campaign in Flanders. Repeated warnings from Pétain, Foch and numerous others that the plan was attended by great danger went unheeded.

Nevertheless, a successful attack would produce positive results. It would incapacitate German submarine bases in the west; restore to Belgium her occupied territory, thereby depriving Germany of a prime bargaining asset at a future peace conference; and disrupt German communications to the Western Front from their depots in the lower Rhineland.

While Pétain strove to reanimate the French Army, many units of which had mutinied after the collapse of Nivelle's ill-judged offensive, Haig moved the weight of the BEF to Flanders to pursue his plan. This entailed, first, an attack on the Messines Ridge to straighten the salient just south of Ypres which included the towns of Messines and Wytschaete.

The main attack, entrusted to General Sir Herbert Plumer, was to prove one of the few in the war that was immaculately planned and achieved all its objectives. Preparations had started almost a year earlier, but it was not until winter 1916/17 that they were fully implemented.

The Messines-Wytschaete Ridge, some 24km/15mls long and at most 76m/250ft high, lay between the towns of Ypres and Armentières. Since 1914, it had been fortified high ground from which the Germans could overlook and bombard British positions. The ruined village of Messines, on the southern spur of the ridge, commanded a dominating view of

the Lys valley, while Wytschaete overlooked Ypres itself.

The Germans were fully cognisant of the strategical importance of this high ground and had developed the position to the utmost, using forced labour and

The view across the Douve Valley, *top*, shows the artillery bombardment of Messines; the distant shellburst on the ridge marks the site of the church. Huns' Walk and the German pillbox, *above*, after capture reveal the havoc of shelling.

Mutiny in the French Army

His offensive in ruins, General Nivelle was relieved of his command on 15 May 1917 and replaced by General Henri Pétain. The new Commander-in-Chief was faced with a disastrous situation: mutiny.

Revolutionary propaganda inspired by events in Russia had an effect, but the chief cause for mutiny lay in the soldiers' disgust at their commanders' inept leadership, Nivelle's in particular. There were other

A French mutineer about to be executed by firing squad. The adjutant on the right has read out the death sentence and the officer in command is about to drop his white flag. Only 23 mutineers were executed after Nivelle's disastrous offensive, but many others were deported to the colonies.

grievances: leave was difficult to get; their women at home were struggling to keep small businesses and farms going, while thousands of fit young munitions workers were exempt from military service.

The first outbreak of mutiny occurred on 3 May, and it spread rapidly until 16 corps were affected. The men claimed that they were willing to hold the trenches but not to advance against German machine-guns to their certain death.

Pétain travelled along the entire French front, addressing the dispirited, surly men and inspiring them with his solid resolve and sense of discipline. He restored morale by instituting equal and regular tours of duty at the front and leave periods for all units, as well as improving rest camps behind the line. By mid-June the danger was past, but Pétain had still to nurse the army back to full health.

that of unwilling prisoners. Not only were the two villages—Messines and Wytschaete—heavily fortified, but so, too, were the surrounding woods, derelict farmhouses and clusters of cottages. A British attack on the Messines Ridge would meet with the most resolute and entrenched defence. General von Laffert, the German commander on the spot, had ordered that both villages 'must be defended to the utmost and be held to the last man, even if the enemy cuts the connections on both sides and also threatens them from the rear.'

The German front line was a network of trenches, concrete dug-outs and pillboxes. There were also artillery batteries and thousands of yards of interlocking systems of barbed wire defences. To overcome and penetrate this formidable barrier, the British would have to devise some new tactic. They found it in the simultaneous detonation of 454,000kg/ 1m lb of explosives in deep tunnels under the German front line.

Since January 1917, engineers had been employed, quietly but persistently, in tunnelling into the ridge. The Germans were aware of this, but not of its extent, and they, too, dug tunnels. Some eight weeks before the assault on 7 June, Plumer was informed that German engineers were within 46cm/18in of a British mine under Hill 60 in the north of the sector, but it was never detected. In fact, the Germans detonated only one of the British Army's mines before the massive explosions that were to herald the attack.

Of the remaining 21 mines, 19 blew up German fortifications on a curving front of just less than 16km/10mls, running from St Yves to Mount Sorrel. Forming the chord of this arc lay the so-called Oosttaverne Line, some 4km/2½mls in length – the German trench system that had been selected as the final objective of Plumer's attack. For roughly a week beforehand, this area had been the object of concentrated bombardment, with the purpose of cutting German wire entanglements and demolishing gun batteries and strongpoints.

By the concentrated bombardment the element of surprise was relinquished, but at Messines this was of no moment, for surprise was to be achieved by the detonation of the mines. Although forewarned by the bombardment, the Germans had not temporarily withdrawn from the heights; so the troops in their trenches were bombarded for the best part of a week and could receive no food or relief from the devastating artillery fire.

The British plan allocated nine infantry

Mining the Messines Ridge

Limited British mining operations in the Messines Ridge were stepped up in September 1915, and galleries began to be dug that reached a depth of 27m/90ft. Eventually they ran so far that mines were sited as much as 55m/60yds behind the first German line; the longest, at Kruisstraat, ran for some 658m/720yds.

The soil formation of the ridge was of crucial importance. The top sandy layers were underlain by a deep layer of blue clay, into which the tunnels were dug. Great care had to be taken to hide this tell-tale clay, since its detection by aircraft would have betrayed the mines' position and depth.

Tunnelling was a laborious and dangerous job. Most of the work was done by gangs of miners, many of them 'claykickers' who sat in the tunnel, leaning against a wooden backrest with their feet at the face, and dug out the clay with a light spade. Apart from lack of oxygen, there was the constant hazard of earth collapsing and of German bombardment or breakthrough into suspected shafts.

Soon, however, sophisticated listening instruments, such as the geophone, and silent air and water pumps were produced, and ammonal was used in place of the more volatile gunpowder and guncotton. Nevertheless, it is a tribute to the miners' ingenuity and perseverance that 19 of the 21 mines laid were successfully detonated.

'British Mine Exploding' by Adrian Hill

1 Sandbagged trench. 2 Barbed wire. 3 No man's land. 4 Shaft. 5 Tamping. 6 Explosives chamber.

Osttaverne Wood, whose remains are seen, *below*, with the trenches that had formed part of the third German line of defence, was taken by the British on 11 June.

The ruined village of Wytschaete, *above*, was captured by troops of the 16th Irish and 36th Ulster divisions.

divisions to the assault, with three more in reserve. On the south, or right flank, stood General Godley's 2nd Anzac Corps; in the centre, General Hamilton-Gordon's 9th Corps; while on the left, or northern, flank, was General Morland's 10th Corps.

Early in the night of 6/7 June there was a great summer storm, with thunder, lightning and heavy rain; when the storm subsided, it was replaced by the uninterrupted flashes of bursting shells. Then, at precisely 03.10, there gushed up, as Gibbs recorded, 'enormous volumes of scarlet flame from the exploding mines and of earth and smoke, all lighted by the flame, spilling over into fountains of fierce colour, so that all the countryside was illuminated by red light. Where some of us stood watching, aghast and spell-bound by the burning horror, the ground trembled and surged violently to and fro.' It was, he wrote, 'the most terribly beautiful thing, the most diabolical splendour, I have seen in war.'

The first German trench system was assailed immediately; then the British and

Women at war

World War I transformed Western society, not least in its emancipation of women, largely because of the enormous contribution they made to the war effort. This was particularly great in Britain after the introduction of male conscription in 1916, but in some other countries, including Germany, many tasks were considered unsuitable for women and initially their employment in war work was discouraged. But later on, the shortage of manpower reversed the situation.

In the field, women proved themselves capable ambulance drivers, and many drove trucks bringing up supplies to the troops. But perhaps their most important role was as nurses, selflessly caring for the wounded, often in dreadful conditions close to the front.

On the Home Front, women's tasks were diverse and often physically taxing. All over Europe they worked in agriculture, producing food, while in Britain many were employed in the shipyards and in the coal fields. In Britain also, in the summer of 1914, some 200,000 women were employed in making munitions, by November 1918, the last month of the war, 947,000. In the other belligerent countries, fewer women worked in munitions, but they played a significant part in the total war effort.

Many women took over men's duties in the public services, operating railway signals, acting as porters, driving buses and working in the Fire Brigade and the Police. By 1916, however, unpaid volunteer service was no longer adequate, and in Britain officially recognized, paid bodies of women were established. The Women's National Land Service Corps, The Women's Auxiliary Corps and the Women's Royal Naval Service and several others were in existence by 1917.

Women's immense contribution during the war led directly to their enfranchisement and to greater professional and social opportunities than they had ever before enjoyed.

Gilbert Rogers's painting depicts stretcher-bearers of the Royal Medical Corps bringing in wounded through a captured German trench at Messines. Stretcher-bearers, many over service age, bravely exposed themselves to danger and suffered heavy casualties.

Anzac troops stormed the crest lines. Within two hours some Allied troops had already reached their second objective, and by 07.00 Messines itself had fallen. The defences of Wyschaete were penetrated early in the morning and British troops immediately began to move down the eastern slopes of the ridge. Guns were brought forward to continue the bombardment and more than 7,000 German prisoners taken, as well as 67 artillery pieces, 94 trench mortars and nearly 300 machine-guns.

In the early afternoon, Allied reserve divisions and tanks passed through their comrades' lines and by about 15.10 the ridge in its entirety was securely held and all objectives taken. For the price of 16,000 casualties, success was complete. British and Empire troops dug in and organized their defences so rapidly that all German counter-attacks the following day were thrown back and even more ground gained by the Allies.

The victory was both immediate and absolute; equally important, it provided a tonic for the Allied civilian population, who were becoming increasingly war-weary and despondent. Messines also provided a sure lesson for future campaigns: surprise and limited, attainable objectives that could subsequently be held should be the tactical aim.

Haig ignores the lesson of Messines

The brilliant success at Messines had a regrettable repercussion. Haig came to believe that what had once been achieved, so swiftly and at relatively little cost, might be repeated. In his mind, it seems, now reposed a conviction that, in Flanders, he could defeat the German armies.

Heavy bombardments of the Ypres area prior to attack had, however, highlighted a singular danger: to the north it was largely reclaimed marshland and once the drainage system was destroyed by artillery fire, it quickly reverted to bog. To this the expectant Germans had devised an answer. They abandoned the concept of several lines of dug-outs and instead relied on machine-guns in strongpoints, while husbanding their troops for counter-attack.

In the flattering afterglow of Messines, Haig's confidence was unbounded. He had not learned the right lesson, however, nor did he have a solution to the problem that would be posed by the mud created by rain and his own artillery. Once more he was resolved upon a decisive breakthrough; once more he was to be disabused and thousands of his men laid low in the mud of Passchendaele.

Austrian women make uniforms, *left above*, by cannibalizing old garments; *far left*, a French woman doing light engineering work in a factory. Edith Cavell, *left*, an English nurse working in Brussels, was arrested for hiding Allied soldiers and shot.

Women undertook varied war work: *far left*, an English bus conductress; *left*, a group of workers in a German factory; *below*, women making gears at the Krupp's armament works in Essen.

Battle of *Passchendaele* *July–November 1917*

Field Marshal Sir Douglas Haig's plan for the British attack in Flanders was to break through the German line from the Ypres salient and then encircle the German right flank resting on the North Sea coast. He was not dissuaded from this strategy by the awesome losses of the Somme offensive in 1916, nor by the doubts expressed regarding the scheme by his Intelligence staff and his fellow commanders. Pétain thought Haig's attack toward Ostend was 'certain to fail', while Foch described the enterprise as 'futile' and 'fantastic'.

Nor was Haig deterred by the fact that German U-boats operated in the main from home ports, and even if Zeebrugge and Ostend were taken, the submarine peril would persist. As early as June 1917, the Germans were aware that Haig intended to strike in Flanders, probably from near Ypres, for imprudent, almost public debate by Allied politicians had made this evident. In any event, the land near the mouth of the River Yser, flooded by the Belgians in 1914, now provided the German right with a defensive barrier.

There were further objections to the plan. The French Army was still in a state of convalescence following the mutinies, and there was the inevitable problem of mud in terrain dependent on artificial drainage. But in his euphoria, Haig had become convinced that he could defeat Germany with the BEF alone before the Americans arrived to steal his glory.

Haig had one compelling argument in favour of attack—the decisive, though limited, victory at Messines, although the credit for that was rightly ascribed almost entirely to General Sir Herbert Plumer. Despite all the irrefutable objections to his

Strategy for disaster

By the middle of 1917 the Allied military situation was grave. The German submarine offensive was at its height; Italy was unable to make progress against Austria; and Russia, on the point of collapse, would shortly unilaterally sue for peace.

There was only one hopeful prospect: the unrestricted sinking of neutral and unarmed ships by German U-boats had brought the United States of America into the war. But her contribution could not be felt in full until her troops arrived in France in considerable numbers.

The German U-boat offensive had a profound effect on Allied military plans in the second half of 1917, for the German submarine base at Bruges was within 48km/30mls of the Allied front line. An advance through Flanders was, therefore, resolved upon, in part to deprive the Germans of this sanctuary for their submarines.

Field Marshal Sir Douglas Haig's other concern was to dislodge the Germans from their dominating positions on the ridge of high ground running from Westroosbeke to Broodseinde before winter set in.

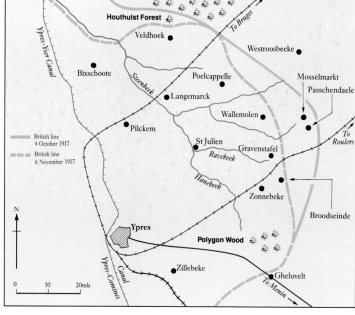

plan, Haig astonishingly got his way and the Third Battle of Ypres (commonly known as Passchendaele) was reluctantly sanctioned by his political masters.

The new offensive was launched north of Messines, on a 32-km/20-ml front between Warneton and Dixmude, on 31 July 1917. Speedy success was essential, since records gathered over the previous 80 years showed that at best only three weeks of rain-free weather could be expected at that time of the year. In the event, there was to be an early and continuous downpour.

The preliminary bombardment was the heaviest so far mounted: over two weeks 3,100 guns fired some $4\frac{1}{2}$ million shells. It served, however, only to churn up the sodden land, whose drainage system had long since been destroyed by years of artillery fire, into a vast morass of craters

The featureless desolation of the battlefields near Passchendaele is well conveyed by the panorama, *below*. In this wilderness, both the British soldiers, at Pilckem in August 1917, *left*, and the German storm troops, *right*, sheltering in a shell hole with their pouches full of grenades, had to struggle to survive.

filled with water, through which the British were expected to advance.

Because of the nature of the terrain, the Germans had abandoned the building of lines of defensive trenches in the northern part of the Ypres salient in favour of concrete pillboxes housing machine-guns. The advancing British—if advance they could through the craters and mud—would, therefore, come under remorseless, raking fire.

The principal part in the attack was given to General Sir Hubert Gough's Fifth Army, with one corps of Plumer's Second Army on its right flank and the French First Army, under General François Anthoine, on its left. The German forces in the area—Prince Rupprecht's Fourth Army—were commanded by General Sixt von Armin, who had led them at Messines.

The Lewis gun

One of the most successful machine-guns of World War I was the American designed, air-cooled, drum-fed Lewis. It was bi-pod mounted, which kept its weight down to 11kg/25lb, so increasing its mobility. Its weight could be further reduced by removing the cooling jacket, and it was like this that the Lewis gun was used as a hand-directed weapon on Allied aircraft.

The Lewis's lightness and versatility made it useful in close-support infantry attacks also. It did, however, tend to jam in damp or muddy conditions, and it suffered from feed blockages caused by the spring mechanism of the 47-round ammunition drum which fitted over the breech. It fired the ordinary British .303 round and had a rate of fire of 500–600rpm.

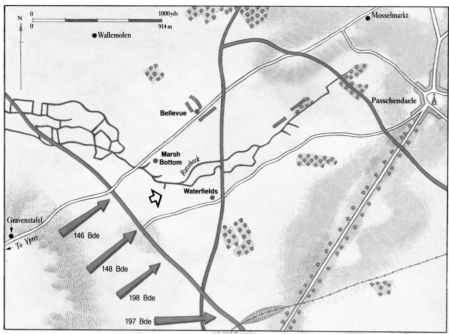

British front line
German positions
Ypres-Roulers railway

Torrential rain fell for two days before the attack and it was still raining on the inky-black night of 8/9 October while the troops struggled, through mud that was often knee-deep, the 4km/2½mls from their assembly areas to the front.

Whole battalions fell behind and did not reach the jumping-off point on schedule, so there were greats gaps in the line when the advance went forward at 05.20.

The weather began to clear as the troops struggled forward; by 09.30 visibility was good.

On the left, 146th Brigade (2) managed to cross the flooded Ravebeek using the raised Gravenstafel road. In the bright, almost transparent light, they were perfect targets for the German machine-guns, in pillboxes (4) on the spur of higher ground near Bellevue, and also concealed in shell holes.

The British advance of 4 October 1917 had created a bulge in the front to the north of Ypres. Five days later, so as to bring up his left and straighten his line, Field Marshal Haig ordered another attack, on a 16-km/ 10-ml front. The units deployed facing Passchendaele were 146th and 148th brigades of the 1st West Riding Regiment and 197th and 198th brigades of the 2nd East Lancashire Regiment. Opposing them was a fresh German force, the 16th, or 'Iron', Division.

The main British thrust was to be made toward Passchendaele, lying some 50m/165ft up on the ridge that ran south from Westroosbeke to Broodseinde, with several spurs, like fingers, extending westward.

Then they came up against belts of wire (3) up to 37m/40yds wide that stretched intact in front of the German defences.

The area had been heavily bombarded before the attack, but the high-explosive shells designed to cut the wire had merely buried themselves in the mud.

The entire brigade was pinned down, and men had to lie in the mud in water-filled shell holes to find any protection.

Messenger pigeons (1), released to take news of the unexpected wire, were too terrified by the noise of artillery and machine-gun fire to fly, and fluttered around their handlers.

148th Brigade (9) made hardly any headway. The Ravebeek, swollen with rainwater, was a morass some 27m/30yds to 47m/50yds wide. Only a few small parties of men succeeded in wading through the water, which was waist-deep in the middle.

In the centre, 198th Brigade (6) made some progress, although hampered by the mud and deep, water-filled, derelict German trenches on the lower slopes of the southern spur of high ground. They, too, came under enfilading fire from the pillboxes at Bellevue.

On the crest of the southern spur, where the earth was sandy, 197th Brigade (7) made good progress, at first along the Ypres-Roulers railway track (8), then along the road.

They came under both machine-gun and shell fire from German batteries south of Passchendaele (5). But by about 10.00, they were approaching their objective, a point some 685m/750yds from the village.

Around midday, finding no support on either side, 197 Brigade fell back to 198's line, and before nightfall a general withdrawal to a line only some 457m/500yds from the start was ordered.

For this meagre gain, almost 6,000 men were lost in this sector alone. Precise German losses are not known, but records state they were 'considerable' and that the 'sufferings of the troops bore no relation to the advantage obtained' in the day's fighting.

A 9.2in howitzer of the 2nd Australian Siege Battery in action at Voormezeele, near Ypres, in September 1917.

The camouflaged gun is in a semi-permanent position, with a platform made of heavy baulks of wood nailed together and laid on hard core. There are duckboards for the bombardiers to walk on, and sandbags handy to compensate for any subsidence during firing.

When rain turned the ground into a quagmire, platforms and sandbags were, however, unable to prevent the guns from sinking. And during the attack on 9 October, the fire from the guns near Gravenstafel was so erratic and so poorly registered that they gave the attacking troops hardly any support.

At 03.50 on the first day of the attack, 12 infantry divisions went forward in heavy mist. It quickly became evident that the attack was not going according to plan. On the left flank, three ridges north of Ypres—Bixschoote, St Julien and Pilckem—were taken in an advance of some 3.2km/2mls; but on the right, the thrust southeast of Ypres, toward the Ypres-Menin road, was halted short of its objectives. Nonetheless, some 6,000 prisoners, including 133 officers, were taken.

Ceaseless rain made further progress impossible, not merely for the infantry, who were sinking up to their thighs in mud, but for the tanks held in readiness to exploit a breakthrough. Gough, earlier a convinced supporter of the attack, now expressed himself uneasy to Haig, but the Commander-in-Chief was fatally confident of a successful outcome. The rain was so heavy and continuous, however, that it was another two weeks before a second thrust could be mounted.

During that period rain fell without pause. 'Even when it stopped on the 5th', the historian John Buchan was to write, 'there followed days of sombre skies and wet mists and mucky clouds. The misery of our troops huddled in their impromptu lines or strung out in shell-holes, cannot be pictured in words.'

Haig, though still hugely optimistic, reported later in a dispatch: 'The low-lying clayey soil, torn by shells and sodden by rain, turned to a succession of vast muddy pools. The valleys of the choked and overflowing streams were speedily transformed into long stretches of bog, impassable except by a few well-defined tracks, which became marks for the enemy's artillery. To leave these tracks was to risk death by drowning, and in the course of the subsequent fighting on several occasions both men and pack animals were lost in this way.' It was a neat description by a commander who had been forewarned of just this certainty.

Farther on in his dispatch, Haig wrote: '... this unavoidable delay in the development of our offensive was of the greatest service to the enemy. Valuable time was lost, the troops opposed to us were able to recover from the disorganization produced by our first attack, and the enemy was given the opportunity to bring up reinforcements.' But despite all this, Haig never deviated from his original plan to renew the offensive at the earliest favourable moment.

Conditions were little better for the Germans. As Philip Gibbs, correspondent for the London *Daily Telegraph* who was

Happy Memories of the Zoo

'What time do they feed the Sea-Lions, Alf?'

The cartoons of the resigned but resolute soldiers in the trenches, by Captain Bruce Bairnsfather, did much to raise British morale at the front. One Member of Parliament wrote of him that he was 'rising to be a factor in the situation, just as Gillray was a factor in the Napoleonic wars'.

Lancashire Fusiliers, *left*, with their Lewis machine-gun, take station in a bay of a captured German trench. The barbed wire apron fence, by which it had been defended, is totally wrecked.

Men of the 16th Canadian machine-gun company, armed with Vickers machine-guns, take shelter in shell holes, *above*. The gunner on the left is firing on a fixed line, the accuracy of his fire ensured by the stakes on either side of the barrel. On the right, one man has contrived to make a roof for his shell hole.

Germany's frontier forts

The building of small, defensive forts, or blockhouses, is as old as the history of formal warfare. Although quite early in World War I both sides moved underground into elaborate trench systems, there were areas where it was not possible to dig deep trenches. This was particularly so in the Passchendaele sector of the Ypres salient, for the ground was reclaimed swamp and water was met at a depth of 45cm/18in.

Since the construction of trenches here was so difficult, the Germans constructed concrete blockhouses, or pillboxes. These boxes stood above ground and were, therefore, visible and obvious targets, but they were so solidly made that only a direct hit by a heavy shell could destroy them. Thus the pillbox garrison was immune to normal shell and machine-gun fire and was to a certain extent protected from the weather. Because the men were serving together in what was essentially a small box with loopholes for machine-guns, their morale was high, for they gave each other mutual psychological support.

The siting of the machine-guns inside the pillboxes provided interlocking zones of fire, which meant that each position had to be attacked and taken out individually. The advantage of a pillbox line was that it could be held with fewer men who could, therefore, be rotated more frequently: another morale-boosting factor.

Coupled with pillboxes, the Germans employed barbed wire to great depth.

Experience had shown early on in the war that a trench line defended by two or three belts of uncut wire (this rose to as many as 18 in some sensitive sectors) held up an infantry attack. Attempts to smash wire defences by artillery barrage were seldom successful.

Later, in addition to the standard type, with barbs every 30cm/12in, the Germans introduced a new type of wire with steel strips cut into sharp-edged and pointed triangles. The *Flandern Zaun* (Flanders hedges) were almost indestructible, and no infantry could penetrate them. It was not until the advent of the tank, which simply rolled over barbed wire, that a counter was found to this simple but effective means of halting an attack.

present at the battles as an observer, wrote: 'The suffering of all the German troops, huddled together in exposed places, must be as hideous as anything in the agony of mankind, slashed to bits by storms of shells and urged forward to counter-attacks which they know will be their death.'

The next Allied blow fell on 16 August when Gough's Fifth Army assaulted the Gheluvelt-Langemarck line, stretching from the Ypres-Menin road to the north-west. The earlier pattern was repeated. The left wing advanced a short distance beyond the Steenbeek rivulet and Langemarck, a village now reduced to rubble. On the right, the advance was once more quickly halted before worthwhile gains could be made or a significant number of Germans captured.

Now the morale of the British Army began to deteriorate. As Liddell Hart observed, men did not 'feel that the enemy's skilful resistance and the mud were the sole explanation of their fruitless sacrifice. Complaints against the direction and staff work in Gough's Army were general and bitter . . .'.

Perhaps for this reason, Haig now extended the front of Second Army northward to include the crucial Menin Road area, thus giving Plumer the principal target: the Gheluvelt plateau due east of Ypres. Plumer determined to take the plateau in four meticulously planned

stages; he opted, as he had at Messines, at each stage to concentrate his effort, going for limited objectives with strong artillery support. This tactic would leave his army capable of repelling the counter-attacks that would surely follow.

Although thick mist persisted so air reconnaissance was ineffective, Plumer's initial thrust was made at 05.40 on 20 September. Four divisions, two of them Australian, went in on a limited front of about 4.5km/2¾mls, with 1,300 guns massed along the line between Klein Zillebeke and Westhoek.

The men of Second Army, pushing either side of the Menin Road, made significant gains. Within 45 minutes the first targets had been seized. By midday, the 23rd North of England Division south of the road was only about 0.8km/½ml from Gheluvelt, while north of the road Nonne Bosschen, Black Watch Corner, Veldhoek and half of Polygon Wood had been taken. Farther north, Fifth Army's forces had advanced astride the Ypres-Roulers railway to a point just short of Zonnebeke.

All objectives had been overrun and counter-attacks thrown back. The Allied line had been pushed forward an average of 823m/900yds and, at the farthest, near Langemarck, about 1.6km/1ml. The southern end of the Passchendaele Ridge, upon which German security there depended, had been taken, although the British were not yet in striking distance of the northern part.

The second phase of the attack went in on 26 September, a day when the weather was unusually fine, although the churned up, sodden ground remained impassable

These four drawings from Jean Lefort's sketchbook depict the terrible conditions besetting the Belgian Army on the River Yser during the autumn of 1917.

Paul Nash was an official war artist with the British forces, whose compelling studies show the war in all its gruesome squalor.

The painting *The Menin Road*, *above*, with branchless trees, shell holes, smashed and abandoned weapons, and scurrying figures, presents an almost surreal landscape.

In *The Ypres Salient at Night*, *right*, bursting star shells briefly light up the scene, giving it an eerie splendour and beauty which add to the sense of pointless conflict.

Canadian capture of Passchendaele

Haig selected the Canadians to achieve his ultimate aim: the capture of Passchendaele and Mosselmarkt and the ridge beyond. The Canadian Corps commander, General Arthur Currie, planned a step by step advance, backed by well-organized artillery support.

The first two phases of the attack, on 26 and 30 October, along the ridges on either side of the Ravebeek Valley, made solid progress. Then at 06.00 on 6 November, men of the 1st and 2nd divisions, covered by a heavy barrage from the guns, made the final spurt forward. Passchendaele, now only a 'brick-coloured stain' in the mud, with just the church recognizable as a building, was heavily defended by Germans with machine-guns in concrete pillboxes. By 08.00, fighting with great bravery, the Canadians had taken both villages for the loss of 2,238 men.

Keeping in contact

Methods of communication during the war, though primitive by today's standards, were diverse and inventive. Telephones were the main means of oral communication. Thousands of miles of cable linked the armies of both sides, but reception was often poor and the cables were repeatedly severed by bursting shells.

Radio technology was still experimental. One British Tank Brigade commander commented: 'Many times it was impossible to hear or be heard when speaking to Corps Headquarters at a distance of five or six miles.' But by the Battle of Cambrai, wireless signalling had become more efficient and proved valuable in keeping the tanks in touch with the rear. On the first day, five tons of cable were towed forward on sledges by tanks, together with 120 poles, numerous telephones and their exchanges. They proved almost useless, for the ebb and flow of the fighting hindered the collection of accurate information, and such as was gleaned was usually out of date by the time of its transmission.

To overcome this, a new method of relaying information was devised: collecting points were established at intervals some 550m/600yds behind the front line. There, specially trained officers correlated all incoming information before signalling a general report to the rear.

Other manual methods of signalling included flags, arc lights operated by gas, and heliographs whose flashing signals could be read by telescope. Tanks again encountered special problems. A hand, or Aldis, lamp for signalling in Morse code was found unsatisfactory; a more efficient method was for tank to signal to tank, or to the supporting infantry, by means of discs of different colour.

British signallers, *below left*, in a shell hole in 1916: the officer observes the fall of fire, and the information is passed back to the guns by daylight lamp.

The German unit, *below right*, is using a heliograph, which operates on sunlight.

Animals played a large part in communications. Pigeons were used to take messages: here, incongruously, a bird is released through a vent in a British tank.

Messenger dogs, seen, *right*, with a German assault squad, were also used by men tending the wounded in the field to fetch supplies from the rear.

and treacherous. The infantry advanced at sunrise, and the Australians had soon captured what remained untaken of Polygon Wood. German counter-attacks, though frustrated, followed, as did more torrential rain.

Then on 4 October, the Allies attacked again, this time on a front of 13km/8mls with 12 divisions (eight from Second Army and four from Fifth Army), four of which were Anzac divisions. The principal ridge east of Ypres, from Gheluvelt to Broodseinde, was gained.

Despite these limited, hugely costly successes, the British strategic situation was now evident to all but the deliberately obtuse as one of stark and undeniable failure. Ten weeks of fighting had achieved what Haig had calculated would take two days. Winter was approaching, and the main British objectives beyond the Passchendaele Ridge had not been attained. There was no longer a possibility of a decisive operation in Flanders, still less the seizure of Zeebrugge and Ostend.

Now was the moment for Haig to abandon his abortive offensive. But, still an optimist and misinformed by his sycophantic staff as to the true gravity of the situation, Haig determined to press on. If October were to bring its usual weather, as indicated by the records, and as it had the previous year on the Somme, conditions would be almost beyond endurance and attack impossible. Moreover, Russia was now out of the war and German divisions were being moved rapidly by train from the east to the Western Front.

But Haig had persuasive arguments to support his inflexible resolve. The French were preparing a great attack on the heights of the Aisne for the end of the month, and so it was, he claimed, essential to keep the Germans occupied in Flanders. In addition, an attack toward Cambrai had been scheduled for November, and an offensive was due to begin in Italy. Haig won his point, although the scale of his attacks was to be reduced.

'The last stages of the Third Battle of Ypres', John Buchan was to write, 'were probably the muddiest combats ever known in the history of war.' This was certainly true. In his memoirs General Gough wrote of a countryside 'battered, beaten, and torn by a torrent of shell and explosive . . . the soil shaken and reshaken, fields tossed into new and fantastic shapes.'

On this already immensely difficult battlefield, then fell the incessant rain. 'Still the guns churned this treacherous slime, the surplus water poured into the trenches as its natural outlet, and they became impossible for the troops . . . men

Rosa Luxemburg addressing a left-wing rally in Berlin, 1918. She, with Karl Liebknecht, was co-founder of the Spartacist Movement, which aimed to end the war and establish a Bolshevik government. Both were arrested in 1919 and, on their way to prison, were killed by soldiers.

staggered warily over duckboards. Wounded men falling headlong into shell-holes were in danger of drowning. . . . Guns sank till they became useless; rifles caked and would not fire; even food was tainted with the inevitable mud.'

Haig, it is only fair to say, was never informed of the ghastly horror at the front; nor did his senior staff know, or choose to imagine, the true situation. The shock of

realization is exemplified by an oft-quoted incident, when Lieutenant-General Sir Launcelot Kiggell, Haig's Chief of Staff, paying his first visit to the front, was reduced to tears as his car lurched and slithered over the battleground. 'Good God,' he muttered, 'did we really send men to fight in that?' He was dryly informed that conditions were much worse farther up.

Convalescent German soldiers in Berlin collecting Christmas cakes, called *Stollen*, for distribution to the troops.

Bread rationing was general in Europe. In 1915, German civilians were allowed 1,400g/ 3lb weekly; by 1919 the French ration was only 100g/3½oz a day.

Despite the appalling conditions and human suffering, despite warnings by meteorologists that the torrential downpour on 8 October would continue, Haig resolved to pursue the attack the next day on a 13-km/8-ml front, stretching from Veldhoek in the north to near Broodseinde in the south. The result was as before: huge losses of men and little ground gained. Nevertheless, and again despite ceaseless rain, Haig ordered yet another attack on the Passchendaele Ridge. Once more the result was certain, with the 'attacking troops . . . back almost on their starting line.'

But Haig, though by now probably at last disabused as to the prospect of a decisive breakthrough, persisted in gaining his objective: the high ground around the village of Passchendaele. An attack by the French First and British Fifth armies was launched on 22 October; another by the Second Army on the 26th; and yet another on 30 October. As before, progress was trivial, losses high. And the already intolerable misery of the attackers was now exacerbated by the Germans' increased use of mustard gas.

Then, on 2 November, a sudden dash by the 1st and 2nd Canadian divisions finally secured the high ground on which stood the destroyed Passchendaele village. Haig was at last content. The Ypres salient, where since 1914 the Allies had been prime targets for the German guns, had been flattened, leaving only a small salient around Passchendaele itself. But Zeebrugge and Ostend had not been taken, nor the enemy rolled back. Still less had the war been won.

Victory for the Allies remained as elusive as ever, despite some 250,000 casualties. Of these, 90,000 were reported 'missing'; almost half that number—a little more than 40,000—were never found. Most of them had drowned and been interred in the mud: even today, more than 70 years later, farmers ploughing the fields unearth the bones of these unidentified men. German losses, though unrecorded, were described by the official history as 'excessive'.

Mud spelt disaster for men and animals alike. Men of the 1st Anzac Corps, *left*, try to free an entrapped horse and light ration cart. For the men of this gunnery detachment going up to the line along duckboards, *below*, to slip or fall off the boards into the liquid mud meant almost certain death.

General Sir Hubert Gough (1870–1963) came of famous Irish army family. He commanded the 3rd Cavalry Brigade in France from July 1914, and in 1915 was given command of the 1st Corps, which distinguished itself at Loos. He became one of Haig's chief subordinate commanders and led the Fifth Army on the Somme.

Gough's operations at Passchendaele were, however, criticised as being needlessly costly of life and when, in March 1918, the Germans broke through despite his strenuous efforts, he was held responsible for the disaster and recalled to England.

Prince Rupprecht of Bavaria (1869–1955) was the eldest son of King Louis III. He commanded the German Sixth Army in Lorraine in August–September 1914, and in October was given command of German forces on the Lys. He came to prominence during the First Battle of Ypres, and thereafter fought mostly against the British in the Ypres salient.

In November 1918, when Bavaria became a republic, he lost his title. Rupprecht was a descendant of the English King, Charles I, and was held by some legitimists to be the rightful British king, as head of the House of Stuart.

Off-duty amusements

The principal hope of soldiers in the trenches was to live long enough to earn a spell of leave, either in a rest centre, in Paris or at home. Men on leave wanted a complete change of environment; some sought the tranquillity of the countryside, others the entertainment of the music-hall or the new 'movies', where for a few hours they could forget the horror from which they had come and to which they must soon return.

Troops also attempted to provide their own entertainment at the front. Card games were popular as, behind the lines, were football and other sports; while in the trenches rat-hunting was pursued with a ferocious glee.

Other sources of amusement were the mouth organ and the gramophone, which by 1913 had been improved to play recorded music. When the bakelite discs became worn out, they were collected to be pulped and reissued with the latest tunes. The songs played and whistled were usually those popular in the music-halls, such as 'If you were the only girl in the world' and 'Pack up your troubles in your old kit bag': songs that became forever identified with a footslogging army on the march.

Patriotic songs and images were often printed on scarves and handkerchiefs.

A scene from *Chu Chin Chow*, a London musical popular with troops on leave, *bottom*.

'Some there be, which have no memorial'
Ecclesiastes 44:9

The Third Battle of Ypres achieved little for the Allies. The casualties, taken with those on the Somme in 1916, almost wiped out a generation of young British manhood. From Ypres the soldiers had ceaselessly marched out to small purpose. '*Boche* is bad', Foch had foretold, 'and *boue* is bad, but *Boche* and *boue* together—ah!' And so it had proved.

In April 1918, the final German attack swiftly overran this area: weary, demoralized British and Empire troops stoically withdrew through the desolation and over the unmarked and unconsecrated graves of their drowned and dismembered comrades. Yet later in the year, the counter-attacking Allies were to retake the Passchendaele ridge in some 30 hours with relatively little loss, as Haig had hoped to do earlier.

But even in August 1917 it was evident that the battle, which was to last for several months more, was a costly, ineffectual waste of life. Before the end of that grim year, however, there was for the Allies a brief spark of promise: the surprise tank attack at Cambrai.

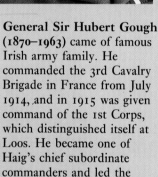

The War in the Air *1914–1918*

At the outbreak of World War I, aircraft were still seen by both sides as suitable for reconnaissance only. In the early months they were used exclusively as scouts and artillery spotters, and their usefulness in this respect was proved at once, during the German offensive in August and September 1914. Reconnaissance aircraft of the British Royal Flying Corps warned Sir John French of the movement of German troops ahead of the BEF before the Battle of Mons, and later of General von Kluck's change of direction, on 3 September, as he wheeled north of Paris.

Nevertheless, mass troop movements often went undetected by spotter aircraft, including the German offensives against Russia in spring 1915, at Verdun in February 1916, and their last offensive on the Western Front in March 1918. But Allied troops, too, soon learned to scatter and take cover at the sound of aircraft engines, and negative reports from German pilots who had failed to detect enemy forces often seriously misled their general headquarters staff.

A pilot flying at 20,000ft and more over Flanders could see to the Alps in one direction and to East Anglia in England in the other. This wide range of vision made aircraft of particular service where the war was one of movement. In East Africa, they played a vital role because, though enemy troops could vanish into the bush, dust clouds caused by their progress could not be disguised. Aircraft were also extensively used to monitor shipping, but their

'The aeroplane is useless'

Most aircraft were designed for aerobatic displays and contests before 1914, not warfare. Then, in early November 1911, an Italian aircraft dropped grenades on formations in Libya during their conflict with the Turks. Although the explosives produced little material damage, the psychological effect on the victims was considerable.

Even so, senior commanders in Europe were generally dismissive of this new offensive arm. General Foch summed up the majority view of the time when he remarked that 'flying is a good sport, but for the Army the aeroplane is useless.'

Flying was indeed considered a sport prior to the outbreak of war, and aircraft had been designed with the prime object of achieving maximum speed. It is as true of aircraft as of tanks or warships that their design is determined by three factors: speed, armour and weaponry. To enhance one necessitates diminution of one or both of the others.

Thus, in their search for speed, designers had paid little attention to the use of aircraft as a weapon, and, coupled to this, the military establishment was slow to perceive their potential in warfare.

efficacy was restricted by their limited fuel capacity and, therefore, limited range.

Few except the Germans, who had built a fleet of both Zeppelins and 'rigid' airships, had given other than perfunctory thought to a conflict in the air. Most senior Allied navy and army commanders were apathetic to the new arm; many indeed were antagonistic. In Great Britain, for example, the Air Battalion of the Royal Engineers was not formed until 1911. There, as in most of Europe, aircraft were seen as no more than spotters for the army and navy. For this reason, the Royal Flying Corps (RFC), established in 1912, had naval and military wings and was not an independent command.

The French, relying for their defence on the size and professionalism of their

army despite their earlier enthusiasm for flying, had neglected to develop a strong air arm. On the outbreak of war their air service was almost paralysed by the demands of military bureaucracy for discipline and training at the expense of actual flying experience.

The distinguished Italian poet Gabriele d'Annunzio flew over Austrian-held Trento in 1915 in this Fiat-Farman. The aircraft, with its complicated structure and rear-sited propeller, typifies pre-war design.

Hanoverian fusiliers pose in a balloon's gondola in 1910: many such studio shots were produced to show Germany's air power. Note the war flag, cannons, bombs and single lifebelt.

Pilots, when driven by anti-aircraft fire above their observation range, used cameras. The photographs soon proved more reliable and detailed than human memory.

Prints were first assembled into a mosaic, then they were interpreted to make an accurate map of enemy positions and artillery installations.

The kite-balloon: supreme observation platform

'The kite balloon is the ugliest thing man has ever seen when he looks up at the sky', wrote Walter Raleigh in his history of the early years of the air war. Looking at the huge, sausage-shaped body of this French Cacquot, being winched down to its mooring near Fricourt on the Somme by the cable attached to its nose, one must agree. But the cheap, reliable kite-balloon served its purpose admirably.

A German invention, plans had been pirated by the French and Belgians, and by 1914 both sides possessed kite-balloons. They were constructed in two parts, the front end being filled with gas, the rear with air. Wind sails, extending at right angles, helped to keep the rear end up; while another 'inflated sausage', the air rudder, curving around the underside of the balloon further steadied it. Together they ensured that the observers in the basket had a level platform, 6,000ft up, from which they could monitor the enemy's movements and direct their own artillery fire.

Kite-balloons were vulnerable to attack by aircraft. Tracer bullets often ignited the gas and, as the disintegrating outer covering sank shrinking to the ground, the hapless spotters descended with the aid of parachutes attached to the mooring line.

Belgium, Austria and Turkey had made only limited aeronautical progress (the last two were subsequently supplied by their ally Germany). In Russia, the designer Igor Sikorsky had produced some of the most successful four-engined bi-planes then flying. Their impact as military aircraft was, however, hampered by the shortage of engines and spares.

Thus, in August 1914, there were few aircraft ready for action. On the Western Front, the Germans had about 180, and some 20 serviceable seaplanes. The British Royal Naval Air Service mustered some 39 aircraft, which were of little military value, while the Royal Flying Corps had only 48 aircraft in France in August. The French could muster 136 aircraft of all types. The combined British and French strength was, therefore, some 185 aircraft to the Germans' 180. Germany and France were at first better equipped than

Great Britain, which had to rely during the early months on French factories for aircraft and spare parts.

But developments in aerial surveying advanced apace, both in techniques and refinements. Communications from air to ground were at first made by different-coloured lights, later by wireless telegraphy. Photography was also attempted as early as September 1914. Photographing enemy positions and movements had long

The romanticized 'dogfight' of the early days of the war, was, if possible, avoided by pilots unless at the time they enjoyed some advantage over their enemy. The risk of their aircraft being shot down or set on fire deterred most from seeking combat, especially since the British airmen had no parachutes.

German Fokkers had been fitted with interrupter gear by mid-1915, so their guns could be fired between the propeller blades. To counter this, British aircraft were sent out in pairs: one to act as escort and protect the other while it carried out reconnaissance.

On 29 December 1915, a clear winter day, two BE 2cs—stable, reliable aircraft—from No 8 Squadron RFC, took off on reconnaissance from Cambrai to St Quentin. The pilot of the first plane (5), Lieutenant Sholto Douglas, had as his observer and gunner Lieutenant James Childs.

The flight went well, although there was plenty of 'Archie' (anti-aircraft fire) near Cambrai, but then, at about 6,500 feet, the BEs were 'jumped' by six Fokkers.

Lieutenant David Glen, flying as escort, was shot down almost at once (1), and two of the Fokkers followed him down.

James Childs, standing in the front cockpit and firing his Lewis gun over Douglas's head, shot down one of the Fokkers (3).

The fight continued; then, after about half an hour, as Douglas's report stated, 'Petrol began to get low and engine sump was hit' by a tracer bullet, so he decided to dive in an attempt to escape.

One of the Fokkers, piloted by the ace Oswald Boelcke (4), followed him down to 3,000 feet; he ran out of ammunition but continued to circle Douglas. Then the equally famous Max Immelmann (2) came to Boelcke's aid. One of his guns jammed, but he kept on firing with the other.

Douglas decided to run for home, and trusting to the good low-flying qualities of the BE 2c, dropped down to 20 feet. German soldiers in the trenches were amazed when his aircraft ripped by just over their heads, and every machine-gun and rifle was trained on it.

Boelcke's engine gave out, but seeing his enemy 'disappearing behind the next row of trees', he landed, and armed with the only weapon handy, a Verey pistol, 'rode across on horseback' expecting 'to take the fellow prisoner'.

But Douglas, flying about 'like a madman', managed to dodge both German planes and soldiers and to land behind British lines, although his aircraft was hit more than 100 times.

Few fights can have taken place between more distinguished pilots: Immelmann and Boelcke were among the top German aces, and Sholto Douglas later became Marshal of the Royal Air Force.

been possible (balloons were used in great numbers during the American Civil War of 1864–8 and the German siege of Paris in 1870) but this gave a distorted view, since the vulnerable balloons could not be poised directly over the enemy.

As the war progressed, reconnaissance became both more professional and more extensive. The early reports by pilots of enemy concentrations and movements were enhanced by technical advances in photography. At first, pilots merely took individual photographs to be developed later on the ground; but as time passed, vast photographic maps, comprising sometimes thousands of sections, could be assembled of whole areas of the Western Front. These were repeatedly up-dated, giving the side with air superiority a clear picture of their enemy's dispositions.

A subsequent refinement for covering large areas entailed the camera shutter exposing at pre-fixed intervals while the aircraft flew at a constant height and speed. The prints could then be over-lapped to form a mosaic giving a uniform, panoramic view of enemy formations and dispositions.

'Artillery' planes were frequently sent up to assist the guns obtain the range of enemy targets close to the front, while long-distance squadrons on both sides bombed and photographed enemy concentrations and installations to the rear. Since World War I was in large measure a war of massed artillery, this cooperation with the artillery was of prime importance.

The gas-filled 'kite-balloon', so called because it combined the principles of both balloons and kites, was invaluable in this respect. But these balloons were vulnerable to enemy fighters, for they were tethered to the ground and the two observers suspended in a basket beneath the balloon were unarmed. Such an attack would immediately draw the fire of every anti-aircraft and machine-gunner, and even of solitary soldiers, armed with no more than rifles. Almost invariably, the fighter made good its escape.

All this activity in the air inevitably led to combat: the famous 'dogfights' of the early months of the war. The usual weapons were pistols and rifles, although some inventive pilots took with them a brick or heavy stone in the hope of dropping it through the flimsy fuselage of an enemy's aircraft.

Most 'kills' were, however, the result of a pilot's being outmanoeuvred and hitting some prominent object such as a tree, or, when turning too steeply to escape attack from the rear, fracturing his plane's fragile wings. This frequently happened to young

The early informal character of aerial warfare gradually gave way to a highly organized system of local and long-distance patrols by entire squadrons. Life for the pilots, too, took on a regular pattern.

In summer, reveille was at about 02.45. After a light meal to prevent nausea, pilots dressed in flying kit. This comprised silk, then woollen, underwear, then a cellular vest and silk shirt, with a regular army shirt over it.

On top came two pullovers; a wool-lined gaberdine flying suit; gauntlets, fur-lined boots, goggles, silk scarf and balaclava helmet. Only in this garb could airmen tolerate the intense cold in open cockpits at high altitudes.

Once airborne, the first hazard for airmen was enemy artillery fire. Pilots feared high-explosive shells and shrapnel, since an explosion within 91m/

100yds could destroy an aircraft's engine, petrol tank or wings. In 1918, the British lost almost 750 craft this way. Pilots were also confronted by enemy fighters; all wrote of the twin sensations of fear and exhilaration felt during combat.

No two aircraft performed identically and each pilot had his own machine, with instruments, mirrors, and harness all individually adjusted.

In April 1917, the life expectancy of British pilots was $17\frac{1}{2}$ flying hours. But of those who survived through skill and luck, many became 'aces', the qualifying number of 'kills' varying from country to country.

Two notable aces were the British **Albert Ball (1)**, who destroyed 43 aircraft before being killed when not yet 21, and Canadian **William Bishop (2)** who scored 72 kills. The American

Eddie Rickenbacker (3) scored 26, while **Georges Guynemer (4)** a Frenchman who always took a camera in his 'Vieux Charles', despite its weight, scored 54.

The most famous German pilot was **Manfred von Richthofen (6)** with 80 kills, closely followed by **Oswald Boelcke (5)** and **Max Immelmann (7)**, who shot down the first (unarmed) British aircraft.

SE 5a British single-seat scout preferred by many aces for its notable qualities as a fighter and its stability.
Maximum speed: 217kmh/135mph at 6,500ft. Endurance: 2½hrs. Armament: 1 Lewis gun above centre section; 1 Vickers machine-gun above cowling. Ceiling 20,000ft.

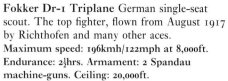

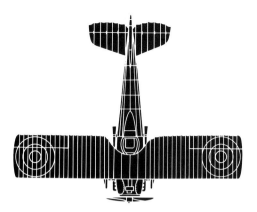

Fokker Dr-1 Triplane German single-seat scout. The top fighter, flown from August 1917 by Richthofen and many other aces.
Maximum speed: 196kmh/122mph at 8,000ft. Endurance: 2½hrs. Armament: 2 Spandau machine-guns. Ceiling: 20,000ft.

Spad S-7C 1 French single-seat scout first flown in July 1916; more than 5,400 S-7s were built in all. Both Ball and Guynemer flew Spads.
Maximum speed: 193kmh/120mph at 6,500ft. Endurance: 2½hrs. Armament: 1 Vickers machine-gun. Ceiling: 17,500ft.

137

British pilots who had been sent to France with insufficient training: even in 1917 this amounted to only about 17 hours of solo flying.

Particularly in the early days of the war, the shortage of established aerodromes proved a problem. Temporary airfields had to be improvised and were usually selected by an officer travelling by car. During the retreat from Mons especially, airfields changed almost daily, and a pilot could not be sure that the field from which he took off would not be in enemy hands by the time he landed.

Cloud and the convection currents that are associated with it were another hazard, for they always disorientated pilots. Often when they emerged, they found themselves upside down and unsure in which direction they were flying, as well as being soaked with moisture. The experience was also scaring, for in cloud the engine made eerie, deafening echoes.

In May 1915, the Germans achieved air supremacy, absolute though temporary, with a new device: the so-called 'interrupter gear'. Hitherto, although machine-guns were carried on many aircraft, it had

been impossible for the pilot to fire straight ahead—the most obvious and lethal direction—for fear of destroying his own propeller. Numerous mechanical expedients were devised to overcome this.

The Moranne-Saulnier 'deflector gear' was an early French invention, designed to deflect those machine-gun bullets that would otherwise have struck the propeller, while permitting the remainder to pass. It was, however, hugely wasteful of ammunition.

Then the Dutchman Anthony Fokker, who designed two of the Germans' most

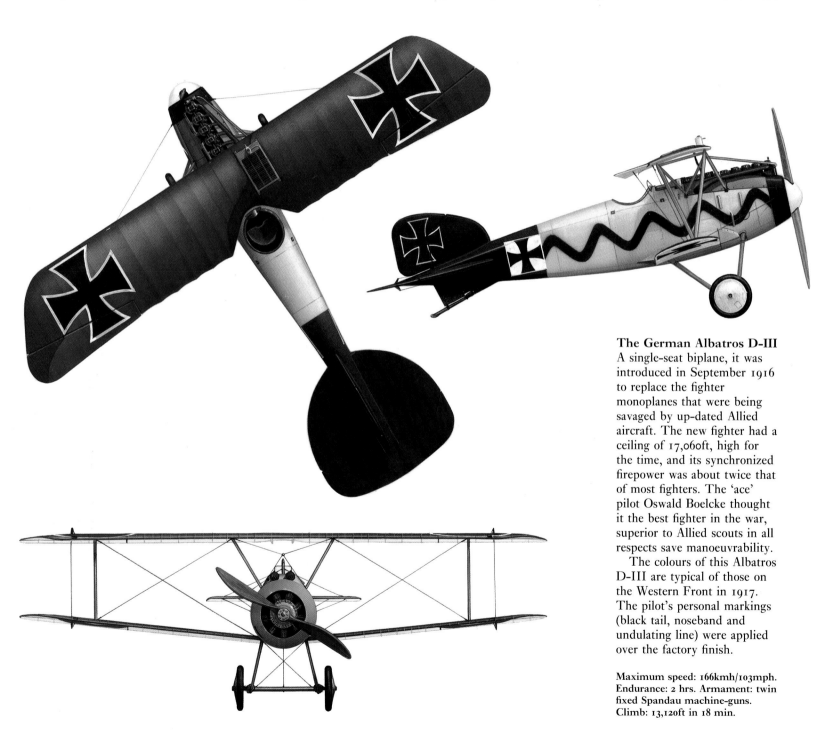

The German Albatros D-III
A single-seat biplane, it was introduced in September 1916 to replace the fighter monoplanes that were being savaged by up-dated Allied aircraft. The new fighter had a ceiling of 17,060ft, high for the time, and its synchronized firepower was about twice that of most fighters. The 'ace' pilot Oswald Boelcke thought it the best fighter in the war, superior to Allied scouts in all respects save manoeuvrability.

The colours of this Albatros D-III are typical of those on the Western Front in 1917. The pilot's personal markings (black tail, noseband and undulating line) were applied over the factory finish.

Maximum speed: 166kmh/103mph. Endurance: 2 hrs. Armament: twin fixed Spandau machine-guns. Climb: 13,120ft in 18 min.

successful aircraft—the Fokker and the Albatross—developed (if he did not invent) the synchronizer, or interrupter gear. With this refinement, the cam was aligned with the propeller blades so that the gun temporarily ceased firing when a blade was directly in front of the muzzle.

Since the blades rotated, and machine-gun fired many times every second, the burst of ammunition seemed continuous. The Germans had manufactured the interrupter gear in great numbers by May 1915, with the result that Fokker fighting machines shot down large numbers of British and French aircraft with little loss to themselves.

The 'Fokker scourge' constrained the Allies to rethink their strategy in the air. Soon they, too, had interrupter gears, but in the meantime they had evolved a method of offensive patrols, whereby fighters were assigned to special squadrons with the object of destroying their opponents behind enemy lines, so leaving the reconnaissance craft to work unmolested. In this way, in 1916, the initiative reverted to the Allies.

Their domination did not last for long, for the Germans produced not only more sophisticated single-seater aircraft but evolved the 'circus' system. This entailed the formation of special squadrons which could be moved rapidly from one sector of the Western Front to another, as the need

The Sopwith FI Camel
The most successful fighter of the war went into service in mid-1917 and claimed 1,294 'kills'. Its high acrobatic performance was the consequence of its compact design, with pilot's seat, engine and guns all sited over the aircraft's centre of gravity.

By the Armistice, some 2,500 Sopwith Camels were in service with the RAF on all fronts. In some instances, the whole aircraft was painted dark green/brown. British pilots painted their machines with personal colour schemes, but the practice was far less widespread than on German machines.

Maximum speed: 196kmh/122mph at sea level. Endurance: 2¾hrs. Armament: 2 Vickers machine-guns. Ceiling: 24,000ft. Climb: 15,000ft in 17 min.

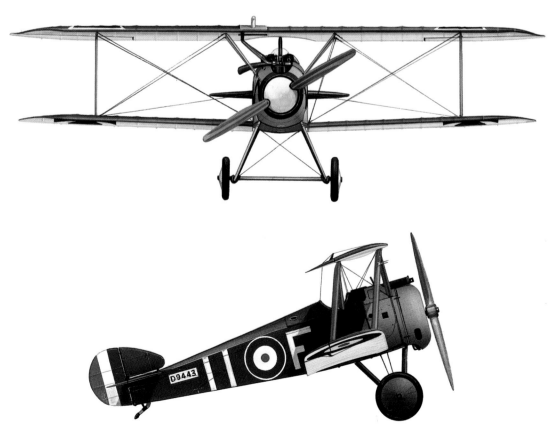

Air raids on Britain

Having occupied large areas of Belgium and northern France in 1914, the Germans possessed a great geographical advantage in respect of aerial bombardment—range. London was far closer to the German aerodromes there than Berlin was to British airfields in France, and the Germans were quick to exploit this advantage.

Towns in southern England, notably Dover, were raided from December 1914 onward by both Zeppelins and bombers. Later, as aircraft became capable of longer flights, sorties were flown against East Anglia and, subsequently, the Midlands, Britain's industrial heartland.

The first Zeppelin raid on London was carried out on the night of 31 May/1 June 1915. Incendiary bombs and some 30 grenades were dropped; seven civilians were killed and almost 40 injured. The damage inflicted was light, but the fact that the raid could have penetrated to the capital at all caused consternation among the British people.

The largest German airship raid took place on the night of 2/3 September 1916, when 14 airships managed to cross the Channel. One of the craft, the wooden-framed Schütte-Lanz 11, was destroyed over Cuffley north of London (the first to

be shot down) by Lieutenant W. Leefe Robinson flying a BE 2c. The descent of the blazing airship could be seen from as much as 80km/50mls away. Leefe Robinson received the Victoria Cross for his exploit, and the British public a considerable boost to their morale.

German raids on Britain reached their peak in 1916, when 22 sorties were flown, nearly 3,500 bombs were dropped and about 1,000 civilians killed or wounded. As British air defences became more effective and German strength sagged, the raids declined: in 1918 only four took place and fewer than 200 bombs were dropped.

German air raids made headlines in British newspapers, especially when a Zeppelin was shot down. The Germans made great propaganda use of their raids, as in the postcard, *above*, where St Paul's and a tranquil Thames are menaced by a disproportionately large airship. The searchlight beams come from the Zeppelin; in fact, they would have been operated from the ground.

arose. Each of these squadrons was led by a skilled 'ace', the most celebrated of whom was the 'Red Baron', Manfred von Richthofen, who personally selected the pilots in his squadron.

In this way, although outnumbered 3:1 in the air, the Germans once more had the ascendancy over the Allies in the spring of 1917. But by then individual duels were things of the past; aircraft now flew in formations, often numbering 50 or more, with the aim of sweeping the enemy from the skies. They operated in this way to particularly good effect in Palestine, where Turkish aircraft were prevented even from taking off, with the result that the Turks remained ignorant of Allenby's army's change of front.

Aircraft were also employed to attack enemy infantry and artillery on the ground, as well as supply bases and road and rail communications in his rear. Yet surprisingly, this was attempted in only a haphazard way; no decisive aerial bombardment was mounted by either side. Here was a great opportunity overlooked.

The Germans tried to demoralize the British 'Home Front' by air raids on London and the east coast, but the Allies had within easy flying range a more

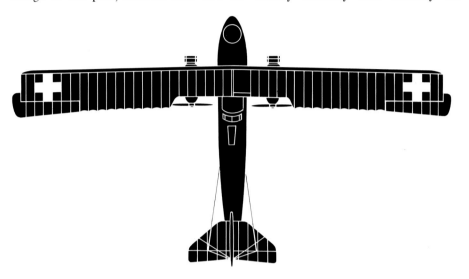

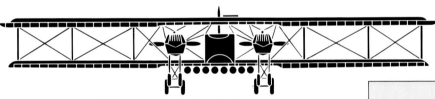

Gotha G-V heavy, twin-engined bomber. The most effective German bomber of the war. On 13 June 1917, 14 Gothas made the first daylight raid on London, killing 162 people and injuring 432. Day and night raids continued until summer 1918.
Upper wingspan: 23.7m/77¾ft. Maximum speed: 140kmh/88mph at sea level. Endurance: 6hrs. Armament: 3 Parabellum machine-guns; up to 14 10-kg/22-lb bombs under the fuselage. Ceiling: 21,300ft.

Handley Page v/1500 British heavy, four-engined bomber. The huge 'Berlin Bomber', intended to take the air war into the heart of Germany, was developed from the successful 0/400. Only three were built by the end of the war.
Wingspan: 38.4m/126ft. Maximum speed: 156kmh/97mph. Endurance: 8hrs. Armament: Up to 5 Lewis guns; bombload of 3,405kg/7,500lb. Ceiling: 10,000ft.

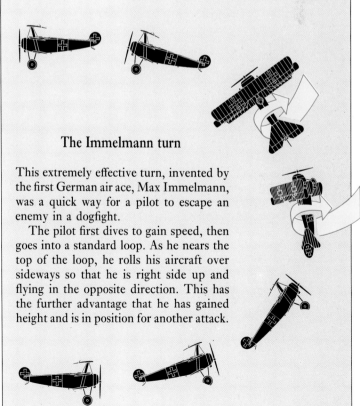

The Immelmann turn

This extremely effective turn, invented by the first German air ace, Max Immelmann, was a quick way for a pilot to escape an enemy in a dogfight.

The pilot first dives to gain speed, then goes into a standard loop. As he nears the top of the loop, he rolls his aircraft over sideways so that he is right side up and flying in the opposite direction. This has the further advantage that he has gained height and is in position for another attack.

Formation of the RAF

In April 1918 the naval and military wings of the British air corps, the Royal Naval Air Service and the Royal Flying Corps, were combined to form the Royal Air Force: the first independent air service.

The driving spirit in the creation of the RAF was Major-General Sir Hugh Trenchard. From the time of his appointment as officer commanding the RFC in August 1914, he had worked towards this end. In 1918, as the RAF's chief of staff, he planned a massive bombing offensive against Berlin, but the Armistice was signed before the raid could take place.

In 1927 Trenchard was the first RAF general to be promoted marshal. Between the wars he formed the nucleus of Britain's Bomber Command which was so instrumental in destroying the German industrial might in World War II.

Aerial propaganda

The dropping of propaganda leaflets from aircraft was practised by both sides, though some considered it illegal under international law. Largely because shot-down Allied pilots were brought to trial for carrying such leaflets, from February 1918 the British used balloons, each carrying up to 1,000 pamphlets, to distribute them.

Cotton-wick, which burns at an even rate, was attached to a wire suspended from the neck of the balloon and lit. The leaflets, held in packets along the wire, were thus released a few at a time 16–80km/10–50mls behind enemy lines, depending on the strength of the prevailing westerly winds.

Captain Albert Ball, VC, DSO, MC, was one of the small band of flyers whose exploits and heroism captured the imagination of the British public. The watercolour, *right*, by Norman G. Arnold depicts his last fight on 7 May 1917, when his SE 5a was attacked by German Fokkers and he was shot down near Annoeullin.

Flying boats of the Royal Naval Air Squadron, such as the Curtiss 'Large Americas' in the painting, *below*, by C.R. Fleming-Williams, were used well out to sea to carry out sweeps, escort shipping and to hunt submarines. Here they are shown bombing and machine-gunning a crippled German U-boat.

significant target: Germany's industrial heartland, the Ruhr and the Saar, where most of her munitions were manufactured. However, as Basil Liddell Hart observed, 'this immense opportunity of crippling the munitions supply of the German armies was sacrificed in favour of air fighting over the trench front.'

Nevertheless, the Allies had arrived, albeit belatedly, at an understanding of the air arm's deadly potential. On 1 April 1918, the British government created the Royal Air Force, completely independent of the army and navy. Now, for the first time, aircraft could be employed as a separate, autonomous force. Thus, when the Allied front was smashed by Germany's last offensive in March 1918, all British and French squadrons that could be spared combined to strike at the advancing Germans. This proved to be a

highly significant factor in their repulse.

Air power played an even greater part when the final German onrush was destroyed by massive Allied counter-attacks in the autumn. But perhaps the greatest contribution of the independent force was its belated part in the strategic bombing, both by day and at night, of German targets, including factories and airfields. Some 665 tons of explosive were dropped between October 1917, when the strategy was adopted, and the end of the war.

The material damage caused was limited, but German industrial output certainly suffered, and the effect on the already war-weary civilian population was further to sap their morale. This new concept in war—to defeat an enemy not by frontal attack but by destroying his industrial heartland—was to be used to awesome effect in future wars.

Lieutenant Hermann Goering, with 22 kills, in July 1918 received Germany's highest award, the *Pour le Mérite*. His fame was sufficiently widespread for a postcard, *above*, to be issued, showing him in the cockpit of his Fokker D-VII.

By July 1918, the Allies had great air superiority on the Western Front, with dozens of aircraft and well-trained pilots and aircrew, as this impressive line-up of SE 5a fighter-scouts demonstrates.

Weapons of the future

By 1918, air warfare had been transformed: pilots operated in squadrons; concentrated bombing raids were mounted; and production lines were disgorging huge numbers of increasingly sophisticated aircraft.

In the last month of the war, the Royal Air Force, formed less than a year earlier, had become the largest in the world, with a strength of 291,750 personnel operating 22,170 aircraft of all types organized into 200 squadrons.

No one in 1918 could dispute that a new

dimension in warfare had come into being. But during the inter-war years, the democracies, no longer faced with the prospect of war, developed their commercial airlines, while neglecting their air services. However, the fact was seized upon and exploited after 1933 by the German *Luftwaffe* under Hermann Goering.

So confident was he of the power of these new weapons that during World War II, in the Battle of Britain, Germany tried to destroy Britain with this arm alone.

Battle of *Cambrai* *November 1917*

The main obstructions to an infantry advance—almost always entailing huge losses for little territorial gain—were the deadly combination of barbed wire and machine-guns. Even when the machine-guns could be accurately located, they could not be obliterated by artillery fire because that in turn left enemy artillery positions undamaged.

The answer to both wire and machine-guns, at least in the minds of their more enthusiastic advocates, lay with tanks, employed *en masse*. For their full potential impact to be achieved, however, suitable terrain was essential. On the Somme, where a few tanks were used during the later stages of the battle, many had become engulfed in the mud or had sunk helpless into shell holes.

Plans for a mass tank raid

The fighting in the Ypres salient had been prolonged into November 1917, when it petered out in a hopeless struggle in the autumn mud. The cost in life had been stupendous and the Allies had taken the Passchendaele Ridge but little else. The need to keep up the forward momentum was great, largely to sustain morale at home, and to dominate the approaches to the U-boat bases at Bruges.

In August 1917, Colonel J.F.C. Fuller of the Tank Corps staff had written a paper in which, having outlined the futility and cost of the Ypres offensive, he advocated a raid by tanks *en masse*. Although he was later overruled by his superiors, this was accepted in principle by General Sir Julian Byng, who had assumed command of the Third Army when, in June 1917, Sir Edmund Allenby was appointed to lead the Egyptian Expeditionary Force.

But in October, as the fading prospects of the Ypres campaign became evident to even the most stubborn-minded, the plan was revived. A new era in military history was to open on 20 November 1917, when in the thick autumn mist of early morning the British tanks lumbered forward.

This underside view of a Mark IV male tank crossing a trench vividly conveys what a terrifying, and often fatal, experience it could be for anyone still in the trench.

These tanks weighed 28 tons and had a 6-cylinder engine, giving them a top speed of 6kmh/ 3.7mph. Male tanks were armed with four Lewis guns and two short 6-pounders; ammunition included both high-explosive and case shot.

Each tank carried a crew of eight: driver, commander/machine-gunner, two more machine-gunners, two gunners and two men to operate the gears.

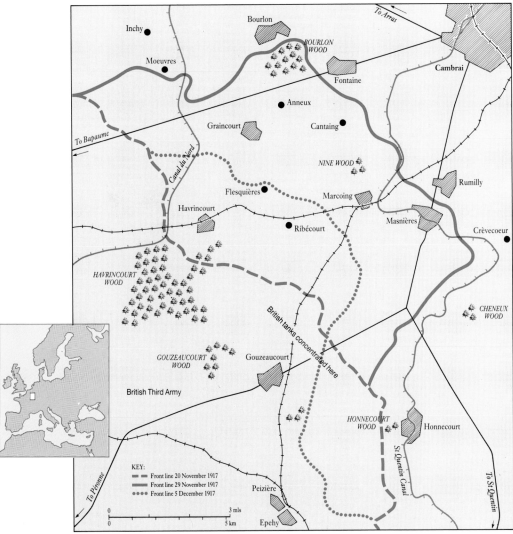

The **Mark IV** female tank, *right*, with two captured German field guns in the foreground, was probably on its way to Bourlon Wood when this shot was taken on 23 November. The female differed from the male tank in that it carried six Lewis guns but no big guns.

Mark IV tanks were armoured with steel plates up to 12mm/½in thick, which were cut and drilled before being hardened. They were then riveted to an iron frame. When the tank came under heavy machine-gun fire, molten metal would penetrate any gaps between the plates and spray the occupants.

Three conditions conducive to the tanks' effective use were to be found in the area of Cambrai. The going was firm; the German positions here were mostly undermanned because they considered it a quiet sector; and, lastly, an immediate breakthrough would open the routes to the bridges on the River Sensée. Once these were gained, the Germans would be obliged to retreat, for their communications to the rear would be threatened.

One further, crucial, ingredient was needed: surprise. This was to be achieved not only by the first use of tanks in great numbers but by the absence of a prolonged artillery barrage, the harbinger, as both sides knew, of attack.

The object of the offensive was to be the prime function of war: to destroy the enemy. Territorial gain was a lesser consideration, the capture of enemy personnel and destruction of his equipment being paramount. The Hindenburg Line (known to the Germans as the Siegfried Line) which at this point comprised three systems of trenches and an outpost line, was to be penetrated and the principal action completed within 24 hours.

The initial plan, therefore, envisaged a raid; unfortunately, however, Byng's enthusiasm for the scheme had become inflated during the weeks of planning and he now contemplated, as have so many commanders before him, a glorious breakthrough. For this he intended to employ in his first attack all his infantry and all his tanks, leaving himself—with disastrous consequences, as it proved—without any reserves of men or machines.

The preliminaries to the attack were made with thoroughness and foresight. Since the tank was an unexploited weapon, secrecy was the keynote of the British offensive plan. Even senior officers were kept in ignorance of the operation until the last moment, and rumours were spread to confuse the troops who were about to take part in the attack.

The concentration of machines and men began some two weeks before the battle opened. From 7 November onward, artillery was brought into position and covered with camouflage netting, while the infantry was moved up by both road and rail. Roads were strengthened and widened, and thirty-six trains were needed to transport the tanks, at night, to within striking distance of the enemy.

From there, under cover of darkness and heavy ground mist, they moved up to their assembly points, without lights and at a maximum speed of 6.5kmh/4mph so that the noise of their engines would not alert the Germans. Tank commanders walked ahead of their tanks, following white tapes that had been laid earlier, and often only the glowing tip of a cigarette indicated where the men were and saved them from being run down.

The tanks lay up in the woods, where many of the low-growing trees had not yet lost their leaves; others were shunted into ruined buildings and the roofs allowed to fall in to disguise their outlines with rubble. At the same time, temporary shelters were erected in the woods for the gathering troops.

Fortunately for the British, conditions

from 10 November remained very misty, giving welcome additional concealment and helping to deter the German reconnaisance aircraft. At the same time, however, daily flights were undertaken by the RFC to check the effectiveness of the cover. By the morning of 19 November, all

The atmospheric painting, *Dawn, November 20, 1917*, by W. L. Wyllie, illustrates the historic moment when the massed tanks rolled forward over the tussocky open grassland toward the trenches of the Hindenburg Line.

'I'm going over in this tank'

The attack at Cambrai was remarkable not only for being the first real tank battle in history but also because Brigadier-General Hugh Elles, the Tank Corps' commanding officer, led his men into battle: not the usual action of a modern general. But in the opinion of Colonel (later Major-General) J.F.C. Fuller, the corps' historian, this valiant gesture signalled the coming of age of the corps and gave it is spirit.

Elles elected to lead his men in a tank from H battalion—'Hilda'—in the centre of the line near Ribecourt. He was a conspicuous figure, standing with his head and shoulders through the manhole in the top of the tank and holding aloft his walking stick to which he had attached the Tank Corps flag. The brown, red and green horizontal stripes, signifying 'Through mud and blood to the green fields beyond', cheered on his already eager men.

When the tanks reached the first German outposts, Elles reluctantly left 'Hilda'. Still smoking his pipe, and followed by batches of bewildered German prisoners, he walked back to Beaucamp, behind the British lines, to direct operations. 'Hilda' later became trapped in a trench but was pulled out by another tank and went on to take part in the capture of Ribecourt.

Elles's 'Special Order No 6', issued on the eve of the battle.

King George V and General Elles watching a demonstration by Mark V Star tanks and infantry in Flanders on 10 August 1918.

New tactics for a new weapon

Each tank carried on top a massive bundle of brushwood to enable it to cross the German trenches, which was here impossible despite the Mark IV's length of 8m/26ft 5in. The brushwood fascine was tightly compressed and bound with chains to support the tank's 28-ton weight.

The tanks worked in groups of three: an advance guard tank and two infantry tanks. The task of the advance guard tank (1) was to smash through the Germans' wire defences, then, without crossing the front-line trench, to turn left and sweep it with machine-gun fire.

Meanwhile, the two infantry tanks made for the break in the wire. The tank on the right (2) dropped its fascine into the trench, turned left and also worked down the trench. The second infantry tank (3) crossed on the right-hand tank's fascine, made for the German support trench, dropped its fascine and crossed. It then turned left and fired on the trench.

Having performed its task, the advance guard tank turned round and, crossing both trenches on the fascines already laid, dropped its own fascine into the third trench. The entire manoeuvre was repeated along the whole front by waves of tanks.

The infantry, too, was organized in three formations. The first, following close behind the tanks, cleared the German fire trench; the second sealed the trench at suitable points, and the third garrisoned it until the next wave of tanks arrived, when it became their advance guard.

Tanks were brought up close to the front by train before the Battle of Cambrai. Each tank carried a brushwood fascine to enable it to cross the wide trenches in the Hindenburg Line.

All tanks were given names beginning with the letter of their battalion. Here 'Hyacinth' of H Battalion has failed to negotiate a captured German trench and slipped back into it.

The ability of tanks to plough through and crush barbed wire defences, *opposite top*, was of paramount importance. It would have taken millions of shells to achieve what the tanks accomplished at Cambrai.

The disabled wire-cutting tank, *below*, is being used as an artillery platform. If the tank stuck fast on its belly, the unditching beam lying across the top could be chained to the tracks. When they turned, the beam was pulled underneath the tank, often enabling it to free itself.

the tanks had reached their final assembly points some way behind the forward infantry line.

These positions were dictated by the fact that, however slowly they moved, the tanks' engines could be heard within 914m/1,000yds of the enemy. Five British divisions and 374 fighting tanks, supported by some 1,000 artillery pieces, were poised to attack an unsuspecting enemy of less than two divisions and, at the most, 150 guns.

The Germans on the ground were taken wholly by surprise. They were taken equally by surprise in the air. Unaware of what was shortly to befall, German aircraft had that day been grounded because of poor visibility, while 14 squadrons of British aircraft—some 275 Sopwith Camels and Scouts, Bristol Fighters, and DH4s and 5s—flew eastward on their missions. They flew so low in the dawn light that the pilots were able to wave to the infantry beneath them and shout words of encouragement.

The 72-km/45-ml long Hindenburg Line, stretching from near Arras to Soissons, was unbroken because there had been no prolonged artillery barrage. It was extremely strong—in some places more than 6.4km/4mls deep—with three lines of trenches, many deep dug-outs and self-contained, mutually supporting centres of resistance sited in a chequer-board fashion. Some of the trenches were as much as 4m/13ft wide, and all the fortifications were protected by belts of barbed wire up to 45m/50yds thick. These, together with the many German machine-guns in concrete gun positions, were intended to make it impossible for infantry to cut a passage

through; at Cambrai, that task had been allocated to the tanks.

The infantry were to follow the tanks closely, pouring through the gaps cleared by them in the enemy's wire defences. Meanwhile, dummy tanks were sited, and gas attacks mounted, north and south of the proposed area of penetration, to deceive the Germans as to the point of the main British onslaught.

The area chosen for the attack lay just south of Cambrai, across open, rolling chalk-land covered in rough grass. From the northwest to the southeast—the line of the British front—ran a series of low ridges. To the northeast, however, lay the dominating height of Bourlon Wood, due west of Cambrai and, therefore, a prime British target. Bounding the area of attack ran two canals: the Canal du Nord and the Canal de l'Escaut.

The staff plan of Third Army was, in essence, first to smash the German defences between the two canals, then to

seize Cambrai, Bourlon Wood and the bridges over the River Sensée. Once this was accomplished, the Germans could be cut off south of the Sensée and west of the Canal du Nord; then Third Army could thrust in the general direction of Valenciennes. For the initial attack, two corps, each of three infantry divisions, the Tank Corps, a corps of cavalry and 1,000 guns were allocated. Opposed to them stood, unsuspecting, units of the German Sixth and Second armies of Prince Rupprecht's Army Group.

Thick mist made it difficult for the men to see when the tanks were deployed some 914m/1000yds from the front German positions, with the infantry units formed up behind them. The tanks moved off at 06.10, and 10 minutes later, at zero hour, they were already rolling slowly across no man's land on a front of 10km/6mls. The British guns opened their barrage so that their shells fell 183m/200yds ahead of the advancing tanks.

The main objective of 40th Division, after the breakthrough of 20 November and the capture of La Fontaine on the 21st, was to take the great 243-ha/600-a mass of Bourlon Wood. But it was not until the 23rd that the tanks were ready to fight again and preparations were completed for an artillery barrage.

It was cold and windy with rain and sleet showers and fitful sunshine as the eight battalions of 119th and 121st Brigades, with 13 tanks of D Battalion, assembled near Anneux. The artillery, sited near Graincourt, put up a heavy barrage for 20 minutes before zero hour at 10.30, and as the troops advanced, it lifted 183m/200yds every 10 minutes. By 11.30, it was nearing the top of the ridge, and starting fires in the wood.

The three battalions of 121st Brigade were supported by 9 tanks. The 20/Middlesex (7) made toward the southern edge of the village, led by six tanks, while the 13/Green Howards (1) with the three remaining tanks advanced toward the west of Bourlon, where the château (4) stood. They at once came under heavy rifle and machine-gun fire from the woods and the trenches of the Marquion Line, to the northwest.

On the right, 119th Brigade extended the British line along the road and pressed ahead through the dense wood, which was criss-crossed by rides and paths. With the help of four tanks, they took out all enemy machine-gun nests and resistance posts, and by 11.30 the South Wales Borderers (6) were approaching the crest of the hill and the Bourlon-La Fontaine road (5).

The village, too, was heavily defended, and for a time men and tanks were brought to a standstill by shell fire from a two-gun battery (2) in the village. But these guns were quickly silenced by Lieutenant F.G. Huxley, the pilot of a DH5 (3) from 68 (Australian) Squadron, who dropped four 11kg/25lb bombs on them from a height of 100ft.

Seven tanks managed to enter Bourlon and heavy fighting took place. But as the Germans brought up reinforcements over the next few days, their counter-attacks grew in strength and by midday on the 27th, with no fresh reserves, the British were forced to withdraw.

The Battle of
Cambrai, which had
started so brilliantly,
petered out with little
territorial gain,
although some 10,500
prisoners, 142 guns,
more than 300
machine-guns and
ammunition and stores
of all types were taken.

This squadron of tanks, with an 18-pounder in the foreground, is moving forward to the attack on Bourlon Wood. Columns of infantry advance on the right.

A German bombing patrol, *below*, takes cover in a shell hole. The soldier on the right holds a stick grenade, while another takes disc grenades from a special carrier

which has been attached to a messenger dog.

Infantrymen devised many original methods for attacking tanks. One was for soldiers to carry a *geballte Ladung*

(concentrated charge), a collection of hand grenade heads, that could be thrust into a tank's tracks and detonated, blowing it off its wheels.

Combating the tanks

Although the Germans were taken by surprise by the British tanks, they saw no need to produce a special anti-tank weapon, relying instead upon their field artillery to combat the tanks by firing at them with high-explosive or solid shot. Late in the war they made a large-bore anti-tank rifle with armour-piercing bullets, but few of these went into front-line service.

The task of fighting the tanks fell largely upon the individual soldier; and, as one officer wrote, 'A ferocious passion for hunting them down is growing.' A favourite method was to attack with flame throwers in the hope that the fire would penetrate the driver's observation slit and blind him.

In many places, the crews of anti-aircraft guns loaded them on trucks and pursued the tanks, shooting at them as they went. The Germans also made primitive anti-tank mines, using shells or bombs which they detonated either electrically or by remote control.

Surprise was complete; the German troops were quickly demoralized everywhere, except in the area of Flesquières. But this slight rebuff was overlapped by thrusts that bore down upon Marcoing, Anneux to its north, and to the edge of the dominating Bourlon Wood. 'The attack was a stupendous success,' Colonel J.F.C. Fuller, the historian of the Tank Corps wrote, '. . . the enemy completely lost his balance and those who did not fly panic-stricken from the field surrendered with little or no resistance.'

Now an opportunity presented itself to the Allies as never before. The German front had been penetrated in 10 hours to a depth of some 8km/5mls—the same distance that had been gained, with immensely heavier losses, only after months of ghastly struggle on the Somme and at Ypres. Ahead loomed an unfinished, and therefore easily overcome, German defence line, then open country, precisely the most favourable terrain for a tank advance. Why was this superb, and potentially decisive, opportunity not at once exploited?

As Colonel Fuller was to observe, problems quickly arose. 'By 4p.m. on November 20, one of the most astonishing battles in all history had been won and, as far as the Tank Corps was concerned, tactically finished, for, no reserves existing, it was not possible to do more than rally the now very weary and exhausted crews, select the fittest, and patch up composite companies to continue the attack on the morrow.' This was effected but, as he noted, 'November 21 saw, generally speaking, the end of any co-operative action between tanks and infantry . . .'.

Nevertheless, further considerable gains were made and—for the only time during the war—church bells in the United Kingdom were rung in salute. The euphoria was premature. By 27 November the tank crews were totally exhausted and two brigades had to be withdrawn from the front. The cavalry, hugely vulnerable to sniper and machine-gun fire, proved ineffectual. Moreover, the 3rd and 4th corps were now situated in a dangerous salient, since most fighting in the previous few days had taken place around the wood and village of Bourlon, and La Fontaine.

On 30 November, General Georg von der Marwitz, commander of the German Second Army, launched a ferocious counter-attack. His object was to capture the 3rd and 4th British corps by nipping off the salient with thrusts southward from Bourlon and westward from Honnecourt. The attack from the north

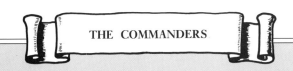
BYNG

MARWITZ

General Sir Julian Byng (1862–1935) had served in India and South Africa. In 1914 he commanded the 3rd Cavalry Division at Ypres, and in 1917 the Canadian Corps when they took Vimy Ridge: their most famous exploit. After the war, he became Governor-General of Canada (1921–6) and was made field marshal in 1932.

General Georg von der Marwitz (1856–1929) was active on the Eastern Front early in the war, and in May 1915 was advancing on Przemysl. In November 1917 he was in command of the Second Army in France, defeating the British at Cambrai in December and leading it in the March 1918 offensive. He later commanded Fifth Army in the Verdun area.

was held, but to the south the German left-wing strike made great headway.

In one day, 20 November, the British had penetrated along a front of some 10km/6mls and taken 10,000 prisoners and 200 guns; now, 10 days later, they in turn suffered almost equal casualties and lost a large part of their captured ground. The great tank breakthrough had been squandered through lack of reserves.

An undervalued weapon

The brief battle of Cambrai ended in bitter disappointment for the British. Questions—penetrating, critical—were asked, and the blame, as so often during the war, was laid on the junior officers and NCOs. This was blatantly unjust, for it was precisely they who had been most insistent that the German Army was poised to counter-attack, warnings that the staff ignored. Nor, as was claimed, did they show lack of 'offensive spirit'.

The initial attack had been a brilliant success. 'But', as Winston Churchill later asked, 'if that was so, why not have done it before?' He had constantly stigmatized the Allied offensives of 1915 through to 1917 as 'wrongly conceived' and held that here, at Cambrai, in surprise and the tank in tandem, lay the key to ending the terrible stalemate of trench warfare.

Although tanks were used successfully during 1918, the British High Command had not recognized that mechanized troops and tanks used *en masse* had become the supreme offensive weapon. During the 1930s, a parsimonious British parliament and pacifist sentiment deprived the army of the weapons and training needed to develop tank warfare. But the Germans, after 1933, were given both, and they used Panzers to deadly effect in 1940, 23 years after their worth had been proved at Cambrai.

Battle of Caporetto *October 1917*

Seldom has a country entered a major conflict so disorganized and ill prepared as was Italy. When Field Marshal Luigi Cadorna assumed the supreme command in July 1914, he found that all staff campaign studies had been exclusively defensive, and that no plans had been evolved for attack. Moreover, the Italian politicians were so secretive about their simultaneous negotiations with both sides that it was only on 5 May 1915 that the military staff was told of the change of Italy's alliance. They were, thus, given less than three weeks to prepare for war against Austria, their erstwhile ally.

But there was worse. In May 1915, Italy believed Austria-Hungary to be reeling into oblivion under remorseless Russian blows. This was far from true, for after Russia's defeat at Gorlice, in the same month, she withdrew from Galicia, enabling Austria to transfer more troops to the Italian Front. Nevertheless, although Italy was short of munitions, she had at least a 4:3 superiority in men.

The Italian-Austrian front ran through the Alps for its entire length, and both sides fought to drive through those mountain barriers and reach the open plains beyond them. Despite two years of war and great loss of life, neither side had, by 1917, achieved that ambition.

Successive minor battles on the River Isonzo during 1915 and early 1916 left the Italians virtually in their original

Steep, serpentine roads made bringing up supplies an arduous, time-consuming task for both armies. This Austrian supply column on the Moistroka Pass near Tolmino, in October 1917, is returning to base to reload. The stationary truck is a war photographer's vehicle.

Monfalcone and Gorizia were taken by the Italians in August 1916. During the Tenth Battle of the Isonzo in August 1917, they were again engaged in difficult and bitter fighting in the area, as this painting of the crack Italian troops, the *Bersaglieri*, vividly conveys.

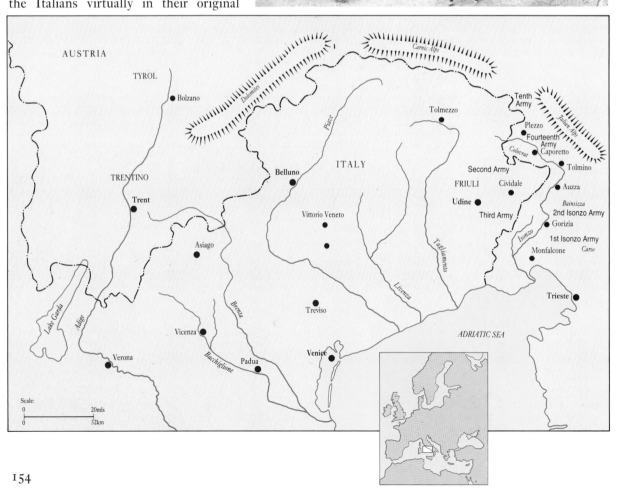

From the early 1880s, treaties between the European powers had been repeatedly made, revoked and reworked. In 1882, Italy, aggrieved at France forestalling her advance in North Africa by occupying Tunis, signed the Triple Alliance with Germany and Austria-Hungary.

In consequence, France, for her safety, made overtures to Russia. Meanwhile, in 1904, an understanding—the *Entente Cordiale*—was established between two traditional foes: Great Britain and France.

Then, in 1907, an Anglo-Russian pact was signed, creating what was known as the Triple Entente.

By 1914, however, Italy's interests more nearly coincided with those of the Allies. Thus, despite her treaty obligations to the Central Powers, Italy at first stood neutral. When Germany failed to gain victory in the early months of the war, Italy, seizing what she perceived to be a favourable moment, joined the Allies and on 23 May 1915 declared war on Austria-Hungary.

positions. Then, in May 1916, a year after Italy had entered the war, the Austrians mounted an offensive from the Trentino region that almost reached the Venetian plain. In the following months, the Russian Brusilov Offensive and the British attack on the Somme brought Italy some respite. Nevertheless, the civilian population was badly demoralized; the expected quick, easy victory, with all its rewards, seemed suddenly beyond Italy's grasp.

Italian morale was slightly enhanced when an attack in the Carso—the Sixth Battle of the Isonzo—resulted in the capture of Gorizia on 17 August. Ten days later the 75-year-old prime minister, Paolo Boselli, declared war on Germany. He was fearful that Great Britain and France would partition the Turkish Empire after the war, without reference to Italy, and thought in this way to secure his country's interests in that region. But this

move was instrumental only in bringing about an Italian military reverse of the severest proportions in 1917, although in the intervening period the war on the Italian Front degenerated into stalemate.

Then, in August 1917, the Italians initiated a general offensive along the River Isonzo: the eleventh battle there. Some local gains resulted, but none of the strong Austrian positions was overrun, and Cadorna lost 40,000 dead and 108,000 wounded, although 25,000 prisoners were taken. Nevertheless, it seemed to Cadorna that with one more effort the military power of Austria could be broken. But there remained a problem of weaponry, for Italy had insufficient artillery for what was predominantly a war of guns.

Cadorna sought assistance from Britain and France; some British batteries were sent to Italy, but neither of his allies could spare troops to reinforce him. Haig was preparing for his great attack in Flanders, and the French Army, demoralized by the huge losses suffered in Nivelle's fruitless assault on the Aisne, was still being nursed back to high morale by Pétain. Cadorna had to make do on his own.

The omens were not auspicious. There was much domestic unrest and pacifist sentiment in Italy, as well as industrial disputes in the great manufacturing cities of Milan and Turin. Even more ominous, the Russian collapse was now as imminent as it was inevitable, permitting the bulk of Austria's élite troops (and now also German units, following Boselli's imprudent declaration of war) to be moved to the Italian Front.

The Eleventh Battle of the Isonzo had ended on 13 September 1917, and almost immediately Archduke Eugene, the Austrian Army Group Commander, decided on a counterstroke which would catch the Italians off balance. The operation, code-named 'Waffentreue' (Brothers in Arms) would be a joint Austro-German offensive, mounted by 15 infantry divisions, seven German and eight Austrian, grouped as Fourteenth Army.

Cadorna seems not to have been aware of the enemy's troop concentrations, and he allowed a thinly held area to degenerate into an unmanned gap between his armies near Tolmino. And it was against this sector that the great mass of Austro-German artillery and infantry was being assembled.

The most significant element in the ensuing campaign was the hand, yet again, of General Erich Ludendorff, for the German General Staff had assumed direction on the Italian Front. While the nominal Austrian Commander-in-Chief,

CAPORETTO/2

Mountain warfare posed great problems. The men of the Italian Alpine artillery unit, *right*, could well have taken all day to lower their 75mm gun down the sheer rock face. The troops, *below*, must have hauled up their field gun in the same manner. The sledges (top left) were used to bring up ammunition and supplies, or they were man-portered; the ropes aided in climbing the icy slopes.

Conrad von Hötzendorff, and the Archduke Eugene remained as commanders of army groups, the alpine strategy was entirely the brain-child of Ludendorff. It was to be executed by one of his ablest commanders, General Otto von Below, and the Fourteenth Army.

The Austro-Italian front ran from Switzerland to the Adriatic Sea near Trieste. Along this line was stationed, in the north, Hötzendorff's Tyrol Group, consisting of the Tenth and Eleventh armies. On their left was Below's very well-equipped 14th Army, and reaching from its left flank to the Adriatic shore lay General Boroevic's Isonzo Group: the Second and First Isonzo armies. Along the entire front 1,550 guns and more than 400 medium and long-range mortars had also

been brought up into strategic positions.

They were opposed on the Isonzo Front by the Italian Second Army, under General Luigi Capello, which was made up of 34 divisions to the Central Powers' 35. The discrepancy in strength was, in fact, far greater than it appears on paper, for many Italian units were understrength and they did not have as many guns as the Austro-German armies.

Ludendorff planned a massive offensive between the towns of Tolmino and Plezzo, with the intention of breaking through into the region of Friuli and the Venetian plain. From there, the Austro-German armies, with their left flank resting on the River Po, would be poised to trap the Italian forces in the Carnic Alps. He had sound reasons for choosing this area, since here the Italian front line crossed and recrossed the Isonzo and looped dangerously northeastward along the crest of Monte Nero, while to the west of Monte Nero lay the town of Caporetto (called Karfreit by the Germans), where the Isonzo Valley broadened, giving an easy avenue of advance.

The German's tactics in the mountains entailed detachments of infantry, accompanied by light artillery and machine-guns carried on trucks, thrusting down the roads and valleys but ignoring the high peaks. This would enable the Fourteenth Army both to sever Italian communications and to outflank troops on the high ground, who could then be picked off at their leisure.

The Austro-German blow, which was to be dealt mainly by Below's Fourteenth Army, was planned to fall upon northern formations of Capello's Second Army. If by surprise and vigour Below could seize Cividale and Udine, he would be well placed to cut off the rest of Second Army and all of the Third Army to the south.

It had been intended that Operation 'Waffentreue' should begin on 22 October, but bad weather caused it to be postponed for 48 hours. Then, at 02.00 on the 24th, still in pouring rain, the Central Powers opened a sustained bombardment on a front of some 40km/25mls between Monte Rombon and Auzza. They fired mainly gas shells because it was common knowledge that the Italian gasmasks were ineffective. At this moment, Capello succumbed to fever and took to his bed, but although incapacitated he most unwisely retained command of Second Army.

The following day, 25 October, dawned cold and misty with snow everywhere on the high ground. This was more than Below could have hoped for, since the low cloud gave additional cover to his surprise

attack. The Austrian artillery barrage opened with intensity and the infantry was thrown in along the entire front from Monte Rombon to the southern end of the Bainsizza. The Italian right and left wings held, but the centre, from Saga to Auzza, was overrun and Below's troops were across the river by early afternoon.

It was now evident to the Italians that they were threatened by three hammer blows: one from the area of Plezzo toward the town of Saga; another from Tolmino, and a third at Caporetto, between the two. The struggle, in freezing conditions, continued throughout 25 October and into the following day, by which time the Bainsizza plateau, which the Italians had earlier taken three weeks to capture, was quickly overrun. Cadorna, dismayed by events, moved his headquarters from Udine to greater safety in Padua.

Well he might, for the two Italian corps

in the Caporetto area, faced with certain encirclement, evaporated in their rush to escape their enemy. This enabled Below to thrust more and more of his men into the fight for the Colovrat and Monte Matajur, which were taken in their entirety by 19.00 on 26 October.

This sector of the Italian front line now disintegrated, some claiming, Cadorna conspicuous among them, that units of the

The man on the right in this front-line Italian unit, *above*, is equipped with a Perelli two-barrelled 9mm assault pistol. A fast-firing weapon, it held 22 rounds but had only a short range. It was copied by the Austrians who called it the Villar Perrosa.

In the Alpine region many front-line trenches, such as the one, *below*, manned by the Austrian infantry, were high on the mountain sides. Having a commanding view over the valleys, they served also as excellent forward observation posts.

The attack by the Stein Group of the Austro-German 14th Army was made at the weakest point in the Italian line: just north of Tolmino.

On 24 October 1917, the 12th German Division moved up the valley of the Isonzo and seized Caporetto. At the same time a strong force struck into the mountains, which were held by the 4th and 24th Italian corps.

Among the troops of the German Alpine Corps was the Württemberg Mountain Battalion under Captain Erwin Rommel, who was to win fame in World War II.

Rommel's detachment was soon through the first Italian line and, meeting little opposition, by the night of the 24th had breached their second defensive line.

Rommel decided not to try to widen the breach but to go straight for the top of the Colovrat ridge. His bold action paid dividends. He picked off the Italian positions one after another and by 07.15 on the 26th had taken Monte Cragonza.

Without resting, the Württembergers set off for the assault on Mrzli and Matajur. But they were held up by attacks on isolated Italian strongpoints, and when Rommel reached the southeastern slopes of Mrzli, he had to wait until 10.00 to assemble the one machine-gun and two rifle companies needed for the attack.

The Italian garrison rapidly withdrew from the peak, but then Rommel noticed a mass of enemy soldiers gathering on the saddle between Mrzli (4) and Matajur (3). This was the 1st Regiment of the Salerno Brigade, which had been drafted into the area only a few days before, without orders or direction from the high command.

As the small German force approached, they threw down their arms and surrendered. Rommel detailed two riflemen to escort the 1,500 prisoners down the road to Luico.

The German force of 100 riflemen and six machine-gun crews then moved on Monte Matajur, held by the 2nd Salerno Regiment. Some of these troops resisted strongly, but soon a further 1,200 men surrendered and were also sent off to Luico (5), while their disconsolate commanding officer 'sat at the roadside and wept with rage and shame' (6).

The garrison on the summit put up a brave fight, firing on their attackers with rifles and machine-guns well placed among the boulders on the bare face of Matajur.

German gunners returned fire, forcing the Italians to dive for cover as bullets struck splinters off the rocks. Led by Rommel himself (1), a few men worked their way around the mountain to the east and then westward along a ridge toward the guardhouse on the summit (2).

Surprised by this attack and still under fire from machine-guns on the south slope, the Italians finally gave up. As Rommel wrote: 'At 11.40 on 26 October, 1917, three green and one white flare announced that the Matajur massif had fallen.'

Monte Matajur was taken 52 hours after the start of the offensive. Rommel ordered an hour's rest on the summit for his troops, saying, with good reason, 'It was well deserved.'

They had captured '150 officers, 9,000 men and 81 guns' for the loss of only 6 dead and 30 wounded, helping to bring about the collapse of all hostile resistance.

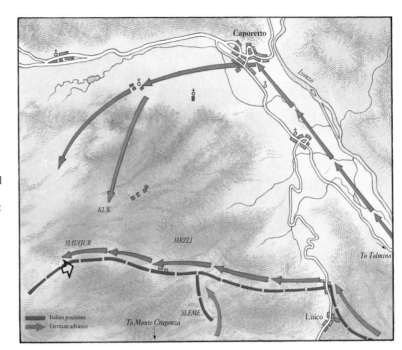

CAPORETTO/4

The Austro-German method of attack at Caporetto was quite new on the Italian Front. Instead of launching the main assault against the enemy's defensive positions high in the mountains, specially trained troops, such as the Württemberg Mountain Battalion, were first sent in. Armed with machine-guns, grenades and flamethrowers, they overran the Italian lines on the Colovrat, picking off the well-defended heights one by one.

In the meantime, the 12th Division, with light artillery mounted on trucks, advanced rapidly up the Isonzo Valley and took Caporetto. Swinging round, they then attacked Monte Matajur from the north and poured down the Natisone Valley, surrounding and isolating a large part of the Italian Second Army.

 1 Monte Matajur
 2 Monte Mrzli
 3 Monte Cragonza
 4 Caporetto
 5 Peak 1192
 6 Luico
 7 Monte Kuk
 8 Tolmino
 9 12th Division
10 Württemberg Mountain Battalion
11 Monte Hum

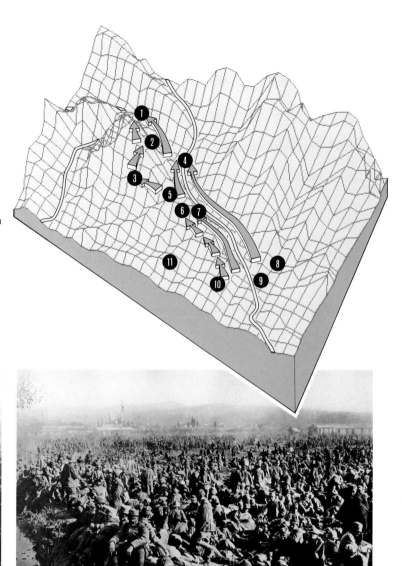

Demoralized Italian soldiers surrendered in their thousands.

Austrian *Schwarzlose* machine-guns had an incision in the shield to allow for elevation, a useful feature in mountain warfare.

Second Army had shown 'insufficient resistance' to the enemy. The implication was clear: it was a matter of cowardice or treason. The truth, however, lay more nearly in the Italians' inept use of their three defensive lines.

The first, heavily manned position was in fact the weakest, for it ran along the line of Italy's farthest advance and was as a

---

'Tin hats' and body armour

The introduction of steel helmets in 1916 significantly reduced the losses from head wounds that all armies were suffering. They quickly became general issue in the Allied armies, but the Central Powers initially distributed them only to front-line units and storm troopers.

The standard British helmet, the Mark I 'Brodie', had a liner and a dished brim. The German 1916 pattern helmet, weighing about 1kg/2¼lb, was a deep bowl-shape,

with a neck flare and two lugs on the side from which were suspended reinforcement plates; the 1918 version weighed 1.5kg/3⅓lb. The addition of brow plates increased these weights, so unbalancing the wearer that they were issued mainly to snipers.

From 1916, British tank crews were issued with a rivetted fibre helmet, to be worn with goggles and a visor of chain-mail as a protection against any particles of hot metal flying around inside a tank under fire.

A few specialist German units were issued with body armour: four overlapping metal plates, connected by webbing straps. They weighed 8–10kg/17½–22⅓lb, and although adopted by the Austrian Army, they proved too cumbersome in mountain warfare.

CADORNA

Field Marshal Luigi Cadorna (1850– 1928) had risen to the highest military rank in some measure through the fame of his father, a general in the wars of the Risorgimento who had captured Rome in 1870. In effect, commander of military operations in Italy before the war, Cadorna showed great strategical insight, but his qualities of leadership were marred by lack of concern for his men, which led to their low morale and to wholesale desertions after Caporetto. He was also intolerant and dismissive of the views of others on military matters.

DIAZ

General Armando Diaz (1861–1928), who succeeded Cadorna, had made a profound study of the science of war and was, in the words of the British Prime Minister, David Lloyd George, 'the brains of the Italian Army'. A determined but cautious commander, he did not undertake the offensive toward Vittoria Veneto until, in late autumn 1918, the collapse of the Central Powers was inevitable. He possessed, however, one supreme talent, which proved invaluable after the disaster of 1917: an ability to inspire confidence in his troops.

BELOW

General Otto von Below (1857–1944) was commissioned in the German infantry in 1875. He was made a general in 1909. After commanding the troops who captured Libau, Windau and Mitau during the Riga offensive, he was transferred in 1916 to the west, where he led the German forces between Arras and Soissons. In October 1917 he commanded the Fourteenth Army, which was largely responsible for the victory at Caporetto. He subsequently led the Seventeenth Army during the German offensives in the spring of 1918.

result erratically located. The second, everywhere stronger, was only patchily defended, as was the third, and ammunition and food stores were sited close behind the lines. These dispositions would have been correct for an offensive, but they were hopelessly inappropriate for defence.

For Italy, the calamity—so sudden and unexpected—was absolute. Although many men resisted fiercely, others gave up without a struggle, and Second Army became largely a terrified rabble. The panic intensified on 28 October when Below struck into Friuli. Cividale had been seized and Udine and Gorizia would shortly fall. The Teutonic avalanche gathered momentum and within three days 60,000 prisoners had been taken and hundreds of guns.

On 25 October, the Italian Third Army had begun its essential hasty retreat to save itself from encirclement; and Fourth Army in the north also fell back, fighting doggedly all the way. One question only

remained: where, if at all, could the Italians stem the seemingly irresistible advance of their enemies?

They were, in fact, aided by Below's now limited power of only six divisions and the general surprise of the Central Powers at the extent of their victory. These two factors, together with the Italians' stubborn resistance, enabled

them to hold their enemy 130km/80mls west of Caporetto, on the River Piave.

Nevertheless, the Italian Second Army had virtually ceased to exist as a fighting unit. Some 2,000 guns had been captured and certainly more than 800,000 men had been lost through death, wounds, capture or desertion. German and Austrian losses were in the region of 5,000.

A new unity evolves

The Italian defeat at Caporetto was, for the Allies, one of the gravest moments of the war. There were, however, several redeeming developments in Italy herself. On 1 November 1917, Vittorio Orlando, the Minister of the Interior, became Prime Minister in place of the inept and aged Boselli. And Cadorna was replaced by a younger man, General Armando Diaz.

The Italian people now found a new comradeship and unity of purpose. Except

for the political extreme left, who stood to gain from failure, the parties combined for the first time in the war. Italy also received help from Great Britain and France, who hurriedly sent troops to her support.

On 24 October 1918, an invigorated army crossed the Piave and drove toward Vittorio Veneto, splitting the demoralized Austrian Army in two. Austria's retreat degenerated into rout and, on 30 October, she sued for an armistice.

The campaign in East Africa *1914–1918*

The war against Germany's colonies in Africa commenced in West Africa. Togoland was hemmed in on three sides by British and French possessions, and her military force consisted of fewer than 4,000 men, of whom at most 250 were German. On 27 August 1914, in the face of combined British and French attacks, the Germans surrendered unconditionally.

Overrunning the Cameroons posed a more complex and costly problem. The plan was for French troops to invade from the Congo, while British forces crossed the frontier from Nigeria. But the great distances involved, the advent of the rainy season, and insufficient Allied preparation, enabled the Germans to counterattack successfully and even temporarily to make incursions into Nigeria. The British Navy then seized the major ports, forcing the Germans to retreat inland. All their wireless stations were captured or destroyed, and by February 1916 the campaign was over.

When war was declared, the Germans in South West Africa abandoned their main coastal bases at Swakopmund and Luderitz Bay and pulled back most of their troops and weapons to the inland capital of Windhoek. They then committed a major strategic error by sending raiding parties across the border into the Cape Province, thus uniting almost all the people of South Africa in a resolve to repel the aggressors. Slowly the South Africans

War in Germany's colonies

The conflict quickly spread from Europe to Germany's territories all around the world, notably to Africa. Here her four colonies—Togoland, the Cameroons, South West Africa (Namibia), and German East Africa (Tanzania)—all adjoined those of Great Britain, France, Belgium or Portugal.

By far the largest and most prosperous of these was German East Africa, whose frontier with British East Africa (Kenya) ran just north of the Kilimanjaro mountain group. The colony was almost the size of western Europe, and the Germans had made great engineering and financial investment in it. Railways had been built and modern seaports constructed, notably at Dar-es-Salaam, the capital.

While the principal campaigns were fought in western and eastern Europe, Africa also became a significant theatre of war as the Allies, especially Great Britain with her naval supremacy, sought to seize Germany's imperial possessions.

The military forces in the colonies were usually locally raised native levies, and in East Africa the terrain was largely bush. These factors made it ideal for guerrilla operations but unsuitable for conventional warfare, entailing the laborious movement of wheeled transport, to which the British were accustomed. Though far fewer men were involved than the millions in Europe, the consequences and eventual spoils in Africa were great.

The vigorous drawings of Askaris were done by Lieutenant von Ruckteschell, Lettow's adjutant. Native troops made up a large part of the German force, as the shot of a column in open country shows. Behind the officers on mules, an NCO carries the cased regimental colour.

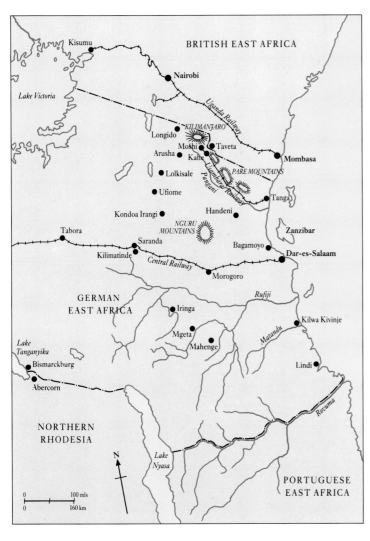

gained the upper hand, and Windhoek was occupied on 12 May 1915.

A more serious danger was developing in East Africa. The Uganda Railway, the single line of communication between Uganda and the British port of Mombasa, ran virtually along the northern frontier of German East Africa, providing an obvious military objective. While Germany's tactics were largely for hit and run raids, her main blow would surely be designed to cut the railway line and seize Mombasa.

Exact German strength is unknown, but it was probably around 10,000, including native infantry, German residents and reservists. However, they were well armed, particularly with machine-guns, of which there were usually four to each battalion. The British were heavily outnumbered at the outbreak of war. There were fewer than 1,500 white fighting men in Uganda and British East Africa, including local settlers serving in volunteer formations, police and scout detachments and some 2,300 African troops.

At sea the British were in a commanding position. On 13 August a cruiser bombarded Dar-es-Salaam and a landing

The King's African Rifles (KAR), made up of recruits from all Britain's East African colonies, was the largest force employed against the Germans.

From three infantry battalions in 1914, it had grown to 22 battalions in five regiments by 1918. Each company had a machine-gun and each man a rifle. The KAR trooper, when well trained, was hardy and adept at living and fighting in the bush.

party destroyed the wireless station, and on Lake Nyasa a German steamer and her crew were captured. The Germans, however, were concentrating their best troops for a decisive campaign against the Uganda Railway.

From mid-August into September, several vigorous German attacks toward the railway were held by the British, who were now receiving limited reinforcements. These attacks died away by the end of October, but the British could do no more here than stand on the defensive. On 25 February 1915, they announced the blockade of the coast, and despite being strong and resourceful, the German garrison was in a state of siege. Although the inequality in numbers was gradually being rectified, the British still had insufficient troops to exploit this promising situation.

The *Schutztruppe*, the German army in the colony, though blockaded by the

A British forward supply camp beside the Ruvu river, seen in half flood. In normal conditions, trucks could drive through the water. The suspension bridge was built by Indian sappers in 1917.

The fiasco of the Tanga landings

The first step in Great Britain's conquest of East Africa was to be the capture of the port of Tanga, from where an advance could be made up the Usambara Railway. Two Indian brigades—8,000 men—under Major-General A. E. Aitken sailed from Bombay on 16 October 1914. They were ill equipped, with obsolete rifles, and had had no experience of bush warfare.

The invasion fleet appeared off Tanga early on 2 November, but no landing was

The rout of the Indians, by an unknown artist.

attempted until next day. The Germans were by now aware of British movements, and the first Indian units ashore came under heavy machine-gun fire from the *Schutztruppe*; they wavered and rushed back to the beach (1). While the bulk of the British troops was disembarking (2), German reinforcements were rushed by rail from Moshi.

Fearing encirclement, the local German commander had withdrawn most of his force from the town (3), but early on 4 November, while reconnoitring on a

bicycle, Lettow found that Aitken was waiting for daylight before attacking. When he did, his men were met by fierce, accurate fire, and the 63rd Palamcottah Light Infantry broke and fled. To add to the Indians' misery, they were assailed by swarms of ferocious African bees.

During the night, the Indians were driven back to the point (4), and Aitken had no choice but to re-embark from A Beach. This was completed by 15.20 on the 6th, but half a million rounds and many wounded were abandoned.

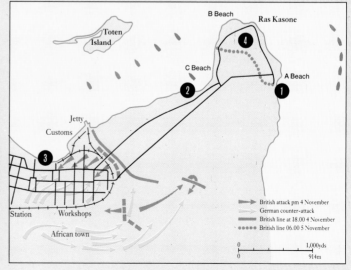

→	British attack pm 4 November
→	German counter-attack
—	British line at 18.00 4 November
•••	British line 06.00 5 November

British navy and surrounded by enemies, had the twin advantages of a greater number of weapons and good interior lines of communication. It possessed yet one more boon in its commander, Colonel Paul von Lettow-Vorbeck, who had had experience of bush warfare in South West Africa. He proved himself a leader of the highest ability, adapting and refining tactics to meet the difficult conditions and terrain encountered in tropical Africa.

The South African Lieutenant-General Jan Smuts, early in 1916, was appointed to the supreme Allied command as replacement for Sir Horace Smith-Dorrien, who had been invalided home. When Smuts arrived at Mombasa on 19 February, his problem was to defeat a well-armed, swift-moving enemy in difficult bush country, and then to occupy the huge territory of German East Africa.

The strength of the *Schutztruppe* at this time was still approximately 10,000 of whom fewer than 2,000 were German, the rest being native 'Askaris'. Smuts had at his disposal some 27,000 men—British, South African, Indian and African—as well as 71 guns and 123 machine-guns. He proposed to penetrate German territory from the north, while other British and Belgian forces were to move eastward from a line running through the lakes of Victoria, Kivu, Tanganyika and Nyasa.

If Smuts were to succeed, he had to force the only gateway through the mountain barrier, the 32-km/20-ml gap between Mount Kilimanjaro and the Pare Mountains to the southeast, where Lettow's strength was concentrated. And Lettow had the considerable advantage of the Usambara Railway to his rear, which would enable him to move his troops rapidly to any point where his enemy might strike.

Smuts's men had a daunting task. First there was a long approach across the dusty, waterless plain; then they had to work their way through a tangle of dense thorn scrub and shoulder-high grass, crossed by a network of dried-up watercourses. Two large rivers, also, bisected the gap: the Lumi, running roughly north to south into Lake Jipe, and the Ruvu, running out of it, which created a great swamp along the steep northern slopes of the Pare Mountains. Established on the high ground overlooking all this, Lettow's position seemed impregnable.

Smuts ordered 1st Division, under Brigadier-General J.M. Stewart, which was stationed at Longido, to march almost 64km/40mls through the thick bush west of Kilimanjaro, to occupy Boma Ngombe. It was then to sweep south of the mountain

The last of the German sea raiders, *Königsberg*, was badly damaged by two British naval gun boats in her hiding place in the Rufiji delta in July 1916. But the Germans salvaged her ten 4.1in and two 3.5in guns and used them on land.

Despite strong, well-hidden enemy positions on the Rufiji, the South Africans crossed the river by stealth in January 1917, to establish a bridgehead.

to sever the Germans' line of retreat at Kahe on the Usambara Railway.

A simultaneous attack was to be made by Major-General J.M. Tighe's 2nd Division, collaborating with the 2nd and 3rd South African Infantry Brigades and Major-General J.L. van Deventer's 1st South African Mounted Brigade. Their objectives were the Chala Heights, Taveta, and Salaita Hill. The two assaults opened on 5 and 8 March respectively, and by 15 March, when van Deventer reached Old Moshi, lying slightly southwest of Mount Kilimanjaro, Lettow's flank had been turned. He was forced to retreat to the River Ruvu, his only hope of escape being toward Lake Jipe.

At this point Lettow faced disaster, but the rearguard actions fought by his troops enabled him to cross the Ruvu to temporary safety. Smuts was determined to give him no respite. Anticipating that Lettow had sought sanctuary in the Pare and Usambara Mountains, he decided to keep the greater part of his force along the Ruvu during the rains, which had just started, and then to strike between the two ranges. In the meantime, he dispatched van Deventer, with the new 2nd Division— 1,200 mounted men and more than 7,000 infantry and artillery—south toward Kondoa Irangi and the Central Railway.

Van Deventer left Arusha on 3 April and by the 13th had taken Lolkisale and

General Jan Smuts's plan in March 1916 was to trap Lettow's army south of Mount Kilimanjaro by a dual advance from north and east.

Although the 2nd Division and the South African Mounted Brigade successfully forced the Kilimanjaro gap and took Moshi, Smuts's hopes of encirclement were frustrated by the tardy advance of 1st Division from the north. By 14 March, when the two forces met, the Germans had fallen back toward the River Ruvu.

To prevent their escape down the Usambara Railway, Smuts ordered the 2nd South African and 2nd East African brigades to advance on Kahe, while van Deventer's mounted troops swept south from Moshi to take the Germans in the rear.

The advance of 1st Division to Kahe began at about 12.00 on 18 March; by the 20th they had taken Masaai Kraal and Store. At about 16.30 that day, van Deventer's mounted brigade set off, covering the 40-km/ 25-ml march through the thick scrub under a full moon. Their only hazardous encounters were with rhinoceros.

Before sunrise on 21 March they were in position some 8km/ 5mls south of Kahe.

The twin peaks of Kilimanjaro (1) and Mawenzi rose high above the plain as the column moved north. Spotting German troops on Kahe Hill (4), van Deventer detached a squadron each from the 1st and 3rd South African Horse (5) and ordered them to cross the Pangani River (3) and clear the enemy out.

The crossing was extremely dangerous, for the banks were swampy and the river, about 18m/20yds wide, was in half flood.

Men and horses were swept down like leaves against overhanging trees by the swift current. As they scrambled out on the far bank, they came under a hail of rifle and machine-gun fire from the Askaris on Kahe Hill. Shells from one of *Königsberg*'s guns, sited near Kahe, also landed among them (6).

The South Africans re-formed, and by 11.00 had seized the hill, driving out the defenders.

As the rest of the column moved up the west bank, it too was shelled by the *Königsberg*'s gun. By 11.30, Kahe Station had been taken and the German force driven back to the railway bridge over the river (2), which they crossed and then blew up behind them.

By 23 March, steady pressure from van Deventer and 1st Division obliged Lettow to abandon the crucial Kahe position entirely and to mount a general retreat into the Pare Mountains.

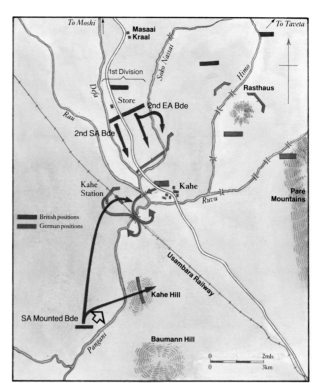

THE COMMANDERS

Colonel Paul von Lettow-Vorbeck (1870–1964) fought in China during the Boxer Rebellion (1900–1) and for two years in South West Africa at the time of the Hottentot Rebellion. This gave him a profound insight into how to train, command and employ native levies in the bush. He was a good administrator and an improviser of genius, gifts that enabled him to hold together and supply his inferior force in siege conditions.

Lettow was promoted general in 1918 and later commanded a Reichwehr division. Becoming interested in politics, he resigned from the army and served as a Reichstag deputy; but loathing Hitler and the Nazis, he retired in 1930. He died, a forgotten figure, at the age of 94.

Lieutenant-General Jan Christiaan Smuts (1870–1950), although a guerrilla leader during the Boer War, realized that his country's future lay in cooperation with the British, and helped to establish the Union of South Africa in 1910.

He was called to London from East Africa in 1917 and became a member of the Imperial War Cabinet. A signatory to the Versailles Treaty, he nevertheless believed its harsh terms would only

alienate Germany. He was twice South Africa's prime minister: 1919–24 and 1939–48. In 1941 he was made field marshal in the British Army.

Smuts and Lettow had a high mutual regard. Indeed, Smuts arranged for a group of wealthy South Africans to provide Lettow with a small pension and, in the aftermath of World War II,

for food parcels to be sent to him.

Major-General Jacob Louis van Deventer (1868–1922), calm, courageous and well versed in bush warfare, was an ideal lieutenant to Smuts and took over from him in East Africa. In 1919 he organized the military garrisoning of what became Tanganyika and was knighted in 1921.

Colonel von Lettow-Vorbeck (second from right), with friends on a plantation verandah near Moshi in 1914.

In 1917, General Smuts visited the South African troops in France; here, *far left*, he is inspecting Bantu soldiers.

General van Deventer (right) with an aide at a bush camp. It was his tenacious pursuit that finally cleared the German forces out of East Africa.

Ufiome. Torrential rains had already turned the previously dusty plains, or *pori*, into gigantic quagmires, in which guns sank to their axles and the horses of the mounted units were hardly able to move. Progress became nightmarishly slow; bridges were swept away, swollen rivers were impassable and, worst of all, hundreds of horses and mules died because the area was a tsetse fly belt.

Even so, on 19 April, van Deventer's depleted force of about 3,000 weary, hungry and sick men seized the strategically important Kondoa Irangi. Lettow mounted a counter-attack on 7 May, but this was repulsed, and the Germans did not renew the attack.

At the end of May 1916, Smuts's main force—the 1st and 3rd Divisions now divided into three columns—began to move southeast on parallel courses down the Pangani River, the Usambara Railway and, in the east, through the Pare Mountains. At the same time some 2,000 British troops stationed near Lake Victoria, and Belgian forces from Lake Kivu, began to cross the border from the west.

Smuts's plan was for his main force to entrap the *Schutztruppe* to the north, and at the same time, by the capture of Handeni, which fell on 19 June, to establish a companion strategic base to Kondoa Irangi in the west. The Germans were obliged to move out of the Usambara Mountains, and on 7 July the port of Tanga was finally captured. The Allies now planned an attack on Bagamoyo and Dar-es-Salaam, which they entered on 4 September.

On 24 June, van Deventer's force had begun to move southwestward again, and on 14 July it took Saranda and then, on 12 August, Kilimatinde, thereby cutting the Central Railway. By the end of the month, some 160km/100mls or more of the railway were in Allied hands. Lettow had no option but to retreat into the Nguru Mountains, an area some 80km/50mls north to south and more than 32km/20mls wide, with boulders, swamps and forests making it ideal defensive country. The area was cut off by the Allies and fierce fighting took place. On 8 August the strategic town of Morogoro was captured, but once again the Germans had slipped away.

Smuts still entertained hopes of forcing Lettow to a decisive battle, but the wily German leader fell back, fighting all the way, on the defensive line of the River Mgeta. His forces were being steadily crowded into the southeastern corner of the country; they had lost all the high, healthy positions, and from now on were reduced to sheltering in fever swamps.

Lettow's surrender on 25 November 1918, at Abercorn in Northern Rhodesia, was painted by an unknown African artist. It appears from the painting that Lettow had to ride to the ceremony; in fact, the British sent a car to fetch him. At the time Lettow's force consisted of some 175 Europeans and 3,000 Askaris and porters. There were 1,500 women and bearers, and also 38 machine-guns, a field gun, and 250,000 rounds of ammunition.

By May 1917, the *Schutztruppe* had been split into two. One group a little under 5,000 strong, commanded by Lettow, was in the Matandu Valley; the other, numbering fewer than 3,000, under Captain Tafel, was based on Mahenge some 240km/150mls inland. Unable to link up with his commander, and with no way of escape from the pursuing Allied forces, Tafel surrendered unconditionally on 28 November. Before then, to avoid the destruction of his main force, Lettow had crossed the River Rovuma into Portuguese East Africa (Mozambique). From here he continued to wage a guerrilla campaign until after the Armistice of 11 November 1918.

German East Africa was now free of its former masters, and some 90 per cent of the original German force, both black and white, had been killed or taken prisoner, but the British had suffered about 60,000 casualties. For more than three years the remarkable Lettow had tied down some 130,000 troops at a cost to the Allies of around £70 million.

Mandates: a colonial solution

After the war, the League of Nations devised a system of mandates for Germany's former colonies. The basis of the system, which was largely the inspiration of General Smuts, was that responsibility for the local inhabitants' welfare should be invested in the League, under the stewardship of one of the Allied powers.

The mandated territories fell into three groups. The 'A' category applied to territories, such as Syria, which were deemed to be approaching viable independence. 'B' mandates applied to former German areas of tropical Africa not yet thought capable of self-government. Great Britain was granted mandates for German East Africa, renamed Tanganyika, while Togoland and the Cameroons were divided and placed under British and French mandate respectively.

'C' category mandates applied to areas so underdeveloped as to need administration almost as an integral part of the responsible power. South West Africa, therefore, came under the aegis of South Africa.

Germany was banished from Africa: one of the sources of grievance exploited by Adolf Hitler and the Nazi Party, who repeatedly demanded the restoration of German African possessions for reasons of national prestige. Since World War II, all mandated territories in Africa, including it seems certain South West Africa, have gained their independence.

Battle of Megiddo *September–October 1918*

General Sir Edmund Allenby's 1918 campaign in Palestine was one of the most boldly planned and decisive in World War I. In his remarkable achievement, Allenby was helped by a major miscalculation in his enemy's strategy. Early in 1918, the Turks saw that Russia's collapse was irreversible and, gambling on a swift and conclusive German victory, went in search of territorial pickings in the Caucasus, instead of reinforcing to the maximum the strategically important Palestine theatre.

Allenby had at his disposal some 12,000 cavalry, 57,000 infantry and nearly 550 guns. His men—British, Anzac, Indian and Arab—were experienced in battle, fit, and well supplied with food, clothing and weapons. Against this, the weary, ill-provisioned Turks in Palestine, with starving transport animals and at odds with their German partners, could muster only 2,000 cavalry, 32,000 infantry and about 400 guns of all types. Allenby, therefore, possessed an overwhelming superiority in cavalry; an arm he intended to use to the full. He had also two further advantages: superiority in the air, and King Feisal's Arabs, masterminded by the wayward genius of T.E. Lawrence.

The Turkish front line in Palestine ran from just north of Arsuf on the Mediterranean Sea to the Jordan Valley. It was held by three armies, each of which comprised hardly more than the strength of a conventional Turkish division. The Eighth Army held the coastal sector and inland for about 32km/20mls to Furkah; it was headed by Djeud Pasha whose headquarters were in Tul Keram.

The Seventh Army, under Mustafa Kemal (later known as Kemal Attatürk), whose headquarters were at Nablus, was responsible for the sector from Furkah to the Jordan. East of the river lay the Fourth Army, led by Jemal the Lesser, with its headquarters at Amman. In overall command, stationed at Nazareth to the rear, was Liman von Sanders, the German general who had filled the same position in the Gallipoli campaign.

Allenby's essentially simple plan was devised to strike at the heart of Turkish road and rail communications. Turkish reinforcements and provisions came down a single line, the Hejaz Railway, running south from Damascus. The Fourth Army relied on this for all its supplies, and a branch of the line, turning roughly west at Deraa, was used to supply Seventh and Eighth armies.

The railway ran roughly parallel to the Turkish front from Deraa, through Beisan to El Afule, and then on to the port of

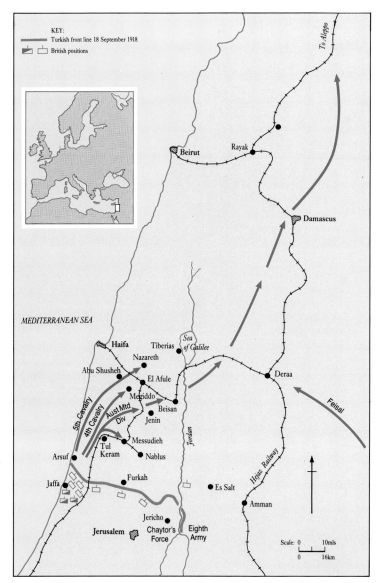

Prelude to Armageddon

In February 1915, the Turks attacked the Suez Canal, the 'jugular vein' of the British Empire. British troops in Egypt were numerically superior but ill equipped, since the armies in France had first call on weapons and ammunition. So, though they succeeded in driving the Turks back into Palestine (Israel), they lacked the means of overcoming the strong Gaza-Beersheba defensive line.

The war against Turkey was taken to the Gallipoli Peninsula in April; but even after the end of that campaign, in 1916 when the fight had shifted back to Palestine, the British were still unable to take Gaza. Then the British War Cabinet decided in June 1917 to strengthen the Allied forces in Egypt. It was obvious that Russia was on the verge of collapse, and her elimination from the war would permit large Turkish

formations to be moved to Palestine from the Eastern Front and the Caucasus.

At the same time, General Sir Edmund Allenby was given command of the Egyptian Expeditionary Force. Allenby re-equipped and reorganized his army, and in October took Gaza and Beersheba. In December he drove the Turks out of Jerusalem, ending 400 years of Turkish rule over the Holy City.

The German spring offensive on the Western Front in 1918 forced Allenby to postpone his own follow-up attack in Palestine, since many of his experienced British troops were withdrawn to bolster the armies in France. They were replaced largely by good Indian units and soldiers from Mesopotamia, but it was not until September that Allenby was once again ready to undertake an advance.

The war artist James McBey's painting, *The Camel Corps: A Night March to Beersheba*, records Allenby's earlier triumph in the desert war in late 1917. When the Indian cavalry arrived in Palestine in May 1918, replacing units transferred to France, the Corps was broken up, and Allenby gave 2,000 riding camels to Feisal. This enabled the Arab Army to form a strong mobile column, whose activities in the desert east of the Jordan confirmed the Turks' belief that this was where the Allied army would strike.

The rugged nature of the terrain is clearly shown in *The Bombing of the Wadi Fara* by Stuart Reid. In flight from Nablus after 10th Division's attack, the bulk of the Turkish Seventh Army was spotted on 21 September as it wound its way down the steep-sided Wadi Fara.

For four hours, aircraft bombed and shot up the column until the gorge was completely blocked by more than 1,500 burnt and abandoned vehicles and 90 guns. The survivors, who had fled into the hills, were rounded up next day and taken prisoner.

The Arab Revolt

General Allenby's campaign in Palestine was greatly aided by the 'Arab Uprising', a haphazard but ultimately general, though disunited, revolt of the Arab tribes against their Turkish overlords. The movement was largely inspired and sustained by Feisal ibn Hussein, later King of Iraq (1921–33), and one of the most controversial figures to emerge during the war, T.E. Lawrence.

An English scholar who had travelled widely in the Middle East, Lawrence was, when war broke out, attached to the Intelligence section of the British Army in Egypt. He joined Feisal in 1916 and became a dominant leader in the Arab struggle.

Feisal was the third son of the Sherif of Mecca. A tall, physically frail man, he had a burning desire to rid the Arabs of the fetters of Turkish control. He had been educated in Constantinople and had served in the Turkish Army, so had an understanding of Turkish thought and, crucially, of tactics. This knowledge, coupled with his skill in

'Lawrence of Arabia', portrayed by James McBey in October 1918.

Feisal ibn Hussein, a portrait painted by Augustus John in 1919.

Haifa. At El Afule, the main line turned south to Messudieh junction, where it again divided, one branch going to Tul Keram, the other (as yet incomplete) to Nablus. Deraa, Beisan, El Afule and Messudieh were also junctions on the road system. If Allenby could seize these key towns, he would cut off the Turks' lines both of supply and retreat.

In outline, Allenby's plan was to delude the Turks into believing that his attack would come in the Jordan Valley, while in fact striking hard in the west. The bulk of his cavalry was to ride north along the coast before they swung in behind the Turkish Seventh and Eighth armies and took their communications centres.

Deraa was beyond rapid reach by cavalry, although vulnerable to raids by Lawrence and the Mobile Column of the Arab Army, who were operating from the desert east of Amman. El Afule and Beisan, however, were only 72km/45mls and 97km/60mls respectively from Allied forward positions. These distances the cavalry could cover in a single ride, interrupted only to water their horses, particularly since their advance was to take them over the comparatively easy going of the plains of Sharon and Esdraelon.

The only problem that might arise was during the crossing of the low mountain range, the Samarian Hills, that ran south-east from Mount Carmel and separated the plains. There were two possible routes through the hills: one leading to Abu Shusheh, the other, the Musmus Pass, that would bring the cavalry out at El Lejjun, near the high mound of Megiddo, or Armageddon. Neither pass was diffi-cult, but both could be easily defended and held by relatively few men, so it was essential that the Turks did not become aware of Allenby's intentions and move troops into the passes.

To prevent the cavalry being exhausted by heavy fighting in the early stages of the battle, Allenby planned to punch a hole in the right of the Turkish line with infantry and massed artillery. He intended to build up a large enough force to ensure the success of his assault by bringing both infantry and cavalry by stealth from his right wing to reinforce his left.

To keep the Turks guessing as to his movements, it was necessary to deprive them of reliable overall reconnaissance; so Allenby employed his air arm systemati-cally to drive his enemy's aircraft from the skies—indeed in many instances, to pre-vent their even taking off. So effective was the Air Force that during the time he was concentrating his troops in the olive and orange groves just north of Jaffa, only four enemy aircraft flew across Allenby's lines.

He also employed Lawrence and his Arab guerrillas to the full. Lawrence had for months been blowing up sections of the Hejaz Railway; then on 16 and 17 September, he and his followers destroyed the railway lines to the north, south and west of Deraa. At the same time, British and Australian pilots bombed the track and station buildings in the town. As a result, all railway traffic to Palestine from the north ceased.

Allenby's subterfuges were far more subtle, however, As he moved troops to his left wing, dummy camps and rows of dummy horses made from wood and canvas were set up in the Jordan Valley. The same few soldiers were marched back

Feisal's men were photographed by Lawrence as they rode into Wejh on the Red Sea, *left*. Captured in January 1917, the town was used as a base for attacks on the Hejaz Railway. The British gave the Arabs arms, *above*, and, almost more valuable, pack camels: a heavy animal could carry 159kg/350lb of stores or explosives.

diplomacy, enabled him to undermine his enemy and also to control the disparate elements within the Arab Army.

This army never numbered more than a few thousand men (who constantly came and went) serving under their tribal sheikhs, who were themselves controlled by local sherifs. Given the irregular nature of the force, Lawrence advocated using 'a highly mobile, highly equipped striking force of the smallest size' to attack 'distrib-uted points of the Turkish line, to make them strengthen their posts'.

Allenby provided Lawrence with money and weapons and gave him almost a free hand. Often operating far behind Turkish lines, Lawrence's Arabs made frequent, swift attacks, mainly on the Hejaz Railway. They repeatedly blew up sections of track and trains, disrupting supplies and tying down thousands of labourers and their guards in the railway's repair. The raids confused and harassed the Turks out of all proportion to the force involved.

Lawrence's ambition to see independent Arab states set up after the war was frustrated both by Arab disunity and by the self-interest of some European powers.

Prior to Allenby's final offensive, three cavalry divisions were secretly moved from the Jordan Valley to the coast. The activity was disguised by the troops moving only at night and by various subterfuges. One of these was the erection of rows of dummy 'horses', made of wood and canvas and complete with 'tails' made from palm fronds. The ruse completely deceived the Turks, since their air reconnaissance was almost nil, and their Intelligence faulty.

MEGIDDO/3

At about 05.30 on 20 September 1918, the Gloucestershire Hussars, the advance guard of 13th Brigade, rode up the El Afule road and stopped on the rim of the hills overlooking Nazareth.

A well-built town with a population of 15,000, Nazareth lay in a fertile, cup-shaped valley, dotted with olive groves and fields of grain. The hills rose so steeply that, from a distance, the flat-roofed houses looked in places as though they formed

a ladder. Here the German general Liman von Sanders had his headquarters.

As the sun rose hot in the cloudless sky, the Gloucesters trotted briskly into the centre of the town, which they reached at around 06.30, to search for Sanders and, they hoped, capture him. The unsuspecting, sleeping enemy was taken completely by surprise.

The cavalrymen had been in the saddle for just on 24 hours, with only brief breaks to rest and water their horses. But they were still keen and ready to exploit the confusion and disbelief that greeted them.

Despite the surprise of their attack, street fighting, in which mounted men are usually at a disadvantage, soon developed. But the Gloucesters were armed with swords as well as their short Lee-Enfield rifles; for when the British and Australians had seen that the Indian Lancers were issued with these effective weapons, they had asked for them also.

Machine-gunners opened up from balconies and flat roofs, while German and Turkish clerks and orderlies, roused from their sleep by the noise, fired from upstairs windows. The fighting rapidly became a mêlée.

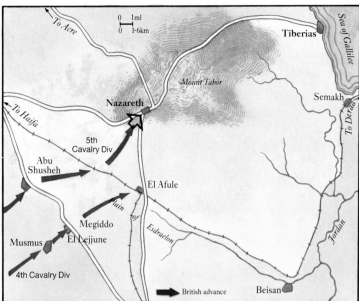

Soldiers stationed in the Latin Monastery (5) soon began to surrender, and all over the town prisoners were rounded up by the score, many still in their pyjamas.

Farther up, the main street was choked by a column of German trucks (2) which their drivers were desperately trying to turn around in an attempt to escape, for the roads to the north had not been sealed.

The Gloucesters ransacked the town in their search for Liman von Sanders, not realizing that the Casa Nuovo (1), a former hospice, was indeed the Turkish General Headquarters. As soon as the attack started, Sanders, albeit in his pyjamas, had fled by car up the street, past the mosque (3) and out along the hilly road to Tiberias (4).

At about 08.30, the Gloucesters were joined by other units of 13th Brigade. But weary and depleted in numbers, they did not have the strength both to hold the town and to guard their 1,500 prisoners, so about mid-morning they withdrew to the plain, taking the prisoners with them.

Many important documents were seized, but the general staff office in the Casa Nuovo was never found, and crucial papers there were burned by the Germans and Turks.

The brief action cost the Gloucesters 13 casualties and 28 horses killed.

The 13th Brigade returned to Nazareth and reoccupied it, this time permanently, on 21 September.

and forth to give the Turks the impression that there was a huge build-up of troops in the area, and mules trailing sleighs were led about continuously to create dust clouds and suggest intense activity and an imminent attack.

So successful were these ruses that, when the bombardment opened in the west, some 35,000 infantry, 9,000 cavalry and almost 400 guns had been secretly deployed along a front of some 24km/15mls. The Turks, supposing the attack would come in the area of the Jordan, mustered a mere 8,000 infantry and about 130 guns. As Colonel (later Field Marshal) Wavell was to write: 'The battle was practically won before a shot was fired.'

Immediately prior to the attack, the Air Force bombed the Turks' exchanges at El Afule, Nablus and Tul Keram, dislocating their telegraph and telephone communications. Thus Liman von Sanders, in Nazareth, was deprived of early and accurate reports of the attack that was shortly to take place. Allenby had one more card to play: during the night of 18/19 September, he ordered 53rd Division, stationed on his right wing, to advance. This not only confirmed the Turks in their belief that the attack was coming in that area, but took 53rd Division some way toward a position from which it could cut off the Turks' retreat eastward once their right-wing armies had been outflanked.

Haifa: ensuring a supply route

After the fall of Nazareth, attention turned to the capture of the port of Haifa. On 23 September the 5th Cavalry Division converged on the town and a sharp action took place.

Haifa lay close to the steep northern slopes of Mount Carmel, and the only access was a strip 1.6km/1ml wide between the mountain and marshy ground, on which ran both the road and railway to El Afule. These were strongly defended by Turkish machine-guns, and there were several field guns on the mountain at Carmelheim.

Two regiments of 15th Brigade, the Jodhpur and the Mysore Lancers, were ordered into action. One squadron of Mysores was sent up a

steep path near Balad-es-Sheikh to ride along the ridge and silence the guns. A little later, two more squadrons of Mysores and the Jodhpurs fell on the Turks guarding the town entrance.

The forces attacked almost simultaneously and both succeeded: the Jodhpurs swept into Haifa and the Mysores, reinforced by a squadron of Sherwood Rangers, seized 17 guns and took some 1,350 prisoners.

1 Road to Jaffa
2 Carmelheim
3 Haifa
4 Balad-es-Sheikh
5 Jodhpurs and Mysores
6 Mysores and Sherwood Rangers

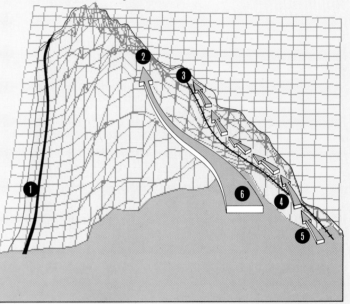

Major-General Sir Harry Chauvel, escorted by a squadron of the 2nd Light Horse, entered Damascus on 2 October 1918. He and his bodyguard were followed by units from his three cavalry divisions, including men of the United Kingdom, Australia, New Zealand, India and France.

Chauvel was one of many commanders to have occupied Damascus, for this rich trading city, lying on a plateau between desert and mountains, and well served by rivers, lies astride one of the main trade routes between Europe and Asia, making it not only a valuable prize in itself but of great strategic importance.

JEMAL PASHA

ALLENBY

General Ahmed Jemal Pasha (1872–1922) in 1913 became Minister of Marine and, with Enver and Talaat, virtually ruled Turkey. Inept as a soldier and diplomat, but a gifted administrator, he was hugely ambitious, even megalomaniac, and retained his position as Governor and Commander-in-Chief of Syria and Palestine throughout the war. Determined to crush Armenian and Arab nationalism, he put many leading Arabs in Damascus to death: one of the main causes of the Arab Revolt. He died in Tiflis (Tbilisi), Georgia, shot it is generally believed by an Armenian.

General Sir Edmund Allenby (1861–1936) was commissioned into the Inniskilling Dragoons in 1882 and saw action in Bechuanaland (Botswana) in 1884–5 and Zululand (1888). He was in command of cavalry operations during the Boer War (1898–1902) and in 1909–10 was Inspector-General of Cavalry.

In 1914, Allenby commanded the BEF Cavalry Division, eventually taking over Fifth Army in 1915. Then, in June 1917, he was appointed to lead the Egyptian Expeditionary Force. A man of violent and unpredictable temper (although he is said never to have borne a grudge), he paradoxically had a lifelong interest in, and love for, birds and plants. Field Marshal Wavell claimed that he was 'the best British general of the Great War'.

In 1919 he was created a peer and promoted field marshal, and until 1925 served as High Commissioner for Egypt.

The main engagement began at 04.30 on 19 September, when Allenby's 383 guns opened fire on the inferior Turkish formations near the coast. The cannonade lasted a mere 15 minutes, then the infantry—a French detachment and the 54th Division on the right, Indian divisions in the centre, and 60th Division by the coast—attacked their unsuspecting foe. The assault overwhelmed the Turks, creating a gap in their lines through which the cavalry could pass unmolested.

The Desert Mounted Corps—the 4th and 5th Cavalry divisions and the Australian Mounted Division—under Major-General Sir Harry Chauvel, swept through the gap without opposition. By 02.00 on 20 September, the 5th Cavalry Division had crossed the hills to Abu Shusheh and 13th Brigade was trotting briskly toward Nazareth. Liman von Sanders, who had had no warning of their rapid advance, only just made good his escape from the town before it was overrun.

The crucial junction of El Afule was taken by the 14th Cavalry Brigade at 08.00; and at 16.30 the 4th Cavalry Division, which had covered almost 129km/80mls in 34 hours, rode into Beisan. The Australian Mounted Division, which had followed the 4th Division through the Musmus Pass, struck eastward at Jenin, to plug the Turks' line of retreat.

This left them with only the dangerous crossing of the fast-flowing and treacherous River Jordan as an avenue of escape. As the Turkish armies fell back in confusion toward the river from Nablus, they were repeatedly attacked by the Air Force, which bombed the fleeing columns until they ceased to exist as fighting units.

The Turkish Fourth Army, east of the Jordan, remained intact though demoralized. Their retreat was inevitable but did not begin until 22 September. By then, however, they had the wrecked Hejaz Railway and Lawrence with the Arabs between them and sanctuary to the north. Part of the Fourth Army surrendered near Amman, which was taken on 25 September, and the remainder near Damascus, which the Desert Mounted Corps and the Arab Army occupied on 1 October.

Turkey sues for peace

Allenby's absolute victory was achieved through his observance of three of the proven maxims of warfare: surprise, mobility and the destruction of all enemy lines of communication.

Within a few days Allenby had destroyed Turkey's military power. Between 19 September and 26 October his forces had advanced more than 483km/300mls northward and had taken some 75,000 prisoners, 360 guns and all the Turkish transport and equipment, for the loss of fewer than 5,000 of his own men. And the key cities of Damascus, Beirut, Homs and Aleppo had all fallen to his army.

The Turkish Empire, on the point of collapse, sought unilateral peace terms, and an armistice was concluded at Mudros on 30 October. Later, by the Treaty of Versailles, Turkey was deprived of massive areas of land, and from her old dominions emerged a separate Palestine, Syria and Iraq, and an Egypt finally stripped of Turkish suzerainty.

The Final German Offensives *March–August 1918*

Germany's last throw

In the spring of 1918 Germany was well placed to inflict a massive, decisive blow in the west. Russia's withdrawal from the war had enabled Germany to move more than 1 million experienced men and 3,000 guns to the Western Front, where for the first time since Verdun she now had numerical superiority.

The French were exhausted, the British Army had sustained serious losses at Passchendaele, and the Italians had been conclusively thrown back from Caporetto. Even so, Germany's main hope of success depended on an early attack, before American forces could reach the Western Front in any strength. But here the German High Command underrated their new enemy.

First, the Americans transported their troops across the Atlantic, in convoys escorted by the British Navy, far quicker and in far greater numbers than the Germans believed possible. By 1 March, the month Germany's last offensives began, there were more than 290,000 American servicemen in Europe; by October there were to be some 1,760,000. Second, these men were ready for combat much sooner than Ludendorff had expected.

Nevertheless, on 21 March 1918, when the blow fell; it seemed to many that Germany was about to achieve the decisive victory she had so long sought.

In spring 1918, the Allies knew that a German attack was planned, but they were not sure where or when the blow would fall. In the event, the Germans struck early on the morning of 21 March, and their target was the British Army, which they hoped, with their superior numbers, to throw back to the coast.

The main thrust was made between Arras and La Fère, to its south, with the greatest concentration around St Quentin. This stretch of the front was held by the Fifth Army, under General Sir Hubert Gough; the Third, commanded by General Sir Julian Byng, lay to the north in the region of Arras. The group of German armies in this area was under the nominal command of the Crown Prince, those in Flanders being under Prince Rupprecht.

On this front of some 65km/40mls between the Sensée and Oise rivers, the

American volunteers were pictured by Thomas Derrick as they embarked for France. Their high rate of literacy and numeracy enabled them rapidly to acquire basic military skills and become an effective fighting force.

Second-wave German assault troops, *below right*, poured through the streets of Bailleul in northern France without opposition, after their comrades in the first wave had stormed and broken British defences and roadblocks.

Germans deployed 37 infantry divisions and 6,000 guns, with almost 30 more divisions held in reserve. Against this formidable array—the greatest assault force to date—the British mustered only 17 divisions, with 5 in reserve, and a mere 2,500 guns. Thus the Germans, with more than 750,000 men, were opposed by only 300,000 British. In some sectors they were superior by a ratio of 4:1.

The Germans had planned a surprise assault, preceded by only sudden, brief periods of intense artillery fire. Troops were to be massed behind the line so that successive waves of men could keep up a sustained attack. This method of attack, in effect no more than a return to the long-established surprise tactics employed by commanders over the centuries, had been used and refined by General Oskar von Hutier in the Riga campaigns of 1915. Now, with her great superiority of manpower, Germany could afford to try these tactics on the Western Front.

This was a potentially devastating form of attack in 1918, for the Allies had become convinced that entrenched forward positions, more cunningly devised and more strongly fortified than ever before, could not be rushed. They had, therefore, omitted to construct defensive positions in depth behind their front line, to which they could fall back if they were compelled to retreat.

The German divisions selected for the assault had, over the months, been given at least four weeks' intensive instruction in mobile warfare and so were trained to

KEY:

German Front line 21 March 1918

Front line 17 July 1918

exploit a breakthrough. Nature also came to the Germans' aid, for 21 March dawned unusually misty, concealing their troops' deployment.

The opening move of the offensive was an intense bombardment, which included thousands of gas shells. This ferocious barrage lasted for little more than two hours; then it switched to an artillery screen behind which troops could advance, and the German infantry swept forward. This first stage in the campaign is known as the Battle of Picardy, or the Second Battle of the Somme.

The Germans at first made extensive territorial gains and continued to do so as more soldiers of Hutier's Eighteenth Army and General Georg von der Marwitz's Second Army swarmed forward in support. Soon British defences were smashed west of St Quentin, forcing Fifth Army into a costly retreat and, in Lloyd George's phrase, 'crippling it'. The German drive was not able to separate the Fifth Army from the Third, although Péronne and Bapaume and then, on 27 March, Albert, were occupied. Noyon fell to the Germans on the same day.

The situation for the Allies was soon to be perilous, for by early April the Germans were only some 16km/10mls from the communications centre of Amiens and had taken in the region of 90,000 prisoners and more than 1,000 guns.

Even worse, the westward retreat of the Fifth Army had now opened up a gap in the Allied line roughly from Noyon to Montdidier to the northwest. The only troops available to plug the gap were French reserves, who had been held back for deployment in a counter-attack. At this, the lowest point in the Allies' fortunes, there was, however, one redeeming feature: they were at last prepared to appoint a supreme commander. On 3 April, the French General Ferdinand Foch became the generalissimo.

Then, on 8 April, the German armies delivered yet another blow against the British, but this time in the La Bassée and Armentières sector of Flanders. Again a massive bombardment was followed immediately by an overwhelming infantry attack, which swept the British back. This great attack, known as the Battle of Lys, gained the Germans a huge salient, extending from just south of Ypres to Lens. French reserves had, for a second time, to be diverted to stem the tide.

The Germans consolidated all their gains and there followed a period of about a month when there was only sporadic and limited fighting. On 27 May, however, Ludendorff launched the third major attack, this time on the French Sixth Army, under General Duchêne, between Rheims and Soissons. The results were as before: the Germans smashed their enemies' defences and, pouring forward, were four days later once more on the Marne. They had taken not only some 40,000 prisoners but up to 400 guns.

Even more demoralizing for the French, this advance brought German heavy artillery within range of Paris. Near-panic engulfed the city and, according to General John Pershing, Commander-in-Chief of American forces in Europe, more than a million people fled from the city during the spring of 1918.

The German advance in March 1918 was made in accordance with Hutier's tactics, devised in the Riga campaign and tested again at Caporetto. The enemy's positions were no longer first destroyed by heavy bombardment, since this would have forewarned them of the imminence and site of attack and created rubble defences for machine-gunners.

Artillery, *above*, was certainly used to give sudden, brief periods of intense fire, including gas shells, but the assault was made by vast numbers of infantry, massed behind the line, who advanced in waves, *right*, to sustain the momentum.

For almost four months the Germans had been on the offensive and four massive attacks had met with glittering success. The Allied line had been broken and their lateral communications severed; all their reserves had, perforce, been thrown into the battle. Moreover, the Germans had made three great bulges in what remained of the Allied line: in the north, between Ypres and La Bassée; in Picardy, between Arras and Compiègne; and to the south—most dangerous of all because it threatened Paris—in the region of Château Thierry. The salient of St Mihiel, seized on 23 September 1914, remained firmly in their hands also.

Everything seemed to be in Germany's favour; yet the very speed of her advance had brought her armies near to exhaustion. In late June, both Ludendorff and Prince Rupprecht noted that 1,000 to 2,000 men in each division were suffering from flu, the supply system was breaking down, and the troops were underfed.

Germany's heavy artillery

At the outbreak of war, the German Army's heavy artillery pieces, the 30.5 and 42cm mortars, were moved by road. Most of the French Army's big guns were installed as fortress artillery, while those of the British were used for coastal defence. When the Western Front became static, both sides tried to break the deadlock with major offensives backed by heavy artillery. Guns with larger calibres, longer ranges and greater flexibility were needed, and the problem was solved by mounting heavy guns, including naval guns, on flat-bed rail trucks and making use of the extensive French and German railway networks.

Massive guns were closely associated with the German Army, especially the 210mm 'Paris gun', with its 40-m/130-ft barrel. This giant weapon was in action between 23 March and 9 August 1918 and, during that time, from three different locations some 128km/80mls from Paris, fired around 350 high-explosive shells at it. Although material damage was slight, 256 people were killed and 620 injured and French morale suffered.

Extra track had to be laid to make a spur, aimed at the target, for these huge German 38 and 40cm railway guns. When the gun was fired, the recoil was absorbed by the flat-bed, which was sent hurtling along the spur track and had to be retrieved after each explosion.

At the end of July, while the Second Battle of the Marne was still raging, General Foch proposed that three offensives should be mounted, to secure vital lateral railways from German attack. Troops could then be moved freely up and down the front.

One of these was the Amiens-Paris ' line, which outside Amiens ran through a sector held by the Australian Corps. Here the attack was to be made on 8 August, only 10 days after Foch's directive had been received.

In thick mist, at 04.20, zero hour, the 2nd, 3rd, 4th and 5th Australian divisions prepared to advance. They met little opposition and by about 07.15 had reached their first objective, a line from Lamotte to Cérisy. As 4th and 5th divisions passed through at 08.20, the mist lifted and the day became hot and sunny.

Behind them, at last able to play an active part in this battle of movement, followed the men of the 1st Cavalry Brigade, made up of the Queen's Bays, the 5th Dragoon Guards and the 11th Hussars.

The main body of the cavalry—the Dragoon Guards and the Hussars—were ordered at 10.00 to advance in the open country between Harbonnières and Buchanan Wood. If they did not meet much resistance, they were to attempt to reach the Old Amiens Defence Line.

The cavalry came under rifle and machine-gun fire from German strongpoints in the well-treed outskirts of the hamlet of Harbonnières. But, racing ahead, they soon reached the Defence Line, which had been abandoned.

Probing forward, the leading squadron (2) then came upon a train drawing a large railway gun (3), as it was attempting to steam away from Proyart (1). The train had shortly before been attacked by a Sopwith Camel (5), probably from 201 Squadron, which had dropped a 25lb/11kg bomb on it, setting some carriages on fire.

German soldiers on the train, surprised by the cavalry, put up a stiff fight. Some took cover in the barricade of sandbags and bales of straw on the flat-bed behind the housing for the shell-loading mechanism

(4). Others fired wildly at the attacking cavalry, who were joined by their comrades in the left-hand squadron. Within a short time, the Germans were all either killed or taken prisoner.

The leading squadron rode on to take three batteries of guns near Vauvillers, while the left-hand squadron captured a hospital at Moulin de Vauvillers.

Coming under sharp fire from a spinney

south of the village, and much reduced by casualties and by escorts for prisoners, the squadrons linked up again. When the Australian infantry arrived, the cavalry were ordered back into reserve. The action had lasted only an hour.

When the Australians came upon the train, they uncoupled the burning trucks, got up steam, and drove it back to British lines. Almost certainly it was this railway gun that was later put on show in Paris.

The first reverse would, therefore, turn legitimate jubilation into despair. This was soon to be the case.

Early in July, it became apparent that the Germans were preparing another major assault, and it was not difficult to deduce where this would come. An attack south and east from the Château Thierry salient would threaten Rheims and give the Germans control along the Marne toward Châlons. Their attack opened on the 15th.

Foch, who had held the newly arrived American units in reserve, distrusting their quality and lack of experience, now had no option but to commit them to battle. There they acted with the utmost gallantry, and the United States for the first time made a significant contribution to the struggle.

The Germans made some gains, but the French defences held. In great measure this was due to the adoption of the German tactic of 'elastic defence' by General Henri Pétain, French Commander-in-Chief. The idea was to allow the initial impact of an attack to overpower limited forward defences and then, when the enemy was beyond the range of his supporting artillery, to counter-attack from a strong defensive position with every man and weapon available.

For three days, the Americans south and southwest of the salient, and the French to its west, frustrated the German assault. Then, on 18 July, Foch resolved that with his ever-increasing American reinforcements he was in a position to mount a counter-offensive.

Eschewing a prior bombardment, he struck initially toward Soissons on the western face of the salient. The Germans immediately rushed up reserves, but to no avail; by the end of the month they had been thrown back and the line of the salient straightened. These few days of fighting, known as the Second Battle of the Marne, formed the crux of the entire campaign, for Allied morale was restored while German morale declined irreversibly. From this time the Allies remained on the attack.

As German second-wave troops in the April attack between Montdidier and Noyon leave their positions, stretcher-bearers prepare to rescue men wounded in the first assault.

During the spring breakthrough, German pioneer units soon constructed sturdy bridges over captured British trenches so that artillery, such as this 77mm gun, could be moved up as the armies advanced.

The invading Germans made Bruges a U-boat depot in 1914; by 1918 there were docking areas for destroyers and 30 submarines. Each day two U-boats left Bruges by the 9.7km/6ml long canal to Zeebrugge to prey on Allied ships in the North Sea. The entrance to Zeebrugge harbour was protected by a sturdy mole, 2.5km/1½mls long, defended by shore batteries, six naval guns at its northern end, and machine-gun emplacements.

On the night of 22/23 April, the British mounted a sea-borne attack to plug the canal. In the van of the flotilla were 8 motorboats and 24 launches, detailed to lay a smoke screen over the mole. *Vindictive*, an old cruiser converted to carry the assault force of 733 Royal Marines, was accompanied by two ferries, *Daffodil* and *Iris*, to be used if she were disabled.

The battleship *Warwick*, with smaller ships, acted as escort. Two submarines, their bows packed with explosive, were towed; their task was to ram the bridge connecting the mole to the mainland. Then

An aerial view of the mouth of the Bruges Canal at Zeebrugge shows *Intrepid* (in the foreground) and *Iphigenia*, with *Thetis* aground behind them. A dredger is at work clearing a passage through which U-boats were soon able to pass freely.

came three 'blockships'—*Thetis, Intrepid* and *Iphigenia*—which were to steam around the mole's open end to the canal mouth, where they were to be scuttled.

Vindictive, with the Marines, was due to reach the mole at 24.00. At 23.00 it began to rain, clouds and mist further reduced visibility, and at 23.40 the first smoke screens were laid. Ten minutes later, however, the Germans fired a star shell, which revealed *Vindictive*. Immediately she was caught in the beam of a searchlight, and the guns opened up on her.

As *Vindictive* tried to come alongside the mole, her starboard anchor jammed. But *Daffodil* appeared, and her resourceful captain used her bow to push *Vindictive* against the mole so the Marines could get ashore; fierce fighting followed. In all, the

Marines suffered 75 per cent casualties.

Meanwhile, the towline of the submarine C1 broke, but C3 smashed into the mole bridge. Having lighted the time fuse, her crew scrambled into a skiff and rowed away; 12 minutes later a massive explosion destroyed the bridge.

At 24.25 the three blockships rounded the end of the mole. The first, *Thetis*, was raked by fire and later ran aground. *Intrepid* got through to the canal and was scuttled, but did not completely close its mouth; *Iphigenia* collided with *Intrepid* while trying to seal the gap and failed to do so when sunk. Most of the ships' crews got safely away in cutters.

The badly damaged flotilla then set course for Dover. The raid had little effect, for U-boats could get past the sunken ships; a raid the same night on Ostend, also connected to Bruges by canal, similarly failed to stop the submarines. But the exploits provided a boost to British morale, out of all proportion to their only limited success, when it was badly needed.

The Allies next attacked the great salient in Picardy that the Germans had seized in March. This operation comprised simultaneous attacks by 9 divisions of the British Fourth Army—The British 3rd Corps, and the Australian and Canadian corps—and 10 divisions of the French First Army, on a front of 23km/14mls. Between them, they had almost 1,500 heavy guns and howitzers; some 600 tanks, both light and heavy, and more than 1,700 aircraft. Against these, the Germans could field only 14 divisions of Second and Eighteenth armies, although they soon brought up reserve divisions.

The attack was launched in thick fog at 04.20 on 8 August across the Santerre plateau, from near Amiens to just south of Montdidier. The Germans were caught unaware and the Allies, particularly the Australians and Canadians in the centre, made a rapid advance of some 11km/7mls. Although there was some fierce resistance, by nightfall 16,000 Germans had been taken prisoner, some 400 guns captured

The elements of warfare—British and Empire infantry, big guns, horse-drawn wagons and, dominating all, Mark V tanks—are seen together, *left*, behind the front line in the summer of 1918. Ignoring the activity, a British 'Tommy' brews tea at the roadside.

François Flameng's painting, *right*, shows an attack by American troops during the fighting in the Château Thierry salient in July 1918. Despite their lack of experience, they proved brave and resourceful soldiers.

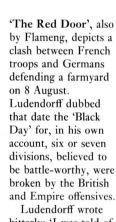

'The Red Door', also by Flameng, depicts a clash between French troops and Germans defending a farmyard on 8 August. Ludendorff dubbed that date the 'Black Day' for, in his own account, six or seven divisions, believed to be battle-worthy, were broken by the British and Empire offensives. Ludendorff wrote bitterly: 'I was told of deeds of glorious valour but also of behaviour which . . . I should not have thought possible of the German Army . . . Retiring troops, meeting a fresh division going bravely into action, had shouted out things like "Blackleg" and "You're prolonging the war" . . . The officers in many places had lost their influence.' On this day, all Germany's hopes of victory were ended.

and 285 sq km/110 sq mls of land overrun. This day was dubbed by Ludendorff the 'Black Day' of the German Army; Liddell Hart was later to describe it as 'the most brilliant [victory] ever gained by British arms in the war.'

Between 8 and 21 August, one side of the Picardy salient, from Arras in the north, through Montdidier to Noyon, was flattened out. This in itself was not tactically decisive, but it fatally undermined the morale of the German High Command. Ludendorff now perceived that it was impossible for Germany to win the war: he made no further offensive plans, and thereafter he fought defensive battles only.

This British success was achieved, as so many victories have been, by exploiting the element of surprise—in this instance augmented by the brilliant deployment of more than 400 massed tanks. Field Marshal Sir Douglas Haig and General Sir Henry Rawlinson (now commanding Fifth Army) whose plan the attack was, ensured surprise by keeping all knowledge of the attack secret from those who were to undertake it. Divisional commanders had a bare week's warning, troops in the line less than 36 hours. And even when the troops began to assemble for the assault, all movements were made at night.

Pursuing his reiterated faith in attack, Marshal Foch, who held that no other strategy could bring victory, now made preparations for a general assault along the whole front, from the fortress of Verdun to the North Sea.

'The war must be ended'

All military history teaches that victory can only be won by surprise, by engaging a demoralized enemy, or by trapping one that is infinitely inferior in numbers or weaponry. The British victory of 8 August was achieved by surprise, and the victory itself, in turn, demoralized the German staff. It also demoralized the ordinary soldiers, who surrendered in their hundreds, sometimes to a single man. Perhaps more fatefully, it led to deteriorating morale in Germany herself, where food shortages had already undermined civilian confidence in victory.

The Germans, as if by reflex action, rushed reinforcements to the front, although this merely reduced their reserves to negligible strength. The war would continue for some weeks yet; but both Ludendorff and the Kaiser had come to the same conclusion: 'The war must be ended'.

Battle of Meuse-Argonne *September–November 1918*

The battle line on the Western Front on 25 September 1918 ran, as it had throughout most of the war, from near Ostend on the North Sea to the Swiss frontier. The strengths of the opposing armies had, however, altered. Between St Quentin and Lens in the north there were 57 German divisions against 40 British and 2 American. In the Meuse-Argonne area 20 German divisions faced 31 French and 13 American divisions. Although German, British and French divisions, after four years of war, comprised fewer men than hitherto, American divisions at full strength contained some 27,000 men.

Marshal Foch's plan for the last great Allied offensive in the west entailed several converging and almost simultaneous attacks in various sectors along the front. These were an assault by the Americans and the French in the Meuse-Argonne and Champagne areas respectively on 26 September, followed between the 27th and the 29th by a British offensive toward Cambrai, a British and Belgian attack in Flanders, and a French attack toward St Quentin. Within four days, the entire front was to be ignited.

These attacks were designed jointly to take out the vast German salient stretching from Ypres to Verdun, so breaking the Hindenburg Line and ensuring German collapse. Their apparently random nature hid the strategy of preventing a build-up of German reserves in any one sector.

In the north, the German defensive lines were widely separated; in the south they ran closer together and were more formidable. This greater concentration was designed to protect two important railway lines that ran parallel to the battle front from Metz, in Germany, to the northwest. These were the Germans' best communication system from east to west of the River Meuse and were crucial for the movement of both troops and supplies.

A successful Allied attack on the Meuse would, therefore, sever Germany's front and disrupt communications between her left and right wings, making their supply routes tortuous. This was especially so since the Germans had ceased maintaining the roads where rail transport was available, due to a shortage of fuel and of rubber for tyres. So the entire campaign depended on Allied success in the Meuse Valley and in the forest of the Argonne.

Because of the limited time available (the overall plan was authorized only on 3 September) the American Army was at once moved into this area and concentrated behind the front line already held by the French. Troops and weaponry were concealed during the day and all moves

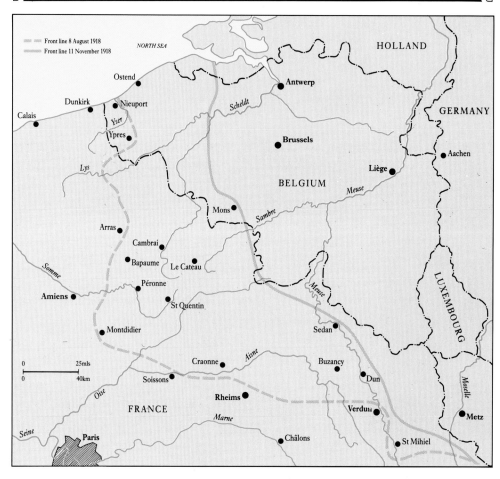

were made at night. Only at the last moment did the French relinquish their positions to be replaced by 12 American divisions, with three divisions in reserve. The Germans remained unaware of the imminent and formidable attack.

Since the German defensive lines were strong and closely packed one behind the other, the Americans' only hope of success lay in driving salients in the German lines and attacking east and west from them.

The first attacks went in at 05.00 on 26 September in dense fog, after a three-hour artillery barrage by 2,700 guns. The American First Army, with 3rd Corps on the right, 5th Corps in the centre and 1st Corps on the left, was led by General John

Pershing. It was supported on the right by French 17th Corps and by the French Fourth Army on its left. The Americans were opposed in the main by the German Fifth Army under General Georg von der Marwitz.

The overall plan demanded a rapid advance of 16km/10mls, which would break through the first three German lines and allow the Americans to occupy the Argonne Forest, outflanking the defences of the strongly fortified hilltop town of Montfaucon. The task of taking the town was given to 5th Corps, while 3rd Corps supported its advance by getting to the rear of Montfaucon from the east, and 1st Corps protected 5th Corps' left flank.

The United States Army

The American Army in 1914 consisted only of a small regular volunteer army of 127,588 men and a National Guard of 181,620. This force was inadequate to play a significant role on the Western Front, so in May 1917 conscription was introduced and the strength of the army rose to more than $3\frac{1}{2}$ million.

As a propaganda move, the 1st US Infantry Division, the advance guard of the Expeditionary Force, was sent to France in July 1917. By the Armistice, more than 2 million men had reached France, although they did not assume a combat role until the last 200 days of the war. Nevertheless, the AEF held 160km/100mls of the front, 29 of the 42 divisions went into battle, and almost $1\frac{1}{2}$ million American soldiers saw combat.

Although Foch and Haig had envisaged American troops serving as replacements for losses in the British and French armies Pershing insisted on keeping US formations 'as a separate and distinct component of the combined Forces'. However, individual units did serve with their Allies' armies on occasion.

America had supplied the British and French with small arms for years, but the factories were not tooled up to produce larger weapons. Thus America had to rely on her allies for most of her aircraft and all her artillery, tanks and machine-guns. In addition, all ranks wore British and French pattern steel helmets in action. The rifle carried was usually a Lee-Enfield of slightly smaller calibre than the British version, or the Garand 1903 pattern, with the M1905 pattern bayonet.

Major-General John J. Pershing (1860–1948) graduated from the United States Military Academy in 1866 and was commissioned in the cavalry. He saw action against the Indian chief Geronimo and the Sioux tribe. Later he served in the Philippines (1899–1902) and led the punitive expedition (1916–17) against the Mexican bandit Francisco ('Pancho') Villa.

Pershing was appointed to command the American Expeditionary Force in 1917, when his genius for organization enabled him rapidly to mould the embryo army into an efficient fighting force. In 1919, he was made permanent general of the American armies.

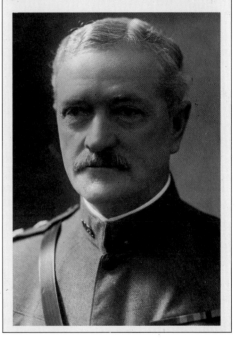

America relied on European weapons, so gunners, such as those manning the British 60-pounder, *above*, were trained in France, where several artillery schools were established.

Fléville, 4km/$2\frac{1}{2}$mls north of Aprémont, fell to the US 1st Division on 9 October. This shot, taken on the 12th, shows men of a divisional field artillery unit in the damaged town.

By 31 October 1918, the right of the American First Army had broken through the Hindenburg Line and taken both the Romagne and Cunel Heights. Its front line stretched from just south of Brieulles on the Meuse River, where a pocket of Germans was holding out, to near Grandpré, north of the Argonne Forest.

Battleworn units had been steadily withdrawn, and rested divisions brought up, so it was an eager, fresh army that resumed the offensive on 1 November. Their primary task was still to cut the Metz-Sedan railway to frustrate the movement of German troops.

The assault went well. In the centre, 5th Corps captured the heights above Buzancy, while on the right 3rd Corps forced the enemy back over the Meuse. Several more or less successful attempts were made to cross the river. Then, on the night of 4/5 November, men of 60th and 61st Infantry brigades managed to establish a pontoon bridge over the Meuse, (4) at a point near Cléry-le-Petit (5) where it ran close to the hillside.

Two footbridges, (2) were also laid over the canal, and by first light, on a cold, rainy morning, a large group of American soldiers was on the swampy ground between river and canal. Some were even crossing to the road from Liny (1).

The Germans, when they saw what was happening, opened fire from the Côte de Jumont (6), so pinning down the Americans, who had little cover among the reeds and no way of retreat.

Realizing his men's predicament, Captain Edward C. Allworth, with the rest of his company (3), leaped into the canal and swam across to join them. He received the Congressional Medal of Honour for his bravery.

The bridge over the Meuse, meanwhile, was heavily shelled and was in danger of disintegrating when three of the pontoons were smashed. But five men from the 7th Engineers plunged into the freezing river and, standing chest-deep in the water, held up the planks until more boats could be floated into place. Their courage, too, was recognized for they were all later awarded the DSO.

Captain Allworth and his men were followed across the canal by many more. As soon as they had regrouped, they launched a fierce attack on German positions on the Côte de Jumont ridge, which was now also under assault from troops who had crossed the river a little to the south near Brieulles. The Germans resisted strongly, but finally they were overcome and many were taken prisoner.

By nightfall, the hilltop town of Dun had been captured, and the Germans were falling back steadily. The Armistice on 11 November found the Americans some 16km/10mls northeast of the river, on the edge of the Woevre plain: the area in which the Germans had assembled their forces for the attack on Verdun almost three years earlier.

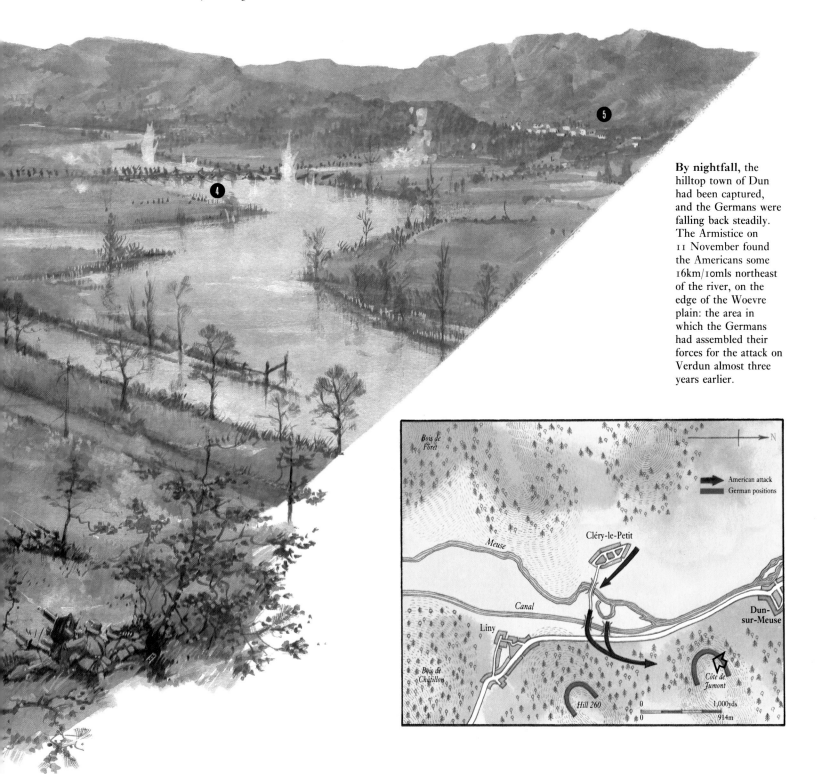

Progress was rapid and uninterrupted except right in front of Montfaucon. The left wing of 5th Corps reached the west of the town and 3rd Corps reached its east and rear. Meanwhile, 1st Corps penetrated the Argonne Forest and along the River Aire. By the evening of the first day, there were American salients on either side of Montfaucon and its capture was inevitable. Indeed, the town was taken by storm at about 12.00 the following day.

North of the hill the Germans rapidly reinforced all of their positions, and on 27 September the Americans made little headway. The infantry had far outrun the artillery, which had immense difficulty in moving its guns over the rough terrain and unmade roads.

On the 28th, however, with strong tank and artillery support, the infantry advanced to a depth of almost 3.2km/2mls along the entire front, bringing 3rd and 5th corps within reach of the Hindenburg Line: the Germans' third line of defence.

But increased resistance the compelled First Army to regroup; reserve divisions were brought up and preparations made for a fresh advance.

Greatly alarmed by the danger of their position, the Germans rapidly drafted in reinforcements from other parts of the front, weakening their defences elsewhere. By 1 October, five days after the opening attack, seven new German divisions had been rushed to the Meuse-Argonne area. So serious was the situation

Running from the Meuse River on the Americans' right to the broken hills of the Argonne Forest, thick with undergrowth, lay a series of east-west ridges. The Germans had made these into a continuous area of trenches, strongpoints and barbed wire, all dominated by Montfaucon, which had been turned into a veritable fortress.

Pershing's initial attack on 26 September was designed to drive deep salients on either side of the hilltop town, then to threaten it from the rear. The

vigorous assault by 5th Corps, with 3rd Corps on the right, forced the Germans to withdraw, within 30 hours, to their strong, prepared positions on the Cunel and Romagne heights. (Most of this area was overrun by 13 October.)

At the same time, 1st Corps on the American left, thrust deep into enemy-held territory along the Aire River, seizing Varennes and, by 3

October, Aprémont.

On the extreme left of 1st Corps, a penetration of about 1.6km/1ml was made into the Argonne Forest, where the fighting was extremely difficult, and it was impossible to make use of tanks. The entire initial attack was backed up by 821 aircraft, which gave valuable support

1 Varennes
2 Aprémont
3 Romagne Heights
4 Romagne
5 Cunel Heights
6 Malancourt
7 Montfaucon

The French 75mm, which had proved its worth as early as 1914, was still one of the guns most commonly used by the American forces in the final months of the war. This rapid-firing weapon, *above*, expelled a spent shell as the breach opened and was at once ready for reloading.

At the height of the battle in the Meuse-Argonne region, US gunners were firing 350,000 rounds of all types per day.

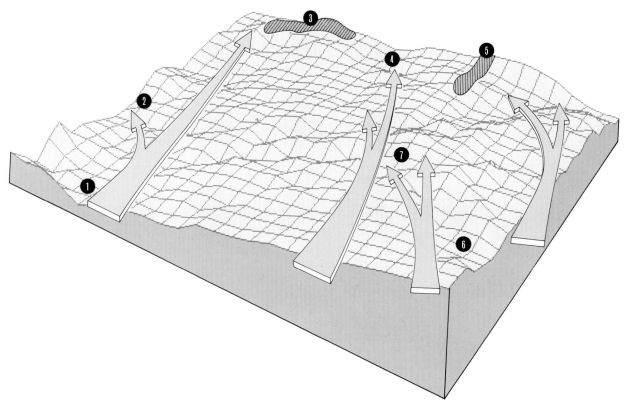

now facing the German High Command that on 4 October it demanded that the Chancellor forward an offer of peace to the Allied powers. This was dispatched on the 6th but was rejected.

The American attack was resumed on 4 October. It met desperate resistance as the Germans poured their most experienced troops into the battle; by 10 October, however, the Americans had overrun the obstacle of the Argonne. The next general attack was made on 14 October, but little

Major George Patton, of World War II fame, who led the US Tank Corps in France, is seen beside his French 'Whippet'. This tank, designed for use as 'cavalry', was fast and light, in contrast to earlier, ponderous versions, and was the first to have a revolving turret.

US troops in the Meuse-Argonne battle operated 2,516 guns, including 14in railway guns, *left* (some manned by naval gunners). They were used mainly against enemy trains and railway installations on the Metz-Sedan line 32km/20mls away, behind the trenches at the southern part of the Hindenburg Line.

was achieved and stalemate seemed to be inevitable. By this time, however, the British offensive on the Allied left wing had broken through the Hindenburg Line. On 8 October, Cambrai was taken and they were at last in open country.

The Americans advanced once again on 1 November. Pershing's strategy had been to throw in his left wing, then his right, which meant that the left would have had to overcome the thickly wooded and heavily defended Bois de Bourgogne due north of the Argonne. But General Hunter Liggett, who had assumed command of First Army on 16 October, advised punching a hole in the German centre and then, in conjunction with an advance by the French Fourth Army, encircling the enemy. His plan was implemented, but it was found that the German forward outposts had withdrawn along the entire American front. Their left flank had been irreversibly turned and the defeat of their armies was certain.

This last American offensive was the final Allied thrust. In one way it brought the war to an end; in another it was superfluous. For Ludendorff, the military architect of the conflict, had already fallen from power, the population of metropolitan Germany was close to revolution, and chaos threatened the country.

Collapse of the Central Powers

The Central Powers held firm and achieved other objectives as long as their spring offensive in the west was successful. Once the tide had turned, disintegration faced the German alliance.

By the summer of 1918, the people of Austria-Hungary, Bulgaria and Turkey were reduced to near-famine conditions, and even Germany was approaching starvation as a result of the British navy's blockade of her ports.

War-weariness was the prevailing mood, and everywhere there were revolutionary undercurrents that threatened to undermine orderly goverment. The revolution of October 1917 had indeed taken Russia out of the war, but radical doctrines had spread, ultimately to Germany herself.

Germany's prestige and, therefore, her ability to hold the Central Powers together had been destroyed by her defeat in France. On 27 October, Ludendorff resigned; on 3 November, Austria-Hungary agreed an armistice with the Allies; on the same day, sailors of the German fleet mutinied at Kiel. Four days later revolution broke out in Munich, and on 8 November German plenipotentiaries were received by Marshal Foch to hear peace terms. On 10 November, Kaiser Wilhelm fled to Holland. The failure of her greatest effort of arms had brought Germany to ruin.

Armistice & Aftermath *1918–1939*

World War I—the 'Great War'—came to an end at 11.00 on the eleventh day of the eleventh month of 1918. In four and a quarter years of fighting there had been more than 8 million killed, with a further 20 million wounded, and many permanently maimed. Human life and material resources had been recklessly squandered on an unprecedented scale.

Three empires, Turkish, Russian and Austro-Hungarian, distintegrated. Communism became established in Russia, and the United States of America finally took her place on the world stage. Such were the changes wrought by the war.

Collectively known as the Treaty of Versailles, there were, in fact, five treaties made following the peace. That between the Allies and Austria, the Treaty of Saint-Germain (1919), dissolved the Austro-Hungarian Empire and instituted the new Republic of Austria, comprised largely of the German-speaking parts of the former empire. Italy gained the South Tyrol,

Trieste, Istria, several islands off the Dalmatian coast and Friuli. The independence of Hungary, Czechoslovakia, Yugoslavia and of Poland was also recognized.

The Treaty of Trianon (1920) between the Allies and Hungary reduced the size of that country by about a third, Romania receiving Transylvania, for which she had entered the war. Hungarian military strength was restricted to 35,000 men. The Treaty of Neuilly (1919) between the Allies and Bulgaria compelled the latter to cede territory and population to Greece, Yugoslavia and Romania, while the Treaty of Sèvres (1920) with Turkey abolished that country's sovereignty over Mesopotamia (Iraq) and Palestine (Israel), which was designated a British mandate. Syria became a French mandate. Turkey also lost territory to Greece and Italy. The Dardanelles became a neutral, international zone for shipping.

But it was the Treaty of Versailles between the Allies and Germany that led

to the greatest resentment. The dominant Allied leaders were Great Britain's prime minister, David Lloyd George (1863–1945), Georges Clemenceau (1841–1929), the French premier, Italy's leader Vittorio Emanuele Orlando (1860–1952) and Woodrow Wilson (1856–1924), President of the United States.

Allied discord at once became evident at the Versailles negotiations. Though Lloyd George provided a moderating influence on both Clemenceau, who demanded the harshest treatment of Germany, and Woodrow Wilson, whose idealistic proposals were impractical, the final treaty was in large measure unsatisfactory.

On 8 January 1918, President Wilson had delivered a speech to Congress in which he outlined his so-called 'Fourteen Points'. This speech was intended as an appeal for peace to the general public of the Central Powers. Among the 'points' were proposals for the reduction of national armaments; changes in European

colonial territories to harmonize with the wishes of the local inhabitants; the preservation of Belgian sovereignty; and the division of the Austro-Hungarian Empire into two separate nations, determined by nationalities.

The final point advocated establishing 'a general association of nations'. This was to lead to the creation of the League of Nations, an organization that, in the event, was unable to affect world affairs and which, in 1945, dissolved itself.

The Treaty of Versailles was signed in the Hall of Mirrors between the Allies and Germany in 1919. Germany, the defeated nation, was dubbed the aggressor and instigator of the war and was not consulted as to the treaty's terms. Alsace and Lorraine were to be restored to France; former German colonies were placed under League of Nations mandates, and most of West Prussia was ceded to Poland. And, for a period of 15 years, the Saar territory was to be administered by the French and the Rhineland occupied by the Allies.

The treaty further stipulated that the German Army could, in future, number no more than 100,000 men and that she was forbidden to build major weapons of aggression, including battleships. But most ruinous for Germany was the imposition, at French insistence, of reparations: payments to be made in money or in goods, notably coal, steel and ships. The United States did not ratify the treaty and waived all claims to reparations.

The devastated German economy made it difficult for the Allies to requisition the amounts due to them, and in 1923, Germany having fallen into default, Belgian and French troops occupied the Ruhr. Almost a decade later, in 1931, the economic situation in the western world had so degenerated that further German payments were impossible, and that clause of the treaty lapsed of necessity.

Germany, crippled by the treaty's terms, became disaffected, her people bitterly resentful. The national mood, aggravated by the chaos caused by gross inflation and the fear of Communism, provided fertile ground from which Adolf Hitler and his cronies were able to reap a dreadful harvest.

In 1935, Hitler, by then Chancellor of Germany, unilaterally cancelled the military sections of the Treaty of Versailles. In the following year he began the remilitarization of the Rhineland, while at the same time ordering the building of a new German fleet and the training of an army far larger than permitted. On 14 October 1933, the year he came to power, Hitler had already withdrawn Germany from the League of Nations. The Allies lacked the will to challenge any of these breaches of the treaty.

Thus the Treaty of Versailles resolved nothing, the very harshness of its terms creating those conditions in which a second world war became inevitable. In November 1918, church bells had been rung throughout the victorious countries of Europe; in fact, they merely rang the intermission gong before round two.

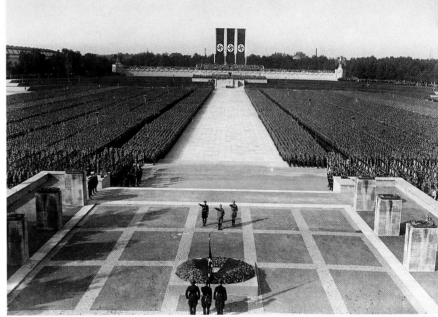

Herbert Olivier's painting, *opposite*, depicts members of the Allied Supreme War Council at Versailles while engaged in drawing up the terms of the armistice with Austria. This was signed just three days later on 7 November 1918.

The crushing cost of the war to the Allies, in purely financial terms, far exceeded that of any previous conflict, as is emphasised by the cover of the French magazine *Le Petit Journal*, dated 31 August 1919. For the Germans the cost was even higher.

Adolf Hitler, *above*, flanked by Heinrich Himmler, head of the SS, and Viktor Lutze, Chief of Staff of the SA, at a Nazi rally in Nuremberg, 1934. Hitler climbed to power in part by playing on the bitter resentment felt by Germans for the harsh terms of the Versailles Treaty.

Gazetteer

The information given here is, of necessity, limited. For more comprehensive accounts of the many battle sites and memorials on the Western Front, readers should consult guide books.

Further guidance may be had from the Imperial War Museum, London, and the Musée de l'Armée, Les Invalides, Paris, as well as the various War Graves Commissions.

Many specialist tour operators offer inclusive excursions to the battlefields and burial grounds.

FLANDERS

Ypres

Ypres is a convenient driving distance from Zeebrugge, where there is a museum in the Palace Hotel with relics from the raid; also near Zeebrugge is Nieuport, where the Belgian War Memorial and a statue of King Albert I may be found.

Ypres was wholly destroyed during the war but has been rebuilt. The new Cloth Hall contains the Salient 1914–1918 War Museum, which is rich in displays of weapons, medals, equipment, documents and photographs, among much else. A fine view of the surrounding country can be had from the belfry.

The most important memorial structure in Ypres is the Menin Gate, which was inaugurated in 1927 by Field Marshal Plumer and is the British memorial to those who died up to August 1915 but have no known grave. Every evening at 20:00 the Last Post is sounded. After the war, the town was awarded the Military Cross and the Croix de Guerre, which may be seen in the Hôtel de Ville. Some trenches that have been maintained can be seen at Sanctuary Wood.

Passchendaele

In the centre of the village stands the church, the west windows of which form the 66th Division's memorial. A short distance to the west is the Canadian Memorial. A number of memorial plaques to the Belgian fallen may be found on the wall of the Hôtel de Ville. The Tyne Cot British Military Cemetery, containing 11,908 graves, and the Memorial to the Missing are 2km/1½mls from the village.

Messines

South of Ypres, near the Armentières road, lies Messines (Mesen). The New Zealand Memorial Park is situated on the outskirts of the village; at one end of the park there are two German pillboxes, which had been part of their defensive line. There is an interesting war museum in the Hôtel de Ville, with much material regarding both the New Zealanders and the Australians. Just north of Messines, is memorial to the London Scottish.

The crater formed by the massive mine explosion at St Eloi has been turned into a lake, as have others.

THE SOMME

The Somme

Albert is in the centre of the Somme sector and makes a good touring centre. Cemeteries abound in this area, the largest war memorial in the world, recording the names of 73,367 British dead, being at Thiepval.

Remains of some British trenches can still be seen in Aveluy Wood, on the road from Thiepval to Albert, while north of Thiepval, in the Newfoundland Memorial Park at Beaumont-Hamel, the trenches have been preserved and there are iron picket bars still in place.

Cambrai

Cambrai is easily reached from Arras on the N39, a distance of 30km/18½mls on an old Roman road. About 1km/½ml out of the town is the Cambrai East Military Cemetery, a German graveyard.

Continuing down the Roman road, the traveller will reach Le Cateau, where members of the 3rd, 4th and 5th divisions of the BEF's Second Corps engaged seven of Kluck's army divisions in August 1914. There are two British cemeteries in Le Cateau: the British Military Cemetery and the Communal Cemetery.

Mons

Mons lies 65km/40mls northeast of Cambrai. It was the scene of four battles (August 1914, November 1918, May 1940 and September 1944), but each was of short duration and no physical signs remain. However, the Musée de Guerre in the centre of the town contains one of the most comprehensive collections of relics from the two world wars in Belgium.

THE VERDUN AREA

Verdun

There are many memorial structures in this ancient city, including a line of statues of the marshals and generals of France near the citadel, and the Victory Monument. A war museum in the Hôtel de Ville contains relics and also extensive literature on the battle area. The outlying forts, such as that at Vaux, may also be visited.

Meuse-Argonne

The Meuse-Argonne and Château Thierry sectors, where the Americans played their greatest part, lie to the east of Rheims. Near Romagne-Gesnes, north of Varennes, is the American Meuse-Argonne Cemetery and Memorial, where 14,000 US soldiers are buried. By continuing eastward to Cunel, 3km/2mls distant, then turning off right to Nantillois, the American Memorial on the top of Montfaucon will be found. This Doric column is surmounted by a figure of Liberty. From a balcony, the entire battle area may be viewed.

War Graves Commissions

United Kingdom

The Commonwealth War Graves Commission, 2 Marlow Road, Maidenhead, Berks.

France

Secretariat d'Etat Charge des Anciens Combattants et Victimes de Guerre, 139 rue de Bercy, Paris (12c).

United States

The American Battle Monuments Commission, 69 rue 19 Janvier, 92 Garches, France.

Germany

Volksbund Deutsche Kriegsgraberfursorge, 35 Kassel, Werner-Hilpert-Strasse 2, West Germany.

PICTURE CREDITS

l = left, *r* = right, *t* = top, *c* = centre, *b* = bottom, *f* = far
IWM = Imperial War Museum, RHL = Robert Hunt Library

1 Camera Press; 4 Private collection; 8*t* Bundesarchiv, Koblenz; 8*b* IWM; 8–9 Jean-Pierre Verney; 13*l* IWM; 13*r* Private collection; 15*l*, 15*r* Private collection; 16, 17 IWM; 20*t* Jean-Loup Charmet; 20*b* RHL; 21*t* IWM; 21*b* James Lucas; 22*t* Hubert Josse; 22*b* Jean-Loup Charmet; 23*t* Renault; 23*bl* Jean Vigne; 23*r* Musée d'Histoire Contemporaine; 24*bl*, *br* IWM; 24*tr* Giraudon/ET Archive; 24*cr* Popperfoto; 25 RHL; 26 Marshall Editions; 27*tl* James Lucas; 27*tr* RHL; 27*b* Ullstein Bilderdienst; 28–9 IWM; 29*t* Novosti Press Agency; 29*c* ET Archive; 29*b* RHL; 31 Bundesarchiv, Koblenz; 32, 33 Ullstein Bilderdienst; 36*tfl*, *tl* Novosti Press Agency; 36*tr* Private collection; 36*tfr* Bundesarchiv, Koblenz; 36, 37 Ullstein Bilderdienst; 38, 39*t* Jean-Loup Charmet; 39*b* James Lucas; 40*t* RHL; 40*c* Popperfoto; 40–1, 41*t* RHL; 44*tl* Heeresgeschichtliches Museum, Vienna; 44*tr* Popperfoto; 44*b* RHL; 45 James Lucas; 47 Jean Vigne; 48*t*, *b* Private collection; 48*c* IWM/James Lucas; 52*t* Hulton Picture Library; 52, 53 IWM; 54–5 Courtesy of Royal Hampshire Regiment; 55*l* Australian War Memorial; 55*r* RHL; 56*l* IWM; 56*tr* – 60, 61*fl*, *l* Australian War Memorial; 61 *fr*, *r* Popperfoto; 62, 62–3, 63*l* ET Archive; 63*r* 64*l* IWM; 64–5 Kriegsarchiv, Vienna; 65*t* RHL; 65*b* Popperfoto; 68*t* Jean Vigne; 68*cl* RHL; 68*cr* ET Archive; 69*t* RHL; 69*c* Musee d'Histoire Contemporaine; 69*b* Memorial de Verdun; 70*t* Jean Vigne; 70*b* Jean-Loup Charmet; 70–1 Hubert Josse; 71*b* RHL; 72*fl* Private collection; 72*l* RHL; 72*r* Popperfoto; 72*fr* Private collection; 73*l* IWM; 73*t* Musée d'Histoire Contemporaine; 73*r*, 76*tl*, *b* Memorial de Verdun; 76*tr* Musée d'Histoire Contemporaine; 77*t* Private collection; 77*b* Jean Vigne; 78–9 Ullstein Bilderdienst; 79 ET Archive; 80–1 RHL; 86, 87 IWM; 87*cr*, 88 Ullstein Bilderdienst; 89, 90*l* IWM; 90*b* RHL; 90–1 Deutsches Schiffahrtsmuseum; 91*b* ET Archive; 92 IWM; 92*b* Popperfoto; 93*t* James Lucas; 93*b* IWM; 96, 97 Novosti Press Agency; 98*fl* IWM; 98*c* Popperfoto; 98*r* Bundesarchiv, Koblenz; 98*b* ET Archive; 99 Novosti Press Agency; 101 IWM; 104*t* Musée d'Histoire Contemporaine; 104–6 IWM; 107*t*, *bl*, *br* Private collection; 107*cl* James Lucas; 108 Popperfoto; 109, 110*t* IWM; 110*bl* Bundesarchiv, Koblenz; 110*bc* Popperfoto; 110*br*, 111*t* IWM; 111*c* Musée d'Histoire Contemporaine; 111*b* James Lucas; 112–13, 113*t* IWM; 113*b* RHL; 116*t* IWM; 116*c* Australian War Memorial; 116*b* Jean Vigne; 117 IWM; 118*t* ET Archive; 118*c* Bundesarchiv, Koblenz; 118*bl* Musée d'Histoire Contemporaine; 118*br* IWM; 119*l* Popperfoto; 119*t* Musée d'Histoire Contemporaine; 119*br* Popperfoto; 120, 121 IWM; 121 RHL; 124 Australian War Memorial/ET Archive; 125 IWM; 126 Hubert Josse; 126–7, 127 IWM/ET Archive; 128 IWM; 129*t* Bundesarchiv, Koblenz; 129*c* Popperfoto; 129*b* Private collection; 130–11*l* IWM; 131*tr* Bundesarchiv, Koblenz; 131*c* ET Archive; 131*b* Mander and Mitchenson Theatre Collection; 132*l* RHL; 132*t* James Lucas; 133, 136, 137 IWM; 137*b* Popperfoto; 140*l* John Frost; 140*r* James Lucas; 142*l* RAF Museum; 142–3 IWM/ET Archive; 143*l* Bundesarchiv, Koblenz; 143*r* Popperfoto; 144 IWM; 145, 146–7 The Tank Museum; 147*t* IWM; 148*t* The Tank Museum; 148*b*, 149*t* IWM; 149*b* The Tank Museum; 152*t* IWM; 152*b* RHL; 153*l* IWM; 153*r* Bundesarchiv, Koblenz; 154 RHL; 154–5 G. Dagli Orti; 156 RHL; 157*t* IWM; 157*b* RHL; 160*l* James Lucas; 160*r* RHL; 160 *b*, 161*l* IWM; 161*c*, *r* Bundesarchiv, Koblenz 162 RHL; 164*t* IWM; 164*b* National Museum of Tanzania; 165 RHL; 168 IWM; 169 National Museum of Tanzania; 170–1, 171 IWM/ET Archive; 172*tl* IWM; 172*tr* Ashmolean Museum; 172*b*, 172–3 RHL; 173, 176 IWM; 177*l* Bundesarchiv, Koblenz; 177*r* IWM; 178 IWM/ET Archive; 179, 180*t* RHL; 180*b* Bundesarchiv, Koblenz; 181, 184 RHL; 185, 186*t* IWM: 186*b*, 187 RHL; 189*l* IWM; 189*r* Popperfoto; 189*b*, 192 RHL; 193*l* IWM; 193*r* Carina Dvorak; 194 IWM/ET Archive; 195*l* Jean-Loup Charmet; 195*r* Bundesarchiv, Koblenz.

ACKNOWLEDGEMENTS
The publishers are grateful to the staff of the Imperial War Museum, London; the London Library; West Hill Library, Wandsworth, London; and the Royal Geographical Society, London, for their assistance.

Figure artwork: **Richard Hook/Linden Artists**
Line artworks: **Janos Marffy**
Profile artwork: **Mike Trim**
Maps: **Technical Art Services**
Colour maps: **Russell Barnet**
Computer maps: **Chapman Bounford & Associates**
Index: **Valerie Lewis Chandler**

Bibliography

This list comprises a selection of those book consulted by the Publishers in the preparation of this volume. In addition, extensive use was made of the official histories of the war on land, at sea and in the air produced by the combatant nations and also of many regimental histories, diaries and personal accounts.
*An asterisk indicates a general work.

American Battle Monuments Commission *American Armies and Battlefields in Europe* United States Government Printing Office, Washington DC, 1938*
Ascoli, David *The Mons Star* Harrap, London, 1981
Aston, George G. *The Biography of the Late Marshal Foch* Hutchinson, London, 1929
Banks, A. *A Military Atlas of the First World War* Heinemann Educational Books, London, 1975*
Barrie, Alexander *War Underground* Frederick Muller, London, 1962
Becke, A.F. *The Royal Regiment of Artillery at Le Cateau* Royal Artillery Institution, Woolwich, London, 1919
Bellairs, Carlyon *The Battle of Jutland* Hodder & Stoughton, London c1919
Bennett Geoffrey *Naval Battles of the First World War*, Batsford, London, 1968
Blond, Georges *Verdun* André Deutsch, London, 1965
Boaraston, J.H. (Ed) *Sir Douglas Haig's Despatches* Dent, London & Toronto, 1919
Bruce, J.M. *The Aeroplanes of the Royal Flying Corps (Military Wing)* Putnam, London, 1982
Brussilov, A.A. *A Soldier's Notebook* Macmillan, London, 1930
Buchan, John *Nelson's History of the Great War* (24 vols), 1914–19*; *The History of the South African Forces in France*, 1920; Thomas Nelson, London
Burt, R.A. *British Battleships of World War One*, Arms & Armour Press, London, 1986
Carew, Tim *The Vanished Army* William Kimber, London, 1964; *Wipers* Hamish Hamilton, London, 1974.
Castle, H.G. *Fire Over England: The German Air Raids of World War I* Leo Cooper/Secker & Warburg, London, 1982
Churchill, Winston S. *The World Crisis* (5 vols) Thornton Butterworth, London, 1921–31.*
Collyer, J.J. *The South Africans with General Smuts in German East Africa 1916* Government Printer, Pretoria, 1939
Coombs, Rose E.B. *Before Endeavours Fade: A guide to the battlefields of the First World War* Battle of Britain Prints, London, 1976*
Cooper, Bryan *The Ironclads of Cambrai* Souvenir Press, London, 1967
Costello, John & Hughes, Terry *Jutland 1916* Weidenfeld & Nicolson, London, 1976
Denton, Kit *Gallipoli: One Long Grave* Time/Life Books, Sydney, 1986
Douglas, Sholto *Years of Combat* Collins, London, 1963
Dupuy, Trevor N. *A Genius for War: The German Army and General Staff 1807–1945* Macdonald & Jane's, London; Prentiss-Hall, NY, 1977*

Edmonds, Charles *A Subaltern's War* Peter Davies, London, 1929
Falls, Cyril *Armageddon 1918*, 1964; *Caporetto 1917*, 1966; Weidenfeld & Nicolson, London
Fredette, R.H. *The First Battle of Britain 1917–1918 and the Birth of the Royal Air Force* Cassel, London, 1966
Frothingham, Thomas G. *A Guide to the Military History of the World War 1914–1918* T. Fisher Unwin, London, 1921*
Fuller, J.F.C. *Tanks in the Great War* John Murray, London, 1920
Gardner, Brian *The Big Push*, 1961; *German East*, 1963; *Allenby*, 1965; Cassel, London
Gibbs, Philip *Battles of the Somme*, 1917; *From Bapaume to Passchendaele 1917*, 1918; *Open Warfare: the Way to Victory*, 1919; Heinemann, London*
Golovine, Nicholas N. *The Russian Campaign of 1914* (Revised edition) Hugh Rees, London, 1933
Gough, Hubert *Fifth Army* Hodder & Stoughton, London, 1931
Grieve, W. Grant & Newman, B. *Tunnellers* Herbert Jenkins, London, 1936
Hafkesbrink, Hanna *Unknown Germany* Yale University Press, Newhaven, 1948*
Hamilton, Ian *Gallipoli Diary* (2 vols) Edward Arnold, London, 1920
Harboard, James G. *The American Army in France* Little Brown, Boston, 1936
Harrington, Charles *Plumer of Messines* John Murray, London, 1935
Hart, Basil Liddell *Foch: The Man of Orleans* Eyre & Spottiswoode, London, 1931; *A History of the World War* Faber, London, 1934*
Hoffman, Max *War Diaries & Other Papers* (2 vols) Martin Secker, London, 1929
Horne, Alistair *The Price of Glory* Macmillan, London, 1962
Hough, Richard *The Great War at Sea 1914–1918* Oxford University Press, Oxford, 1983
Howarth, David *The Dreadnoughts* Time-Life Books, Alexandria, Virginia, 1979
Hoyt, Edwin P, *Guerilla: Colonel von Lettow-Vorbeck & Germany's East African Empire* Macmillan, NY; Collier Macmillan, London, 1981
Hussey, A.H. & Inman, D.S. *The Fifth Division in the Great War* Nisbet, London, 1922
Ironside, Edmund *Tannenberg: The First Thirty Days in East Prussia* Blackwood, London, 1925
Irving, John *The Smoke Screen of Jutland* William Kimber, London, 1966
James, Robert Rhodes *Gallipoli* Batsford, London, 1965
Joffre, Joseph (*et al*) *The Two Battles of the Marne* Thornton Butterworth, London, 1927
King, H.F. *Armament of British Aircraft 1909–1939* Putnam, London, 1971
Knight, W. Stanley *The History of the Great European War* (7 vols) Caxton Publishing, London, (no date)*
Knox, Alfred *With the Russian Army 1914–1917* Hutchinson, London, 1921
Laffin, John *Jackboot: The Story of the German Soldier* Cassell, London, 1965

La Gorce, Paul-Marie de *The French Army* Weidenfeld & Nicolson, London, 1963*
Langmaid, Kenneth *The Sea Raiders* Jarrolds, London, 1963
Lawrence, T.E. *Revolt in the Desert*, 1927; *Seven Pillars of Wisdom*, 1935; Jonathan Cape, London
Lettow-Vorbeck, Paul *Meine Errinerungen aus Ostafrika* Koehler Verlag, Leipzig, 1920
Lewis, Cecil *Sagittarius Rising* Davies, London, 1936; Penguin Books, London, 1983
Lloyd George, David *War Memoirs* (2 vols) Ivor Nicholson & Watson, London, 1933*
Lucas, James *Fighting Troops of the Austro-Hungarian Army 1868–1914* Spellmount, Tunbridge Wells, Kent; Hippocrene, NY, 1987
Ludendorff, Paul *My War Memories 1914–1918* (2 vols) Hutchinson, London, 1920*
Macintyre, Donald *Jutland* Evans Brothers, London, 1927
Macksey, Kenneth & Batchelor, John *A History of the Armoured Fighting Vehicle* Macdonald, London, 1970
Mack Smith, Denis *Italy: A Modern History* (Revised edition) University of Michigan Press, Ann Arbor, 1969
Marwick, Arthur *The Deluge: British Society and the First World War* Bodley Head, London, 1965*
Masefield, John *Gallipoli* Heinemann, London, 1916
Meinertzhagen, R. *Army Diary 1899–1926* Oliver and Boyd, London, 1960
Middlebrook, Martin *The First Day on the Somme: 1 July 1916* Allen Lane, London, 1971
Miller, Charles *Battle for the Bundu: The First World War in East Africa* Macdonald & Jane's, London, 1974
Moorehead, Alan *Gallipoli* Hamish Hamilton, London, 1956
Mosley, Leonard *Duel for Kilimanjaro* Weidenfeld & Nicolson, London, 1963
Munson, Kenneth *Fighters: Attack and Training Aircraft 1914–1919* Blandford, London, 1968
Nevinson, Henry W. *The Dardanelles Campaign* Nisbet, London, 1918
Norman, Aaron *The Great Air War* Macmillan, NY; Collier-Macmillan, London, 1968
Palmer, Frederick *Our Greatest Battle: The Meuse-Argonne* Dodd, Mead, NY, 1919
Pares, Bernard *Day by Day with the Russian Army* Constable, London, 1915
Peel, Mrs C.S. *How We Lived Then 1914–1918* John Lane/Bodley Head, London; Dodd, Mead, NY, 1929*
Pershing, John J. *My Experiences in the World War* Hodder & Stoughton, London, 1931
Pitt, Barrie *The Last Act* Macmillan, London, 1962
Reynolds, Quentin *They Fought for the Sky: The Story of the First World War in the Air* Cassell, London, 1958
Rommel, Erwin *Infantry Attacks* Infantry Journal, Washington DC, 1943
Savage, Raymond *Allenby of Armageddon* Hodder & Stoughton, London, 1925

Seth, Ronald *Caporetto: The Scapegoat Battle* Macdonald, London, 1965
Stacke, H.Fitz-M. *The Worcestershire Regiment in the Great War* G.T. Cheshire, London, 1929
Stallings, Laurence, *The Doughboys: The Story of the AEF 1917–1918* Harper & Row, NY, 1963
Stone, Norman *The Eastern Front 1914–1917* Hodder & Stoughton, London, 1975
Terraine, John *The Road to Passchendaele* Leo Cooper, London, 1977; *White Heat: The New Warfare 1914–1918* Sidgwick & Jackson, London, 1982*
Thayer, John A. *Italy and the Great War* University of Wisconsin Press, Madison and Milwaukee, 1964
The Times History of the War (22 vols) Times Publishing Co, London, 1914–1923*
Toland, John *No Man's Land: The Story of 1918* Doubleday, NY; Eyre & Methuen, London, 1980
Villari, Luigi *The War on the Italian Front* Cobden-Sanderson, London, 1932
Warner, Philip *Passchendaele* Sidgwick & Jackson, London, 1987
Wavell, A.P. *The Palestine Campaigns* Constable, London, 1928; *Allenby: Soldier & Statesman* White Lion Publishers, London, 1974
White, C.M. *The Gotha Summer* Robert Hale, London, 1986
William, Crown Prince of Germany *My War Experiences* Hurst & Blackett, London, 1922*
Williams, John *Mutiny 1917* Heinemann, London, 1962
Williams-Ellis, Clough & A. *The Tank Corps* Country Life/George Newnes, London, 1919
Winter, Denis *The First of the Few: Fighter Pilots of the First World War* Allen Lane, London, 1982
Woolcombe, Robert *The First Tank Battle: Cambrai 1917* Arthur Barker, London, 1967
Woolf, Leon *In Flanders Fields: The 1917 Campaign* Longmans Green, London, 1959
Young, Peter *The British Army* William Kimber, London 1967*

Index

PEACE AND FUTURE CANNON FODDER

The Tiger: '*Curious! I seem to hear a child weeping!*'

Will Dyson's cartoon showing the Allied leaders—Clemenceau (The Tiger), Wilson, Orlando and Lloyd George—leaving the Versailles peace conference appeared in the *Daily Herald* in 1919. It proved uncannily prophetic in its judgement of the treaty's result.